READING *MORE* OF RODDY DOYLE

CARAMINE WHITE

GLASNEVIN
PUBLISHING

First published in 2012 by

Glasnevin Publishing
16 Griffith Parade, Glasnevin, Dublin 11, Ireland
www.glasnevinpublishing.com

based in Dublin, UNESCO City of Literature

A CIP catalogue record for this book is available from the British Library

Papers used by Glasnevin Publishing are from well managed forests and other responsible sources.

ISBN: 978-1-9086890-1-6

CONTENTS

For Mom

In addition to sharing your compulsive genes, you've given me all I've ever needed. You've also gone way above and beyond the call of duty in so many ways, not to mention by reading everything I've ever written. Thank you. I love you.

Acknowledgements

I would like to thank so many people for helping me through the process of writing this book. First and foremost is my husband, whose life, besides my own, has been the most (adversely) affected. The poor man has eaten nothing but meatloaf and pizza for six months now and has never (well, not that often) complained. Additionally, he has supported me in every one of my over-reaching goals, from doing an Ironman triathlon to running marathons, to writing this book. I'd be remiss if I didn't sincerely thank Roddy Doyle and John Sutton, who never hesitated when I suggested an interview to begin this project or failed to answer any questions, no matter how inane, during the project itself. Next, my colleagues Susannah Clements, PhD, Mark Gatlin, MFA, and Bill Ventura, PhD, all deserve medals for having endured my nonstop whining about how busy I was. They never failed to make me laugh even when I felt like crying. Heather Brist was wonderful with helping me research this project; Chelsen Vicari transcribed the interview for me and helped me with some of the early research; and Fellyn Lewis was great when I was figuring out the bibliography. Talking to my grandmother, Amine Kellam, always perked me up because she sincerely thinks that I am the most talented writer she has ever read. Lucy Herman, my grandmother/mother, was always completely understanding and loving, no matter how many times I had to cancel lunch because of my writing. The presence of my other grandmother/mother, surrounded me during this endeavour. I wish she were here so I could properly thank her. Similarly, Radka Heineman never complained that I owe her at least several visits, which I've had to postpone indefinitely because I couldn't find the time to drag myself away from the computer. Laura Foreman, PhD, has been my confidant and advisor, without whom I couldn't have made it through these last seven months (or last three years). My sisters, Somers Farkas and

Kellam White, my cousins, Laura and Ari Anderson, and Lee and Anna Kilduff, and aunt Ginny Foot have all been wonderful to me, and their love and prayers have supported me throughout this and, indeed, all my endeavours. Additionally, Laura and Ari were integral to my overcoming a personal crisis and thus being able to continue to write. The Reverend Canon Win Lewis was also a vital part of my healing from that crisis, and I'll never be able to thank him enough. I wrote almost every word of this book with Virginia White, PhD (Pretty Hound Dog), Phoebe White, MD, (Monster Dog), Mr. Rochester, and Sweet Naomi curled up on my lap (or on the keyboard), expectantly dropping a slobbery ball under my chair, or contentedly snoring at my feet; they made writing much less lonely and much more hairy. Finally, I have to thank my mother, who has read everything I have ever written and seems sincere when she says, "This is the best thing you've ever written!" I'm beginning to catch on—I just hope she never does.

Reading *More* of Roddy Doyle

Chapter 1
Introduction

In 2001, I published *Reading Roddy Doyle*, the first book-length study of the work of the Booker Prize winner, one of Ireland's most prolific, successful, and celebrated authors today. I concluded with a chapter "predicting" what we should expect from Doyle in the coming years.

> Doyle does not (and seems determined not to) repeat himself as an artist. . . .We can also surmise that Doyle's success with both the literati and the public will continue. He has demonstrated his ability to create fiction with artistic depth, but he remains dedicated to making his novels enjoyable to the average reader. . . .Not content to rest on his past successes, Doyle has attempted increasingly ambitious works. Each work shows growing maturity and skill, while retaining the qualities that brought him success. In all his work, Doyle demonstrates his compassion for and understanding of humanity, and his characters benefit from the "lessons" found in his works, namely that humor, some type of family and self-understanding will provide the independence and strength to live a satisfying life in today's difficult world. (143, 145,146)

I was pretty much spot on, if I do say so myself. Doyle's work has remained constant throughout its constant change. Despite the extraordinarily broad range of experimentation, his characteristic humor, compassion for and understanding of humanity have remained consistent.

Doyle fans do not have to fear his ever settling into a rut. In fact, he almost maniacally seems determined to experiment with every genre imaginable, from children's books to motion pictures to historical novels. The books for which he has written

Forwards encompass an eclectic variety, from Charles Dickens's *Great Expectations* to *Cigar Box Banjo*, a memoir about the last seven months of blues musician Paul Quarrington's life in which he travels with his band, records two albums, writes this book, and battles terminal lung cancer.

At times, his ability to navigate the waters of different genres seems to surprise even him. For instance, in a 1999 interview, Doyle said: "I've only written one short story in my life. So, I mean, I'd love to be able to write short stories, but I just don't think they're there, or they're not in me" (Sbrockey interview 542). The handful of stories he's published in *The New Yorker* and in *McSweeney's Enchanted Chamber of Astonishing Stories* and his two collections of short stories, *The Deportees and Other Stories* (2007) and *Bullfighting: Stories* (2011) attest to the fact that he has found at least a couple of short stories in himself and is enjoying the discovery: "Recently, in the last four, five, six, seven years, I've been writing short stories. They're great. I went straight into novels [when I first started writing]. Short stories are more precise. There's a precision to short stories and a little glimpse into a life" (McCann interview.)

The Deportees is comprised of serialized stories previously published in a Dublin, multi-cultural newspaper. These short stories focus not only on the experiences of the recent wave of immigrants to Ireland, the result of the Celtic Tiger economic boom, but also on the typical Irish citizen's experience of the changing population. The ever-changing Doyle says that the stories are "a challenge. It's to make sure I don't get lazy—that I don't decide that the living I did in my twenties and thirties is as much research as I need for the rest of my life" (Drewett interview 346). *Bullfighting*, a collection of thirteen short stories, chronicles the challenges facing middle-aged men— disintegrating marriages, self-sufficient children, regrets over choices, and fear of being redundant, emotionally and economically. The inspiration for this last collection is another change for Doyle. These stories couldn't have been written, says the 53-year-old Doyle (born in 1958), had he not also been experiencing middle age and raising children. In the past, Doyle has avoided writing from experience and has focused on characters and topics not closely related to his world.

Doyle has also begun collaborating with other authors on several "short-story-ish" projects. *Finbar's Hotel*, the brain child of Dermot Bolger (1997), brings seven Irish novelists together, each writing a chapter about events taking place in seven rooms in a seedy Dublin hotel. The characters in the various chapters encounter characters from other chapters, creating a type of unity. While we know that each author writes one chapter, we don't know who writes which as the chapters are unattributed. I would guess that Doyle writes the first chapter, about a married mechanic, in search of adventure and spending his first night ever in a hotel.

Amnesty International sponsored *Yeats is Dead!* (2001), the product of Doyle and 14 other Irish authors, including Frank McCourt and Anthony Cronin, all "hyper-articulate potty-mouths" according to a review on Amazon.com! Each chapter of the mystery, the premise of which is the discovery of an unpublished James Joyce manuscript, is written by a different author. The Amazon review continues: "and each writer seems eager to outdo the last by killing off as many characters as possible. This can be good, bloody fun. It can also lead to some creaky exposition. . . . More successful are the writers who altogether give up the ghost of creating a cohesive mystery, and instead wallow around in literary references and ridiculously purple prose" (1). Doyle writes the first chapter.

Click (2007), also benefitting Amnesty International, is a collaboration with nine celebrated young-adult novelists. This collection, for children twelve and up, "unites this beautiful tapestry of stories which are woven about the life of a photographer and his impact on his family and the world. Not only have ten writers been able to work together to tell a beautiful story, but they have done it for a good cause" (Junyk 37). Each writer contributed one chapter, "all of which mosaic together to form a single snapshot from a multi-generational story" (Farrey 2).

Click is not Doyle's first foray into the young-adult and children's market. He has written a handful of other children/young adult books, and even a cartoon version of one of them. He says that writing children's books is an entirely different process to that of writing for adults:

> My children's books do better than my adult books these days. . . .It's actually a slow process. They're not easier [to write than adult fiction.] They are so in as there aren't so many words. But in a sense, they are not easy. . . . [because] they are not realistically based. Things happen in the stories that aren't feasible, but they have to be within the context of the story. . . .With the three children's books, the idea was to play with reality. . . . It's hard to let your mind go and not damp [ideas] down. The other books that I've written, and I've given them to my editor, finished. . . . The work of us coming together and making final decisions about a sentence here and a paragraph there--you are talking about hours, maybe a day. . . .The children's books . . . [my editor] always thinks they can be funnier. So by the time they are finished, the books are always longer" (Doyle, Personal interview 232).

Doyle had a specific audience in mind for his children's books, namely, his own children. Doyle began writing children's books "after he found himself fed up reading books to his children. He used to make up stories at night, but the writer in him wasn't happy with them so he put them down on paper and polished them" (Dwyer 3). Unfortunately, the writing and polishing came too late: "The problem with my career as a writer of children's books is that I've always written them for my own children. . . .[but]I've got [them] . . . wrong on several occasions [because the children outgrew them before they were finished]" (Doyle, Personal interview 233).

Wilderness (2007) is fiction for young adults, although this not-so-young adult found it a very good read. It is based on a vacation that Doyle took with his sons, then ages eleven and nine.

> It was a holiday that became an idea for the book. [I went with] my wife and two boys, who are now nineteen and seventeen. . . .It was a great holiday. It was a week. And the huskies were great. . . . On the first day we were kind of slow because they drag you wherever. The [primary goal] is to keep them under control. You make them stop by putting your foot on the brake. They follow the lead of the front sled. You know if they turn the corner, you turn the corner, and it's your job to stay on. But there's a point where in the first hour, it's very tiring surprisingly. I suppose you are using muscles you don't normally use, and, considering it is really, really cold, you are perspiring quite a lot. It's [also] hard to see. You're sliding through trees and past a lake. Because it had snowed the night before, it looked like we were the first people who had ever been on that lake. And it struck me then that there's a story to make. I suppose it's because we lived the story, you know. But it was so easy to make. So easy to imagine. It's so glittery and so simple, white. It's just so beautiful. On the way home I suggested it to the boys while we were waiting on the train. I just got a notebook and wrote down all I needed to remember. It was a long ride. . . . .And that one I got wrong. By the time I got around to it, the boys were older and I had to start again and write something. So that's why it ended up being a book for older kids. They were older by the time I finished it. (233)

Doyle was also inspired by the stark, uninhabited beauty of Finland:

> I've been to India and dramatic places like that that are inspiring. But I've never had a book jumping up and down [in me.] But I think the fact that . . . it was

5

virtually uninhabited, it was like a blank page. It allowed me to think like a foreigner and I still got away with writing a book about this place. . . You go to Finland and you've got a couple of hundred people, and you go to India and you've got millions. . . .you feel really underqualified - whereas in Finland, I didn't feel that way. (233-34)

Wilderness has parallel plots, one of which places two boys and their mother on the aforementioned dog-sledding trip in Finland. The boys have an immediate attraction to and understanding of the sled dogs, who help them rescue their mother when she and her sled disappear during one particularly long, overnight trek. Their older half-sister, Grainne, a difficult adolescent, hurt and angry at being abandoned by her real mother yet idealizing her nevertheless, remains at home with her father as her real mother, absent for years, has suddenly decided to schedule an appearance in her daughter's life. Ultimately, the daughter has to play the parent for her emotionally immature mother (which makes her appreciate her half-brothers and step-mother all the more when they return from Finland).

While it seems as if, in *Wilderness*, Doyle is giving a recipe for good parenting, he denies this and won't comment on the type of father he is: "I've never ever written a book about parenting. I don't know what sort of father that I am, other than a loving father. . . .But I don't feel like I have anything to say. . . .if I start talking about it, I fall over. I'm always stunned by the number of people who think they can write books on how to raise children. . . .I just find it quite funny. No, I have nothing to say" (Personal interview 18). In another interview, still protective and private, he opens up a little more about fatherhood in general:

I don't know if fatherhood changes you but it adds. I suppose there are certain lifestyle changes which are a choice, like hangovers become a really bad idea when you've got young kids. They weren't that common but they're far less common now. I find that my role as a father changes. You have to know when to let them go and I'm not sure that I do. You hope that you're doing it right but of course you never can do it right. (Dwyer 2)

The three Rover books, *The Giggler Treatment* (2000), *Rover Saves Christmas* (2001), and *The Meanwhile Adventures* (2004) are entirely different from his young adult fiction. All illustrated by Brian Ajhar, these are best suited for children with a third- to fourth-grade reading level and with a third- to sixth-grade interest level (or adults who appreciate grade-school humor, like myself). They feature recurring characters, Rover, the dog, the Mack family, and Victoria, a neighbor originally from Africa (Victoria is not in *Giggler*.) Though for children, the books are not simply illustrations with a couple of words at the bottom of each page. They range between 100 and 180 pages and are hilarious: I found myself laughing out loud as I was reading to my husband about Mister Mack stepping in a "huge. . .big pile of wet, fresh dog poo" (Doyle, *Giggler* 11).

The Giggler Treatment, which was nominated for the Book Sense Children's Book of the Year, features Gigglers, "babysized and furry creatures. . . . that look after children. . . .so quietly that hardly anybody has ever seen them" (20,21). They punish unsuspecting but deserving pedestrians by placing poo, manufactured and marketed by the entrepreneurial Rover, in their paths. They mistakenly target an innocent Mister Mack, and the plot hinges on whether or not Mister Mack (and his shoes) can be saved in time.

Rover Saves Christmas, the weakest of the Rover trilogy, in my opinion, substitutes Rover for an ailing Rudolph in the reindeer line-up and "may not be the first story of how Christmas gets saved just in the nick of time, but it may be the funniest" (McMahon 4). Doyle also introduces multiculturalism (one of his current pet themes) with the Macks' African neighbors. When the toddler Victoria is helping deliver gifts around the world with the Mack children, she happens upon her grandparents' home in Lagos and sees them sleeping: "She could tell: Their dreams were sad. All of their children lived far way from Nigeria, and they had never held and cuddled any of their grandchildren. Their dreams were full of empty rooms and voices belonging to children they couldn't see" (Doyle, *Rover* 115). I'm not giving anything away when I report that all the presents get delivered in time and Victoria's grandparents wake up with happy dreams.

The Meanwhile Adventures (2004) is the most recent Rover installment in which the hapless Mister Mack is incarcerated for allegedly robbing a bank (in fact, he is only trying to get a loan). Mrs. Mack, his only alibi, alas, is busy travelling the world. The Mack children, Victoria, and Rover split forces, the children tunnelling under the jail to free Mr. Mack, and Rover searching the world for Mrs. Mack. My fourth-grade sense of humor is gratified by plenty of bathroom humor, including Mrs. Mack propelling her make-shift raft across the ocean by passing gas at an inordinate rate.

The books are filled with digressions, random questions that little children might ask, fake advertisements, and even funny glossaries for words with different meanings in American English (like "biscuit" which is a "cookie" to Americans.) Sections delineating "Lessons one should learn from this book" conclude each book: In *The Meanwhile Adventures*, Doyle writes, "All good stories have messages, and this story has none. But here are a few anyway" (168). Critics enjoy the novelty of these books: "Such digressions have a joyous, vigorous lunacy, absolutely in tune with a child's way of thinking" (Crompton). Although "a bracingly rude dose of fun," (*Publishers Weekly* 94), *The Giggler Treatment*, as are its companions, is described as having an "imaginative narrative and clever plotting [which] make this more than just another silly read" (Englefried 119).

The Rover books, although for children, share qualities with Doyle's adult fiction. For instance, the fast, tumbling pace in Doyle's novels is turtle-esque compared to these books, which span continents in paragraphs, begin and end narrative threads in pages, and throw so much at the reader that he can't even find a stopping place to put down the book. I had to read each children's book in one sitting as there are no breaks, despite the fake advertising sections and chapter divisions! Doyle's characteristic humor, while considerably more bathroom-ish here, is even more apparent in these books. For instance, the well meaning but extraordinarily inane Mister Mack has a curious effect on people: "But a Mister Mack slam was the sound of a door being slammed by someone who had just been talking to Mister Mack. . . .Mister Mack was a nice man, but something about him made people slam doors" (Doyle, *Meanwhile Adventures* 117). Additionally, these books share a self-consciousness with the Henry trilogy and some of the short stories. We never get so wrapped up in the Henry trilogy that we fail to notice Doyle's weaving in certain historical figures and events, and Doyle plays up this quality in the Rover trilogy.

Interestingly, despite what Doyle says about writing for his children, these particular children's novels seem to be written for, or at least, edited for, an American or international audience, which his adult novels are not: "I don't look at America. I think if I started looking at America, you'd never see the same type of writing again. If I started rewriting *Woman* thinking, well, Sally Field will read this and she'll want to make a movie, it's goodbye. The book is gone. If it's true to me, if I think it's accurate, if I think it's well put together and well structured, if I'm happy with it, then I'm finished with it. . . .If I start to think about markets, that unique locality will disappear and it will just be bland" (Sbrockey interview 544-5). The aforementioned glossaries included in each Rover book provide a hint to the intended international audience.

The quietly touching *Her Mother's Face* (2008), illustrated by Freya Blackwood, is a different type of children's book. Dedicated to his mother, Ita, the story loosely parallels Ita's childhood, in that Siobhan, a little girl whose mother has died, is upset that she can't remember her deceased mother's face but only her hands.

Ita's mother also died when Ita was almost four years old: "I can only remember her hands. I can't remember her face. I have no memory of her attire whatsoever. I can't remember what she wore on her feet. The only memory I have is her hands, doing things" (Doyle, *Rory & Ita* 13). Upon viewing her mother's body, Ita still only remembers her hands: "I remember being carried in to see her and I remember her hands were white and I remember saying, 'Mammy has new gloves'" (14). Ita knows very little about her mother, Ellen O'Brien: "She is a bit of a mystery to me. My father never spoke of her. Maybe it upset him too much, or maybe he thought it would upset us" (6). Ita says, "I never realized she was dead. I remember being told that she was coming back, which was terrible but I suppose it was done to shut me up; I was told she was coming back. I'm still waiting" (14). Included in the *Rory & Ita* is a poem about her mother's hands:

A hand.
Her hand,
Winding a handle and putting a needle in place,
Only a hand.
I cannot recall a body or face.
Later, I knew that the handle was part of a gramophone.
Newly arrived
And she was still alive.
Later still,
When lonely and blue
I handled that handle,
Remembering she had handled it too. (11)

Siobhan's father is also similar to Ita's. Both fathers give their daughters books for Christmas, and Ita calls her father "a very, very quiet man but, sure, he must have been dead lonely" (43), as is Siobhan's father. Siobhan, however, is visited by a mysterious woman (the ghost of the deceased mother) who tells the little girl to examine her own face to discover her mother's face, which comforts Siobhan throughout her childhood and adulthood.

The book seems to be Doyle's attempt at assuaging the sadness of his mother's childhood. Despite the young audience, this book doesn't have the happy endings of the Rover stories. Indeed, the penultimate lines are, "And that's the end of the story. Siobhan didn't live happily ever after, but she lived a long, long life, and she was happy a lot of the time. Her father lived enough to see Ellen [Siobhan's daughter] grow into a woman" (Doyle, *Face*) *Her Mother's Face* is a sweetly touching book in its own right, but knowing the back story makes it even more so.

In addition to short stories, collaborations, and children's books, Doyle has also tried his hand at memoir writing with the aforementioned *Rory & Ita* (2002). (Rory and Ita are Doyle's parents.) While his influence is definitely present in the memoir (which I discuss in the related chapter), he records and transcribes his parents' stories rather than actually editorializing this memoir of his parents' lives as people, instead of parents. Indeed, neither he nor his three siblings gets more than a mere mention. The book is Doyle "with a mission and a microphone," as he writes in the introduction, and besides a few footnotes explaining the more obscure references, the book is compiled from hours of transcribed conversations with his parents. Although not exactly a he-said-she-said type of book, the chapters do alternate between Ita and Rory and occasionally offer interestingly different commentary on the same occurrence, be it World War II or buying an engagement ring.

Not only does Doyle vary the types of books he writes, he also has worked at keeping his favorite genre - "novels for big people" (McCann interview) - fresh. He has moved from writing novels set in contemporary, working-class Ireland to tackling the three historical novels of *The Last Roundup* trilogy: *A Star Called Henry* (1999), *Oh, Play That Thing* (2005), *The Dead Republic* (2010), which are a mixture of fact and fiction: "I never saw it as strictly fiction as such, and I'm not even sure what that is" (Doyle, Personal interview 234). Doyle decided to write historical novels, in part, for "the challenge of seeing if I could surround myself with images and music and biographical details to create my own picture. It wasn't obviously lived experience, but that's where the challenge is" (Drewett interview 345). His previous novels required little research: For *Paddy Clarke*, his only research was "trips up to my parents' attic to remind me of books and what not" (qtd. in White 161); and for *The Woman Who Walked into Doors*, he "did a hell of a lot of reading while I was writing—I read a lot about women and violence, women and alcohol, sexual fantasy. And I used very little of it in the strict sense. It was just to make the ice I was walking on thicker as I walked along" (qtd. in White 161). He was aware, before he began the *The Last Roundup* trilogy, of the enormity of the research component: "So, I'll have to do a lot of reading to the extent that it'll take years and years and years to write" (qtd. in White 161). Indeed, the bibliographies included in the back of the Henry novels are impressive: As he says about *Oh, Play That Thing*, "Even if I shocked myself now, tomorrow, and finished the novel, I would still have a load of books that I need to read before I'm absolutely happy that I've got it there" (Drewett interview 348).

Doyle has expanded his "novels for big people" concept with his involvement in the Open Door Series, novellas written by Irish authors to promote adult literacy in Ireland. Doyle has written two of these novels, *Not Just for Christmas* (1999), examining the feelings generated when two brothers reunite after a 20-year split, and *Mad Weekend* (2006), telling the story of two childhood friends on their way to a football match event when one disappears from a pub. These books follow strict editorial guidelines, which include aspects such as a readily apparent plot, fairly simple vocabulary, short chapters, and a length not exceeding 10,000 words.

Doyle has also revisited old characters in new ways. First is Paula Spencer, a character whom he is quoted as saying "took about a year to get [her] voice out of [his] head" (Drewett interview 341). On 1 May 2003, the Helix Theatre held the world premier of the stage play of *The Woman Who Walked into Doors*, which Joe O'Byrne adapted, with Doyle's assistance, eighteen months before. Doyle was "wary at first. . . .that it should become a one-woman show. . . .and while it might be quite engaging and it might be very worthwhile, it didn't really appeal to me" (Drewett interview 340). Instead, the play has a complete cast, although Paula narrates the show, "but the whole world is revolving around her. . . .no intermission. It really brings an emotional force" (Drewett interview 341).

He also has written *Paula Spencer* (2006), the sequel to the first-person *The Woman Who Walked Into Doors*. *Paula Spencer* is written in third person because:

> I wanted it to be fresh. If I was to go [from] first person to first person then, inevitably, you're going to be falling back into the character. But if I wrote it in third person, second tense—that was a bit of an experiment. I could stay close to [*Woman*] but I could write alongside it. In first person, I use the analogy that she's holding the camera. In the third person, it's somebody else holding the camera. It was a different perspective and a different vocabulary. (Doyle, Personal interview 241)

Additionally, the third person narrative allows Doyle to present a more chronological narrative.

He also revisits *The Commitments*, except this time in a short story, "The Deportees," which speeds up the narrative considerably. Not untouched by time, Jimmy Rabbitte, Jr, is now middle-aged, married, and a father, but still craving the excitement of a band. Doyle also changes the political dimensions of the band: Instead of empowering working-class Dubliners, the band is comprised of members of the recent population of Central and Eastern European and African immigrants. Finally, he also has worked on a film script of *A Star Called Henry* which he says is "a huge job. The hardest job I've done yet is making a script out of that novel" (Drewett interview 348).

Not concerned with just his own fiction, Doyle has also updated J.M. Synge's *Playboy of the Western World* (1907) with Bisi Adigun, a Nigerian who is the producer and director of

13

Arambe Productions, which, per its website, "introduce[s] classic and contemporary plays in the African tradition by reinterpreting relevant plays in the Irish canon and also by producing intercultural music concert [sic]." Arambe commissioned Adigun and Doyle to rewrite the iconic Synge play in recognition of the centennial anniversary of its first production at the Abbey Theatre for the 50th Ulster Dublin Theatre Festival in 2007. Instead of the Aran Islands, the rewrite takes place "in a rough lounge bar somewhere off the M50, run by small-time gangsters, and the hero arrives off the plane from Nigeria [seeking asylum for supposedly killing his father with a pestle]. . . . It revives the comedy and finds a contemporary edge to it, reflecting Synge's satire unto our own times" (Murphy 1-2). Doyle says that direct collaboration, as opposed to the looser collaboration he had done by writing discrete chapters for various projects, was difficult: "In any writer's head, there is often an argument with the self about what direction to take the story in. When you're working with someone else, you have not only your own argument with yourself but the other writer's with themselves and also the debate with each other" (qtd. in Sanai 4).

Although the play received fairly good reviews which generally praised its humor, cultural sensitivity, and cleverness in updating the material, Doyle says that collaborating with Adigun, in particular, is one of his few professional regrets: "We wrote it back in 2006, and the writing was difficult but it went very well. Line by line, we kept the structure of the play. And it went very, very well, but after that, he claims I've breached contract. . . .And if I could go back and, when he suggested I write with him, just say no, I really would. But now I can't. But it's been very difficult" (Doyle, Personal interview 244). While Doyle (not wanting to spread rumors or indulge in innuendo) was reticent on the topic, , on the front page of the Arambe website, bold, red lettering claims that "Arambe Productions . . . had to disassociate themselves from the most recent (Dec 2008-Jan 2009) rerun of [*Playboy of the Wester World*]. . . .because Roddy Doyle and his agent John Sutton on the one hand, and the Abbey Theatre/Amcharlann na Mainstreach on the other, have refused to honour the contractual agreement they entered into with Arambe Productions in 2006 and 2007 respectively." Doyle vehemently denies breaking any contract, although, again, he prefers not to discuss such a sensitive and hurtful topic on the record.

Finally, although no stranger to the film industry, as his first three novels were made into movies and *The Woman Who Walked Into Doors* sprang from the controversial televised series *Family*, Doyle has also tried his hand at writing and producing an original screenplay. Doyle, "an unabashed fan of motion pictures" (Engall 143) wrote the romantic, screwball comedy *When Brendan Met Trudy* (2000), starring Flora Montgomery and Peter McDonald, and directed by Kieron J. Walsh. Brendan, a cinephile and "quiet non-achiever who works as a teacher with all the application of a stunned mullet" (Engall 143), meets and falls in love with the unpredictable Trudy and finds himself living out iconic motion picture scenes as their relationship develops. Movie references and allusions, obviously, abound in the movie. Trudy turns out to be a thief, which fact Brendan accepts and even embraces. Doyle says:

> If people like what they are watching in the first ten minutes and accept that these are real people then you can get absurd, anything could happen. I've written what may seem a very inappropriate relationship between a hemmed in man and a much more bohemian, wild woman. I was just playing around with some things. The script was very playful; it was part of the mood I was in when I wrote it. . . . I was very keen to mess around. (qtd. in Engall 143)

Interestingly, part of the reason that Brendan is a teacher in the movie is because of the research-heavy *The Last Roundup* trilogy: "Brendan is a teacher because work I have done in recent years has been very heavily based on research. A day of working can sometimes be a day of reading rather than a day of writing. So I was writing Brendan's character as a way of escape, light relief, because I was keen not to have anything to research. I knew I wouldn't have to ask people what's it like in a staff room" (qtd. in Engall). While Doyle's input on film projects has varied from director to director, with *When Brendan Met Trudy* he was intimately involved in the shooting: "I made sure I was there for scenes that were dialogue driven. Often a piece of dialogue may work on paper, but when you are there on the actual location you can find you are one utterance too short. . . .I would want to be there to make sure [any changes] fit" (qtd. in Engall 145). The film received good fairly good reviews, one reviewer calling it "an emerald from the isle" (Rozen).

Doyle has, however, been receiving more than just good reviews. The eleven-minute adaptation of "New Boy" from *The Deportees*, directed by Irish-American Steph Green was nominated for a 2009 Oscar in the short-film category. Green was initially intrigued by the story in that, "It's really interesting the degree to which we are strangers—and not strangers. What does it mean to have to sit next to someone? That's the same in a classroom as on the bus. There is something about the humanity of that which I like looking at" (qtd. in O'Grady 2). The film is available at the "Responsibility Project" website, which reads, "We thought, if one TV spot can get people thinking and talking about responsibility, imagine what could happen if we went a step further? So we created a series of short films, and this website, as an exploration of what it means to do the right thing" (qtd. in O'Grady 2).

Finally, although Doyle stopped teaching at Greendale Community School in Kilbarrack almost twenty years ago, he has reinserted his hand into the educational mix. In 2009, he and Sean Love, the former director of Amnesty Ireland, co-founded "Fighting Words," a creative writing center which, as its website asserts, "helps students of all ages to develop their writing skills and to explore their love of writing." In the neighborhood just outside of Croke Park, multi-aged children can practice writing, editing, and creating projects, receive one-to-one tutoring, and get encouragement for their creativity - all for no cost.

It's very deliberate and in the city of Dublin. It's deliberately bright and new for working class. It is not second-hand or charity, although some people are surviving on a wing and a prayer there. So I have made years and years of work there. And it's open to anybody. It's an open invitation. The vast majority of people who go in there are working-class kids. They are from the locality around Dublin. . . . (Doyle, Personal interview 28)

Doyle, along with other nationally recognized authors, tutors in the school and works on the Fighting Words project two afternoons a week (Dwyer 3).

However, amid his experimentation, Doyle has remained constant and consistent. Firstly, his compassion compels him to give a voice to otherwise voiceless and marginalized characters, although he disagrees with the term "marginalized":

I suppose you can say that the woman who experiences domestic abuse is marginalized. But I suppose writing the book was to drive her back into the center. So I never actually see them as marginalized. I suppose people that are born into that—if you can accept the idea [that the] marginalized . . . are somehow outcasts-- then I suppose there are good stories about that. But I never ask you to perceive them in that way, you know. . . .I'm not particularly interested in marginalized people as such, say, for example, if we decide that recently arrived people are marginalized people. Somehow, that just struck me as an opportunity to tell stories that I hadn't had an opportunity to tell before. It was more an opportunity rather than a crusade. It wasn't a crusade at all. I just wanted to write—that's the way I saw it. . . . It's not so much that I'm driven to the margins. It's the way we perceive it. (Doyle, Personal interview 225-26)

Despite his protestations, impoverished street urchins, alcoholic cleaning women, recent immigrants, and middle-aged men in crisis are not generally society's darlings and often live on its margins.

Although his books are somewhat apolitical, Doyle sees himself as a political writer. "I don't actually force the issue because I write about Irish, urban characters and they drag politics behind them, not the other way around" (Sbrockey interview 538). However, he distinguishes what type of political writer he is: "It's the difference between politics with a little "p" and a big "P." But a book about a woman in a violent marriage is a political book, a book about two unemployed men is a political book" (qtd in White 180). Rewriting the sacred book of Irish history and allowing immigrants voices are also very political things to do, even if they are not party affiliated.

Doyle has little interest in party politics, but he considers himself, not surprisingly, more of a liberal:

> Well, I suppose in a left/right spectrum, I lean towards the left very much. But again I live in Ireland and that raises questions and issues. When I was much younger I would have gone through a communist phase. And I'm kind of wary of "isms" now. Anything that ends in an "ism." But I suppose I am—um, somebody said I was socialist, and I guess I would say that I am--but without going into the various reasons--because it's a term that's as bland as a term "right" and "ice-cream." But my politics always lean towards the left in a European sense. I don't have anything interesting to say politically that thousands of people in this country couldn't say better. I'm not affiliated with any political party. . . . I am very pro-European. . . .You know, you have this notion of [Ireland's being a] little Britain, and I've always voted against that. I like being able to call ourselves European and having another angle to look at. Even though we are not able to speak different languages, [being a part of Europe] has opened us up

and made us less insular. I think it's huge and a great impact on us. But a lot of the left union people are pro-European. In an Irish context I hate the word "republicanism." I am a republican under the notion of electing our leaders and such. I hate the idea of having a head of state that is born. It seems so absurd and silly. But yet most of the other European countries have exactly that sort of system. But "republicanism" in the Irish sense has violent affiliations. [The members of the American Republican party] Bush and Palin seem almost fascists. . . . (Doyle, Personal interview 245-46)

Thus, despite his father's dedication to Fianna Fail and his grandfather's IRA affiliation, Doyle himself remains unimpressed by the political arena.

Although he has threatened to leave Ireland, for instance, had the 1995 Divorce referendum not passed, Doyle enjoys living in Ireland and credits it as being part of the reason he is a writer: He says, "As a citizen, I really like, love, living there. As a writer, it's endless. It changes and shifts—just when you're settling into what Ireland is like . . . it kind of kicks you!" (McCann interview). He also says,

> …say, for example, [if] Quentin Tarantino . . was born and reared in Ireland, he would have ended up a novelist. A lot of young Irish people became, and become, writers because that's one of the few options. I think a lot of writers were drawn to writing because it was one of the good, easy, cheap, accessible ways of expressing themselves. Also, Ireland has always had a very strong oral tradition. We're full of great talkers. (Sbrockey interview 540)

Finally, Doyle "like[s] it here. It's far from perfect, but, by accident or design, we've produced a country that's actually got a lot going for it" (Drewett interview 346).

However, he dislikes hard and fast definitions of Ireland and Irishness, a theme which has become consistent in much of his recent work (although he was also concerned with it when I first interviewed him in 1996):

> One of the themes of the [*Last Roundup*] trilogy [as well as *The Deportees*] was Irish identity: who defines it, who controls it. . . .When I was younger, there was an insistence that you had to be a certain kind of person. Now, there's no pressure because the economy has collapsed, so politicians who can't talk without drooling are now pushing culture, so we're back to being able to be artists, poets and the like. Now, being Irish can be several things at once, as being Scottish can be. (qtd. in Sanai 1,3)

He protests against the stereotypical view of Irishness: "It basically was the Catholic Church against everyone else. It was this insistence that if you're Irish, you're white and you're Catholic as well, and if you're not both of those things, then you're not fully Irish" (qtd. in White 38). Perhaps because of Doyle's strong compassion for the immigrant population as well as his atheism, his work can be seen as "supremely unfaithful to the 'nationalist project' of post-Independence Ireland, a narrative that constructed an artificial Irish identity that was 'Catholic, not Protestant; rural, not urban; Celtic, not Anglo-Saxon; agrarian, not industrial; religious, not secular . . . in the name of tradition" (Whelan qtd. in Moynihan 52). Doyle laughs at the xenophobia inspired by the influx of the immigrant populations: "The Irish did it [emigrated], and do it all the time. . . .What's the threat? Do we need to be white? No! Do we need to be Catholic? Jesus Christ, no! What is it that we'd be trying to protect? I don't see it. All I can see is enlargement" (Drewett 347). Doyle says that the only time he worries about being Irish is when he isn't there: "I only feel Irish when I am not actually in Ireland" (Personal interview 2).

Besides a few derogatory references in *A Star Called Henry,*
Oh, Play That Thing, and *The Deportees,* Doyle continues to ignore
the topic of religion in his work. Doyle believes that religion isn't
a major part of the lives of most Irish, and he may be correct.
Recent statistics show that only 18% of the Irish are regular,
church-going Catholics, compared to the 33% of US Catholics
(Lusembo), even though 90% of the Irish primary schools are
under the Church's patronage. In Dublin, only one in five
Catholics go to Mass, and across the pond in America, a full
third, or 11 million, or those who have left the church are Irish-
American. From 1974-2008, Mass attendance declined 50%. And
many these ex-Catholics are not going to the Protestant
churches; instead, they are just existing in a religious nowhere
land (Fraze 11). Hence, when Doyle says religion isn't really an
issue in contemporary Ireland, he has a point.

Although the Catholic Church has lost some of its power
and credibility in Ireland, nevertheless, it still a strong force in
the country, as Doyle admits when he rails against Catholicism
being a facet of the traditional definition of Irishness.

Doyle himself is an atheist: "I won't be up in a cloud
looking down on it, I'm fairly convinced. Nor will I be down
below! Nothingness I think is what's in store" (Sbrockey
interview 552). His journey away from the Catholicism of his
parents began in his teens:

> [Becoming an atheist] wasn't anything spectacular. . . . I
> wasn't at Mass or anything. I just decided I didn't
> believe. It wasn't that I didn't believe in the routine of
> the liturgy or the various routines of Mass at the end of
> the week. I just didn't believe anything. I was at an
> interview with Woody Allen ten years ago and he
> captured it better than anybody. He said our religion is
> that we live in the city. And I agree with him. It's as
> simple as that. . . . Anyway, nobody's interested
> anymore. You know I married a Protestant woman.
> Twenty-five years ago, or whenever we started going
> out with each other, this was a point of interest. Now

nobody gives a damn. . . . . I don't think it's anti-Christian as such. I've gone past that. . . . .I mean, you know, religion, as I said, is fundamentally silly, but it's entertaining. . . .I kind of don't think about it at all. It doesn't get into the house really and it doesn't interfere. I look at the stories about clerical child abuse that aren't going away--the way the Vatican handles it—it's atrocious. It's horrible and it's stupid . . . .and that's all. . . .I don't feel detached completely. I don't feel it explicitly because I am not a Catholic, but I don't feel detached from it either. It's the country I live in, and, you know, still the majority of people have their children christened even though they're not practicing. It's a cultural thing rather than a religious thing. But I do feel a distance from the church. (Doyle, Personal interview 225)

He seems to dislike the Church for its "arrogance," especially surrounding the child abuse scandals and the "notion that canon law supercedes the law of the country" (Dwyer 2), as well as for its exclusionary practices, its powerful and conservative social stances, and it being so wrapped up in Irish identity, which obviously is alienating for non-Catholics.

Despite his protestations, Doyle's references to religion and religious characters are often negative. Henry thinks of the church: "Fuck her. And religion. . . .And your man on the cross up over the blackboard. Fuck Him too" (*A Star Called Henry* 82); Sister Flow, a religious icon of the period with a tremendous following, is depicted as the consummate con woman in *Oh, Play That Thing*; religion is likened to politics in *The Dead Republic* as merely a tool for inspiring loyalty for the revolution; Micah, the formerly slightly off-balance and violent drummer in *The Commitments*, is, in "The Deportees," a born-again Christian with no compunction about having children by several women; Fat Ghandi of the same story uses his Christianity to disguise his homosexuality and to promote his business: "His loud embrace of Christianity was very good for business. It bored most people, and frightened quite a few, but, even so, Gandhi's weird faith had made him suddenly respectable. Here was a man who could be trusted, a man who took the world seriously. So he took it for what it was: golf without the exercise" (71). Finally, *Rory & Ita* has more discussion of the trappings of religion than of faith, despite his parents being lifelong Catholics. In toto, it seems as if Doyle does have a prejudice against the Church, although, granted, he doesn't dwell incessantly on it in his work. The few instances I've mentioned are insignificant when placed against the sheer volume of his work.

Doyle also remains a working-man's novelist, keeping 9:30 am to 6:00 pm office hours, his office being in the attic of his house: "I'm quite happy to work office hours" (Writers Institute interview). He jokes that he enjoys being his own boss because he often favorably looks upon his requests for a day off. He also says, however, "I'm very disciplined when I'm working" (McCann interview). Being so extraordinarily prolific and successful attests to his tremendous work ethic. In fact, he takes breaks from working by working, just on other projects:

> Ideally, I divide my day in two between the novel and some sort of screen work. Just in terms of one's working life, when you're writing a novel, there's no end in sight. . . .Whereas with screen work, when you become involved in screen, if you like, there's a bit of action just around the corner. If I was working on the novel all day, it'd drive me demented. Two years writing a novel . . . is a small chunk of anyone's life, [but] when you're living it, it's an eternity. (Sbrockey interview 550)

Doyle starts the day with editing his current novel "and I add or subtract and then take it on a bit. Then I leave it aside quite deliberately—when I'm still a bit itchy . . . and do, like, a children's book. . . .I do that for maybe an hour . . . and then I can go back to the novel, and that itch that was there—I can start scratching it" (Drewett interview 348). He also makes sure that he immediately begins another project as soon as he finishes something: "When I finish a novel, it's back to work the day after. . . .there is no creative decompression" (Doyle, Personal interview 247).

Doyle loves the "job" of writing: "Why do I write? Well I suppose the simplest answer is because I love it. And I've written books that I thought—I'd like to think—have entertained people, that have shown them worlds that they didn't know existed or that they sensed, but didn't know. . . .In an Irish context, I'd like to think that people reading my books are seeing their area . . . for the first time between the pages of a book" (Sbrockey interview 550). Doyle even enjoys the editing process:

> It's work, but I love the work. . . .Sometimes, people say that writing, say, *The Commitments*, must have been great fun, but it's work. The sense of fun is [the product of good] editing. . . and taking things out. It's work. I get anxious at times—worried that you're taking out [too many] things. The trick is to make it seem as if you're enjoying writing it. . . . It is, though, a pure form of self-enjoyment. . . .It's our privilege that we get to explore. Starting a novel is lovely. . . . It's like a relationship really—you forget about the original dream and work with what you have. That's why I love editing—because you have a bit of a mess on the page. You have a notion of what it's going to be and then it's not, but the exciting compensation is that you invent something entirely different instead (McCann interview).

Despite the compassion his work shows, writing is not about "giving back" to the community: "No, I hate that. If I didn't like it, I wouldn't do it" (Dwyer 3).

Doyle, although admitting that his work is literature, refuses to judge its literary importance: "I still don't know [it's important]. It's not for me to say. I feel it, obviously, personally—but I don't expect it to be to anyone else, and I'm not being coy" (McCann interview).

It's a nice thought to think that my books would be on the shelf in a hundred years' time, but that's all it is. It's not an ambition. . . .It's a nice thought to think that when I'm in my dotage, on a cane or something, and I go into a book shop, that if I pluck up the courage to go to the 'D' section that my books will still be in print. That's a nice thought, but other than that, I don't really have an opinion. As for people's reactions, I would hope they like it. That perhaps they would be recognized as being books that are both literary and accessible. And that they are creative records of what life was like at the various times, or what a segment of life was like at various times, when I was writing them. (Sbrockey interview 552)

Although some say that writers feel they must stand outside of society to write about it, Doyle says, "I don't think about it." He is similarly nonplussed when asked about his impact on Irish culture: "It's happenstance. I didn't actually think of it. I don't think of consequences until it's too late. Basically, it's between me and the page. If I start thinking of the impact, the book will fall apart" (McCann interview).

Doyle also prefers to remain under the radar publicly. He lives quietly with his wife, three children (two sons and daughter), in Clontarf and works at his home office. He loves movies, exercises a couple of times a week at a local gym, and walks a lot, including to and from Fighting Words (Dwyer 2). While he is perfectly charming when interviewed, he tends:

..to stay away, if I can, from interviews and profiles that hone in on the personality and don't actually get around to talking about the books; so I wouldn't be interested in creating a mythology around myself— either being the hard drinking man or the soft drinking man. I think it's unfortunate that an awful lot of writers are remembered for little, well-advertised traits, and not for what they wrote about, so I've no interest in that whatsoever. (Sbrockey interview 552)

He doesn't do many interviews: "I gave up doing them for five or six years because I got tired of hearing myself say the same things" (McCann interview). When he travels, in particular, he also does not want to be seen as an ambassador for Ireland or a "roving representation of my nation" (McCann interview). Instead, he finds the best thing to do is to "answer questions honestly and not to say what people want you to say. Expectations are hard to escape. . . .and the way to circumvent problems is to always reply to questions honestly and not give stock answers or tourist board answers. . . . Of course, as you get older the answers vary from day to day. It's nice to vary your honest answers, even if only for one's mental health" (qtd. In Sanai 5). He is determined not to become a celebrity: "There's not an awful lot you can do about fame, but there's a hell of a lot you can do about celebrity. Celebrity is a question of choice and the way to avoid becoming a celebrity is just to say 'no'" (qtd. in White 40).

While Doyle himself may be unassuming, his literary abilities are not, as we can see from his work in the last decade. He is talented enough to constantly experiment with genres, themes, and characters, while maintaining his unique wit, style, and empathy, the substance, in the truest, Latinate sense of that word, of his success.

CHAPTER 2
A STAR CALLED HENRY

A Star Called Henry is Doyle's first foray into historical fiction and the initial instalment of *The Last Roundup* trilogy. (The trilogy title is based on a 1947 western in which Gene Autry, with the help of a local schoolteacher, brokers a deal which brings Native Americans and ranchers together.) Published in 1999, this mixture of the picaresque and magical realism traditions introduces us to the resilient Henry Smart as a newborn in 1902 and follows him as he navigates the Dublin slums, fights in the 1916 Easter Rising, and joins the IRA as an assassin in the Irish War of Independence. In the novel, Doyle places Henry, *Forrest-Gump* style, as a witness to important events in some of the most turbulent times of the early-twentieth-century Irish history.

Doyle's novel has quite a basis in history. Piano Annie, Dolly Oblong, and Miss O'Shea are based on real people (Lanters 247), and many of Henry's (and his wife's) war experiences are based on real occurrences. Doyle took the bulk of his information about what happened during the War of Independence from Ernie O'Malley's first-hand account: "In my opinion, he wrote the best IRA memoir, *On Another Man's Wound*" (Doyle qtd. in Sanai 1). Henry even mentions O'Malley, who died in 1957, in the novel: "Drilling the new men on the local big shot's demesne was an idea I'd picked up from Ernie O'Malley . . . .[He had] an intelligence about him, a twist to the lines on his forehead that impressed me. He was a saint who hung up his halo now and again" (220, 183).

However, Doyle is not writing a historical novel: "It is true to say that fiction makes bad history. . . .I'm not a historian and I don't want to be. [Rather] it was like putting a magnifying glass over reality and making something bigger of it" (Doyle qtd. in Lanters 246). Thus, the novel "resides somewhere between myth and history. His account not only makes the events larger than life but also presents them through a late twentieth-century lens that highlights politically correct issues such as class, gender, and ethnicity" (Lanters 248). Doyle's position is closer to the "post revisionist historiography that began to emerge in the late 1980s and 1990s. 'Post revisionists' created historical scholarship that, after meticulous research, endorsed some of the claims of the nationalist narrative that had been discredited by revisionists, while also acknowledging the validity of many revisionist's findings" (Moynihan 53).

Theoretical viewpoints aside, Doyle's agenda in the novel is not to create a myth but to destroy one. His words do not cement the Irish freedom fighters in patriotic immortality but accuse some of them as being power-hungry mercenaries. At the very least, his depiction of the Irish is just as much an indictment of them as of their traditional view of the British, which is a radical change from usual view of that period:

> Despite the fact that he becomes one of the IRA's most legendary and feared killers—his actions immortalized in song and poetry—he gradually decides that his bosses, behind their patriotic rhetoric, are as mercenary as the people they oppose. By the book's end, the rebellion's successful outcome brings little sense of triumph. The hunter has become the hunted, and he regrets the moral consequences of his own violence, as well as the overall circumstances he helped bring about. That view has already caused controversy in Ireland, where it is a given that the uprising against England is a black-and-white tale of heroic underdogs rising against villainous oppressors. Doyle's view is more complex, suggesting that in the short term at least, the new Republic of Ireland simply replaced one set of greedy manipulators with another. The fact the country is now prepared to hear that view, he has said, is a sign of maturity: until recently, it would have been unacceptable. (Wilson-Smith 42)

The demythologized version of Irish history presented in *A Star Called Henry* does not allow patriotism and heroism to whitewash the injustices perpetrated by the revolutionaries. "Doyle's intention is to make his narrator an illustration of the dark side of Ireland's struggle for independence, a relic and victim of the largely unremembered, or at least, sentimentally remembered, savagery that achieved it" (Gordon 1). The novel's actions depict the ultimately successful revolution as "a Catholic, bourgeois takeover . . . [which critique] owe[s] a good deal to O'Casey's view of those events as well as to much subsequent 'revisionist' historical commentary" (Donnelly qtd. in Lanters 2567).

Doyle admits to using the novel to re-present the history he learned as a boy. He remembers memorizing the Easter Proclamation, which "read like an Irish western with this collection of saints and martyrs. . . .When I went to Christian Brothers school, Pearse was a god, a saint - we had to read those shitty sentimental stories and write these glowing reviews of them" (Doyle qtd. in Lanters 246). Doyle's slant on these important historical events is radically different than the version taught to him as a child.

> When I was a kid, less so in secondary school but definitely in primary school and before the IRA started planting bombs and stuff like that, Irish history was presented as doctrine, as religion. And these men who must be complicated human beings with their egos, you know, their ideologies and their egos. They were men who decided, and they were mostly men, to engage in this hopeless war, say, in 1916, who in the last hoorah, they locked themselves in a building in order to jump out. They were there to sacrifice themselves. And one or two of them did. That's what their poetry was about, blood and sacrifice. Which in a different context, it's pessimistic. . . . . .Yet this was all presented to us as deep membership. . . .there is a continuity from the

mythological figures, you know fictional characters like Fionn [Mac Cumhaill] and St. Patrick, historically based, but fiction. . . .right up to these historical figures who shaped the Ireland that we live in now. But they're all presented as being good guys, saints in some shape or form. And I suppose in a changing society you can allow yourself to poke fun at that and to reinterpret that and to satirize it. I'm not interested in satire. To take those old things and make the modern—I wasn't doing it. . . .I wasn't attempting to re-write history. I'm not a historian. I suppose I was telling the story from a different angle. (Doyle, Personal interview 241)

In the context of the novel, Henry's "angle" has the same problems that the traditional version has: We don't fully trust it. "Henry's narrative is a palimpsest in that it is presented as true, but as a truth subsequently erased from official history. This questions the nature of 'truth' itself . . . is Henry's story not to be found in Irish history books because it was subsequently erased from all accounts, or because he made it up" (Lanters 249). Henry's reliability is questionable because he "challenges the accepted view of Irish history by parodying the official version of it . . . [thus] his own position also becomes discredited" (Lanters 246). Additionally, Henry's tall tales and "braggadocio sometimes strain credibility" (Hutchings 44) throughout the trilogy. Significantly, *Castle Rackrent*, an Anglo-Irish historical novel which Henry sees just as he is captured and subsequently imprisoned, features a notoriously unreliable narrator on the margins of history. Thus, we are left in a quandary: "Henry is both gobshite and hero—deluded and self-aggrandizing swaggerer on the one hand, debunker of the official myth and champion of women, children, refugees, and slum dwellers on the other. Even if we go along with him in debunking the received version of the sacrificial myth of the motherland, we are not necessarily persuaded to accept Henry's alternative version" (Lanters 254). Nevertheless, we trust him more often than not (even if his stories of his sexual exploits seem to have a touch of the blarney about them.)

And it is necessary for us to at least entertain Henry's tale as credible because "our narrative of cultural self-identity is itself a fiction. . . .[Revisionism frees us] from the strait-jacket of a fixed identity [and opens us to] other possibilities of being" (Kearney qtd. in Lanters 248,49) as well as "highlight[ing] that every narrative of self-identity is a fiction, allowing each one of us the freedom to re-invent our past" (Lanters 250). Doyle himself says about the trilogy, "If they're about anything at all, they're about identity and who gives us our identity" (McCann interview). Thus, if we as readers are allowed to re-create ourselves and expect others (and ourselves) to believe in it, we should of Henry the same luxury.

Paradoxically, whether we trust Henry fully or not is almost beside the point. Demystifying the past and seeking its truth, even if we can never learn the truth fully (a theme in many of his works, e.g. the Paula Spencer novels) is vital for a successful future. For instance, the seeds of Ireland's current economic crisis can be found in its mythologized history, says economist Michael Lewis:

> When money was made freely available to Irish banks and individuals at shockingly low rates, the Irish wanted to buy Ireland. They created a land bubble. . . They drove up the price of their own real estate to just incredible levels. . . .The Irish turned in on themselves, and it was in some ways poetic because if you look at the history of Ireland, the Irish have always had a very uncertain relationship with their own land. For hundreds of years, it was illegal for an Irish person to own land and so . . [the fact that] they fetishized Irish soil was interesting.

Thus, de-mythologizing the past is essential for Ireland and for the Irish.

By demythologizing the Irish sacred cow of the struggle for independence, Doyle is asking Ireland to face a more realistic view of itself. Ironically, Doyle uses the mask of fiction to show the dangers of masking reality. *A Star Called Henry* asks readers to face a version of truth of the Dublin slums, about the classism and sexism which the glorious versions of the revolution don't address and may even perpetuate.

Plot Summary

The novel is divided into four parts, as are the two other books in the trilogy. We first meet Henry, interestingly, before he is even born. He tells us in his first-person narration about his mother Melody Nash and his father, the one-legged brothel bouncer and assassin, Henry Sr. Henry readily admits to creating the grotesque and oddly touching story about his parents' lives as newlyweds in the Dublin slums. Interestingly, Henry's story shows two people almost entirely in their capacity as absent parents. *Rory & Ita*, another story created by a son, except this time about successful parents, almost entirely ignores Rory and Ita's lives as parents.

Despite the couple's rapid descent into abject poverty, Henry's birth, in the magical realism tradition, is extraordinarily auspicious. His maternal grandmother, Granny Nash, is suddenly able to read, and he is famous: "a healthy, good-sized baby. . I was the Glowing Baby. . . .Only a week in the world and already there were stories spinning up and down the streets and alleys" (Doyle, *A Star Called Henry* 24-5).

Henry is named after his previously deceased sibling, whom, his mother avers, has become a glowing star (hence the name of the novel.) Interestingly, Doyle himself is named after a deceased brother. Doyle's mother Ita says, "A lot of people said it was bad luck, so I said, No, it's in memory of his brother. It keeps the name alive" (Doyle, *Rory & Ita* 236).

Not even the spectacular birth can save the couple as Henry Sr, having become enamored of Dolly Oblong, the, gloriously bewigged brothel's madam, stops coming home and Melody seeks refuge in an alcoholic stupor. Five-year-old Henry and his nine-month-old brother Victor take to the dirty Dublin streets and survive by catching rats, stealing cattle, picking pockets, and selling old newspapers. His life on the streets is punctuated by three notable events: In 1907, during a visit by the English monarch, Henry Sr saves Victor and Henry from the police. He carries them as he limps and floats through the Dublin sewers. This is the last time Henry sees his father, who bequeaths to him a supernatural divining ability and his wooden leg, both of which serve Henry well throughout the novel. Three years later, the eight-year-old Henry decides that he and Victor should attend school, where they meet Miss O'Shea, a young teacher and future revolutionary, who becomes Henry's wife ten years later. Their education is short-lived, however, as the Mother Superior of the convent school rudely and cruelly expels them. Shortly thereafter, on the day of George V's coronation, Victor dies of malnutrition and consumption. Henry never forgets the irony: "The city killed Victor. And, today, the King was being crowned. In another city. In London. Did they cough till they died in London? Did kings and queens cough up blood? Did their children die under tarpaulins?" (Doyle, *A Star Called Henry* 85). He is also present when Countess Markievicz burns the Union Jack and is arrested, although the importance of the event doesn't register to the devastated and lonely little boy.

Part Two spans a three-week period, opening on Monday, April 24, 1916, with the 14-year-old Henry and the other members of the Irish Volunteers and the Irish Citizen Army preparing the General Post Office to withstand a siege by the British regulars in the famous 1916 Easter Rising. Henry is not part of the rebellion out of any particular love of his country. Indeed, as a boy, he thinks of Ireland as "something in songs that drunken old men wept about as they held onto the railings at three in the morning and we homed in to rob them. That was all" (71). Henry joins the Citizen Army because he has nothing to lose: He and his few friends have "nothing against Englishmen either, or Scots or Welshmen. We were fighting a class war. We weren't in the same battle at all as the rest of the rebels" (109). This emphasis on class strife is a consistent theme in the novel and predicates much of what Henry does and much of what is done to him. During the first engagement, Henry, who runs the Dublin streets most often barefoot, directs his shots "at Tyler's, the shoe shop, with its windows full of single shoes, its special corner for children's boots" (101), and he "shot and killed all that I had been denied, all the commerce and snobbery that had been mocking me and other hundreds of thousands behind glass and locks, all the injustice, unfairness and shoes—while the lads took chunks out of the military" (107).

Another running theme is Henry's overwhelming need for family and the desire to belong to something. Thus, in addition to class resentment, he joins the Citizen Army for the feeling of belonging. He is a protégé of sorts of one of the rebellion's hero, the socialist James Connolly, who teaches him to read and even asks his advice on the Proclamation of Independence. Notably, Henry suggests that Connolly include something about children: "There should be something in there about the rights of children. He looked at me. He saw my pain, and the pain of millions of others. And his own. . . ." (99). Henry, who throughout the trilogy seeks acceptance from and is loyal to individuals instead of causes, finds a type of father in the celebrated revolutionary.

The narrative takes us through the first several days in detail, as Henry waits for the fighting to begin and re-encounters Miss O'Shea, now a member of Cumann na mBan and also barricaded in the GPO. Miss O'Shea [improbably] seeks out the fourteen-year-old Henry who, by his own admission, is "six foot, two inches tall and had the shoulders of a boy built to carry the weight of the world. I was probably the best-looking man in the G.P.O." (91). Their reunion is a sexual one, the seeds of which are [improbably] sown in their elementary-school encounter. Amid the atmosphere of the multiple accounts of sexual abuse of minors by Catholic priests, Doyle seems to regret this one aspect of the novel: "You know, whatever afternoon or morning I decided to do that back when or whatever—don't ask me why. It just seemed like a good idea" (Doyle, Personal interview 241).

By Saturday, 30 April, the revolutionaries have surrendered. During a roll call in the parade grounds, Henry escapes by using his divining abilities to find and then leap into a manhole connected to the sewers. He emerges into the arms of Piano Annie, an Irish woman whose husband is fighting for the British in World War I. Piano Annie, in addition to having frequent sex with Henry, cleans him up, gives him new clothes, and provides him shelter. In a *Godfather*-esque Christening/execution montage, we leave the couple having sex while the sixteen senior leaders of the Rising are executed.

Part Three is the most complicated and involved section. For about a year, Henry lives simply, working as a stevedore and living with Piano Annie. Despite the horrendous work conditions, swallowing clouds of coal dust and the soft-tissue-eating phosphorite as he unloads ship after ship for a daily wage, Henry enjoys the uncomplicated existence—hard work, drinking, and sex with Annie. However, after Annie's husband returns, Henry is at loose ends, unable to get work (he previously gets work because Annie has prostituted herself with the dock boss) and without a place to sleep. Still living under a false name because of his connection to the Easter Rising, he reconnects with his grandmother, Granny Nash, a single-minded bibliophile with no maternal feelings, who parcels out information about his past in exchange for books.

However, the most important person with whom he reconnects is Jack Dalton, who is also at the GPO and with whom Henry instantly bonds. The nationalistic Dalton instils his fervor in the impressionable Henry: Henry joins the Irish Volunteers and becomes one of the few who "knew that there was a war" (Doyle, *A Star Called Henry* 174) as they prepare for the bitter fighting of the Irish War of Independence. Henry enjoys this period of his life—baiting the British police, playing spy, and having sex with women who idolize him because of his GPO connection: "The sheer fun of it: for the first time in my life I was behaving like a kid" (175).

From the hints dropped by the narrator Henry, recalling these events, we sense that, in reality, the young Henry is still on the margins and excluded. We get a glimpse of the other agenda of those involved in the new revolution—power for power's sake. Henry, out of his longing both for family and justice for the victimized poor, continues to belong to the organization, even getting in more deeply and, at the behest of Michael Collins, becomes a member of "the Irish Republican Brotherhood, the secret society at the centre of the centre of all things. . . .I was special, one of the few" (186).

Henry is dispatched to the rural parts of Ireland "to train the country lads. And to pick out the best ones for ourselves" (206). He rides everywhere on his bicycle, teaching young men how to drill and enjoying the pleasure of any and all women available, as well as eating cabbage and breathing fresh air, both for the first time. He winds up at the Roscommon home of Missis O'Shea, whom he later discovers to be the mother of his beloved Miss O'Shea, who has continued her revolutionary activities. The two quickly marry, with neither the reader nor Henry learning Miss O'Shea's first name. They are often able to work together, although their wartime activities forces them to spend many nights apart.

All of this is backlit by the highlights of the revolution: the December 1918 Sinn-Fein electoral landslide; the 1919 formation of Dail Eireann (the Irish parliament); the British declaring it illegal eight months later; and the escalating violence with the subsequent arrival of the Black and Tans and Auxiliary Cadets, both groups of British mercenaries. Additionally, Henry waits on the fringes as the other leaders of the revolution, including Jack Dalton, win elections and gain prestige and power.

The strategy of Collins and Company is to "keep at it until it becomes unbearable [for the British.] To provoke them and make them mad. We need reprisals and innocent victims and outrages and we need them to give them to us. To keep at them until the costs are so heavy, they'll decide they have to go" (254). With the increased bloodshed "keeping at it" entails, Henry is "promoted" to assassin, one of the Twelve Apostles, an elite group of the IRA, because of his paradoxical qualities: "dissident and slave, a man who was quick with his brain and an eejit" (242). Henry doesn't question what he is told to do, and, following in his father's footsteps, Henry, ignorant of the reason, is given a name and quickly eliminates the person.

Henry's faith and ignorance last a few years until several occurrences disturb his equanimity. Henry becomes good friends with David Climanis, a Latvian Jew emigree. However, Henry is warned to keep away from Climanis, an order which, for the first time, Henry questions, as he is firmly convinced of Climanis's political neutrality. Also, Alfred O'Ganduin, M.P., formerly Alfie Gandon, brothel owner and gangster, has gained political clout in Ireland and has risen correspondingly in the revolutionary circles, with its highly placed leaders supporting his claim to have been at the GPO, which Henry knows to be false.

Henry also gets severely wounded during a raid with his wife. Miss O'Shea, who is shot several times in the arm, manages to carry Henry to safety. The shooting for Miss O'Shea is liberating: "I knew when the third bullet hit me that I could stand up to anything. I've nothing to fear. There's no stopping me now, Henry" (274). Henry, however, loses his desire to fight. After doing several more assignments, including one of the Bloody Sunday assassinations, Henry privately decides "my war was over" (289). He visits Granny Nash one last time, during which she cryptically tells him that O'Ganduin is still using the same murderous techniques of his former incarnation Alfie Gandon. She also has time to observe "You're just like your father. And that's no compliment" (290) before members of the Auxiliary Cadets storm the room and capture Henry.

Part Four opens with a severely beaten Henry, held in Dublin Castle before being transferred to Kilmainham. Despite the repeated beatings, Henry consistently refuses to admit who he really is. After four months of imprisonment, he is freed when Miss O'Shea orchestrates his oddly uncomplicated escape. Exhausted from his mental and physical turmoil, Henry enters a months-long period of "Great Sleep," a la Jack Burden in *All the*

King's Men, while his wife, now pregnant, continues her ambushes.

Henry's "Great Sleep" is literally disrupted by one of his "country lad" protégés, Ivan, who has risen to prominence in Roscommon and has become just as corrupt and oppressive as any British government. Ivan brokers self-aggrandizing deals with the British forces in return for money and non-interference. Ivan, truthful with Henry despite his corruption, is the first one to articulate the misgivings Henry has been having, admitting that the revolution has allowed him and others like him to control their own tiny portions of the country. Henry has finally awakened to the truth about his comrades.

Although Henry's epiphany has been some time in coming, he reels from it and the news that the heads of the organization are displeased with him, which means "I was dead" (318). He leaves the countryside and Miss O'Shea, and he returns to Dublin, where he finds David and Maria Climanis gone. He confronts Jack Dalton directly, who tells Henry, "If you're not with us you're against us. That's the thinking. And there are those who reckon that you're always going to be against us. And they're probably right. You've no stake in the country, man. Never had, never will. We needed trouble makers, and very soon now we'll have to be rid of them. And that, Henry, is all you are and ever were. A trouble-maker. The best in the business, mind" (327). Jack isn't as crude as Ivan, but the message is the same. Thus, the entire revolution has boiled down to class warfare—the haves against the have nots. The have nots have no property, business, or resources tied to Ireland's success and therefore can't be and won't be trusted. Their ideal of patriotism is too abstract to matter.

Jack tells Henry he is on the list of those to be assassinated, and Henry spends the better part of a year hiding because, even though the Truce between Ireland and Britain is effected, the Irish Civil War is raging. He misses the birth of his daughter Saoirse.

Finally, realizing that he must emigrate to stay alive, Henry first visits Dolly Oblong's brothel, where he learns that Gandon has had the Climanises executed and, long previously, Henry Sr. Granny Nash is correct in that Gandon, despite his respectability, is nevertheless still a murderous gangster, ordering many of the hits for which Henry has been responsible. An enraged Henry clubs Gandon to death, trying to kill the pain of his own past as well as punishing Gandon for being the puppet master in Henry's own sordid life.

Lastly, Henry visits Kilmainham Jail where Miss O'Shea is now imprisoned. The two shout goodbyes before Miss O'Shea is dragged off by the jailers. Nevertheless, Henry leaves us on a positive note: "I'd start again. A new man. I had money to get me to Liverpool and a suit that didn't fit. I had a wife I loved in jail and a daughter called Freedom I'd held only once. I didn't know where I was going. I didn't know if I'd get there. But I was still alive. I was twenty. I was Henry Smart" (542).

Argument

Doyle has carefully constructed "his story" in an attempt to promote his theme: demythologizing "history" in the search for truth. Doyle uses characterization as the primary tool to introduce and further this theme. No one-dimensional heroes or situations exist in the novel. When a character tries to believe or exist in a one-dimensional, mythologized world, such as Henry's initial belief in the purity of the revolution, that character endangers himself and those around him by his self-deceit. History is alive, and failing to realize this—even at the expense of the Irish struggle for Independence--can irrevocably damage the present. Thus, the novel shows that a living history and a living present, no matter how sordid, are ultimately much richer than dead, sanitized ones.

It is through Henry that we see the battle between reality and mythology most forcefully. Henry, a born storyteller, has a penchant for romanticizing events and is able to create a believable reality easily, his inheritance as a denizen of the slums: "Stories are the only things the poor owned" (9). Indeed, names like Silver Alley and Standfast Lane mask dark, filthy, dead-end streets.

The ability to create is also a legacy from his parents. Henry, by his own admission, is descended from fiction-makers: His father "made his life up as he went along. . . .He invented himself, and reinvented. He left a trail of Henry Smarts before they finally disappeared . . .Was he just a liar? No, I don't think so. He was a survivor; his stories kept him going" (9). When he meets Melody and hears her musical name, Henry says, his father immediately begins to imagine: "With a name like that beside him, he'd find his leg, a new one would grow out of the stump, he'd stride through open doors for the rest of his life. He'd find money on the street, three-legged chickens. . . . He saw what he wanted to see" (7).

Her musical name has the same effect upon Henry Sr as Jack Dalton's lyrics have on his son: "Both Melody and the song incite Henry Sr. and Jr. to action, respectively in the form of marriage and joining the IRA—two disparate demonstrations of lifelong commitment and loyalty. These decisions give a sense of purpose to the men's existence, yet, at the same time, each Henry remains quite oblivious to the consequences and context of their actions" (Jacklein 133). When Henry Sr falls in love with Dolly, he repeats his modus operandi: "He'd become devoted to a woman of his own making, as false as her teeth and hair. . . .he fell in love with another of his own creations. . . .she knew how to make money but she was just a big old tart who was too lazy to get out of bed more than once or twice a week" (167). Thus, "his self-creation . . . easily turn[s] into self-delusion" (Lanters 251).

Henry tends to mythologize his father while exposing the folly of his father's own mythologizing: The "tap tap tap" of his father's wooden leg becomes an incantation of sorts. "For both men, the wooden leg becomes "the 'magic bat' of the pantomime capable of transforming reality" (Pearse qtd. in Lanters 250) as well as "both a practical and a supernatural means of dealing with the brutalities of the real world" (Lanters 250). The wooden leg, with its paradoxical brutal killing power and regenerative divining power, is a metaphor for the conflicting nature of mythmaking.

Melody too immediately creates her own fantasy, seeing honesty in Henry Sr the first time she sees him. She likes "the space where the leg should have been," implying that she prefers the thought of the leg—with all the possibilities for that leg—to an actual leg. Later, after the deaths of her children, she assuages her grief at their loss by believing they are stars in the sky.

The fight which destroys the couple's short-lived happiness at Henry's healthy birth is over reality, or rather, whose fiction is dominant. Henry Sr wants to name the newborn Henry, despite its being the name of their deceased first-born son. "Naming me Henry would take the pain and weight away; it would let them start again. It would let them include the dead in their new life" (33). But Melody sees it differently: "We already have a Henry. . . .—But he's dead, said my father. I heard a gasp. My mother shook her head and hid behind her hair" (33). The fight escalates until the newborn is indeed named Henry: "The stars are only stars and his name's Henry, d'you hear me" (34). Although Henry Sr prevails and the infant is named Henry, Melody persists in believing the deceased Henry is a star. She won't be forced into giving up her fictional world.

The downfall of both characters is their respective beliefs in their own created realities. Melody believes in the star called Henry; Henry Sr believes in the star called Dolly. Melody descends into an alcoholic stupor with little grip on reality; Henry Sr dedicates his life to a madam whom he mistakenly believes is the puppeteer of the Dublin slums. However, the reader doesn't judge; any fiction, no matter how desperate, seems better than their actual lives, even though both fictions destroy their lives and the lives of their children.

Getting back to Henry: Despite being drawn to storytelling, the narrator Henry knows how dangerous this inheritance is, although he is constantly seduced by it. Henry is constantly searching for the truth while wanting illusion: The baby Henry "looked for a nipple in his [father's] coat. My lips met with dust and blood. I tasted awful secrets" (34). Imagination can only mask reality. It can't eradicate it, as he knows: "What did Melody Nash look like? She was sixteen. That's all I know. . . I can create a good-looking sixteen-year-old. I can make her a stunner. I can make her plainer then, widen her, spoil her complexion. I can play this game for what's rest of my life but I'll never see Melody Nash, my sixteen-year-old mother" (7). When consciously playing the game of re-creating the details of his parents' lives, he strives for authenticity: though he invents the details of his parents' courtship, he allows reality-type moments to intrude. Note the wedding scene, in which the matrons advise Melody about human reproduction. The innocent Melody is terrified of the horrible stories and is "saved" only by Granny Nash's bloody attack upon the beer-stealing interlopers.

This realistic imagining only blurs the line between fiction and reality for Henry, something he (and we) struggle with. Indeed, his whole existence is an attempt to draw a line in the sand between the two and assert the primacy of truth. Henry loses in this struggle. He, stretching reality, describes his own birth as mythic, "presenting himself as a slum-born heroic alternative to the demi-god Cuchulain, complete with miraculous birth and precocious boyhood deeds" (Lanters 252). However, the living Henry's mythology is not as powerful as his mother's stories of his dead brother, the star, and Henry is relegate to an "also ran" status: "I was the other Henry. The shadow. The impostor" (Doyle, *A Star Called Henry* 34). The dead brother, the star, is the real Henry. Throughout the novel, Henry yells, "My name is Henry Smart" (36), attempting to thrust himself into his story and history, but never quite doing so. Fiction displaces reality in Henry's mind, as it does no matter how hard he searches for reality.

Notably, Henry's alias when he surrenders with the other GPO rebels is "Brian O'Linn," a character featured in many folk ballads. "The song, 'Brian O'Linn, dates back to at least the sixteenth century, is found in England, Scotland, Ireland, and America, and exists in as many variations as Henry Smart has identities. In most versions, Brian's main characteristic, like Henry's is that, poor though he is, he is extremely resourceful and can invent himself and his attributes out of virtually nothing" (Lanters 250). Henry, who comes to have his own songs, becomes as created a character as Brian O'Linn.

Being an inheritor to such imagination, Henry allows himself to be marginalized by his brother the star. However, in actuality, he is already negated by his poverty and class, initially, and the fiction of equality, ultimately, which force him to remain on the fringes of important events. Henry is a smudge on the events of history: At the Richmond Barracks, he is standing next to Eamon de Valera during "the famous photo. The last man to surrender. Hands behind his back, a Tommy on each side of him, another behind. . . .Just all de Valera and his guards, three English kids barely bigger than their rifles" (Doyle, *A Star Called Henry* 140). However, Henry's elbow is the only piece of Henry to make the photo, and even it is eventually cropped out. Henry is marginalized and cut out in the photo as he is most of the situations he encounters. Reality and his failure to see it serve only to make him the pawn of others' ideas, just like his father is.

Henry's next lesson in the danger of believing created realities occurs during Edward VII's visit. Amid the huzzahs and hoorahs, Henry angrily lashes out at the Irishmen who espouse a loyalty to a king who pretends concern. Henry's "Fuck off" lands him and Victor into trouble, from which their father rescues them. During the float down "Swan River," the sewer, Henry's father "invented the world above us" (59) to pacify his young sons. Henry is captivated by the stories and is seduced by the comforts that imagination can bring—in this case, believing his father's paternal concern will last. However, after his father unceremoniously deposits Victor and him onto the street, reality sets in, all the more painful because of his few moments of illusion:

His words burst and disappeared in front of me as I crawled over and peered through the slats and tried to see him. . . .I wished now that he'd never seen me. . . .the royal procession, my perch on the lamppost—I tried to knock them all out of my head. His hands as he lifted me, the crazy escape, his laugh, his hands as he lifted me—I dropped my head onto the cobbles again, and again and again. I made darkness to match what we'd had down below but nothing came back with it. I was absolutely alone. But then Victor was crying, pining for something he'd never had. . . .I tried and tried to forget the last hours and minutes. . .And then I was dead for a while. . . Until something dragged me by the collar, pulled me so that I had to breath, lifted my head and dropped it, and there was pain again. And did it again. (61)

The fun stories, the paternal concern, and the feel of a loving father make Henry believe in the fiction of a paternal relationship, which makes his return to reality all the more painful as he returns home "to the stinking, smoke-choked hollow and the wet basement and our share of our poor mother's lap. I led the way, staring through the dried blood and the agony and the heartache that made a little death of every step away from the rusty shore and the river under it" (62). Henry learns again that believing in an illusion comes with a heavy price, namely, the pain that sets in when that fiction cannot be sustained.

He is able to capitalize somewhat upon this knowledge. He and Victor are "the only beggars who never asked for money" because they trade on people's dreams: "I knew who they were talking about and what they really wanted. I was never a child. I could read their eyes. I could smell their longing and pain. I'd stand right up against them, confuse them, harass them. Guilt would open their purses. And shame threw the spondulix at us" (67). He can even seduce animals: With boiled-rat-baby soup rubbed on his arms, he easily captures adult rats by tricking them into running to him, "sniffing for their children on my wrist and fingers . . .before the rats knew that they were licking the hand of the killer [of their children]" (69). Henry has begun to learn how to write, though, not to believe his own fictions: He is careful not to think that "we'd be allowed up the bright steps and into the comfort and warmth behind the doors and windows." He knows "we would never going to prosper" (68). No matter how many women throw coins at him or how the men applauded his rat-catching prowess, he knows, on some level, that he is destined to be an outsider.

The lesson is beaten into him again during his first brush with formal education, resulting in his refusal to believe in any sort of inclusive God, especially the Catholic God of his fellow Irish. Not willing to believe in an intangible being that seems to have left him on the streets as unceremoniously as Henry Sr does, he wants "less prayers, more information" (76). He sees no reason to study a God that he has never seen, who seems to have left him and all the impoverished behind, and whose hymns would "earn no shillings . . . on the streets" (77). Because he has none, one of the foci of Henry's early life is getting money — even when he "buys" into the Irish Republic, he doesn't forget to make it profitable by skimming 10 percent off the top of all his enterprises.

In the school, he falters, almost believing in the permanence of "the warmth. . .the woman [Miss O'Shea] who'd made him feel wanted" (81). Like the last encounter with his father, the initial comfort of Storyland is followed by a devastating brutality. After being confronted by the harsh Mother Superior, he is finished with God: Miss O'Shea is merely "a lucky knock on the door" and "the nun had been the normal one. . . .Fuck her. And religion. I already hated it. . . .Fuck Him. And your man on the cross up over the blackboard. Fuck Him too. That was one good thing that came out of all the neglect: we'd no religion. We were free. We were blessed" (82). Ironically, Henry uses his imagination to reconfigure what he considers to be the destruction of a figment of imagination, God.

In the novel, nothing occurs to reunite him with religion, which he (and Doyle) see as no more than a formalized system for wish fulfillment and self-deception. The masses use religion in order to get something—be it safety during the bloody Easter Rising or healing from a bloody statue. Henry disdains the prayers of his fellow soldiers: "Behind me, my colleagues and comrades, my fellow revolutionaries, were on their knees—and they'd been on them and off them all day—with their eyes clamped shut, their heads bowed and their cowering backs to the barricades. What sort of a country were we going to create? If we were attacked now, we were fucked. I didn't want to die in a monastery" (114). (Interestingly, Henry is having sex when the real fighting begins—at least the bead counters are at their posts.) The religious soldiers "clung to their beads like their mammies' fingers" when the fighting begins, imperiling the other soldiers and forcing Collins, Henry's mentor, to yell, "Get rid of the beads and pick up your rifles" (114). Connolly is honest with Henry about using the belief in God to win the revolution: "We need Him on our side. And all His followers" (99), although he sees the religious soldiers as "gobshites. . .Catholic and capitalist. . . .It's an appalling combination" (117). Henry observes Catholics believing in God as long as "their will be done," and as Henry's will is never done, he sees no use in prayer. Additionally, Catholics' strong devotion to the Virgin Mother Mary fails to move Henry, understandably as his prolific mother only fails him and marginalizes him. Thus, Henry won't allow himself to believe in something so patently unreal as a benevolent God.

The 14-year-old soldier of the Easter Rising has seemingly learned the lesson, and poverty and misfortune have given the adolescent an adult cynicism. During the Easter Rising, Henry remains unswayed by the illusions of the others with whom he is barricaded and denigrates them privately. He has no compunction about stealing 10 percent from the tills (105) before he distributes the money to the wives of soldiers fighting for Britain in World War I. Because of his poverty, he hates the idealism of the privileged "Volunteers. The poets and the farm boys, the fuckin' shopkeepers. They detested the slummers—the accents and the dirt, the Dublinness of them. When was the last time Collins had been hungry? I knew the answer just by looking at the well-fed puss on him" (105). The hungry don't have the luxury of political ideals, and Home Rule "meant nothing to us who had no homes" (72). As previously mentioned, he doesn't fire upon the Republic's enemy but instead shoots at the stores from which he has been excluded.

Henry is not the pure cynic, however. His one "weakness," which endears him to the reader, is a desperate faith in people who make him feel both important and masculine: He says that Miss O'Shea "made a man of me" (125). Of Victor, whose dependence makes Henry responsible to someone, he says, "I loved him so much. I was able to stand up through the pain and blindness" (61). Finally, Connolly:

> wasn't just a man; he was all of us. We all needed him. He'd made us all believe in ourselves. . . .He'd fed me, given me clothes, he let me sleep in the Hall. He made me read. He let me know that he liked me. He explained why we were poor and why we didn't have to be. He told me that I was right to be angry. He was always busy and distant but there was always a wink or a quick grin as he looked up from his work or passed me. He wanted me there. (128)

Henry won't let the images of his beloveds become tarnished by real life. His desire to remain ignorant of his wife's first name demonstrates his desire to keep those he loves on a pedestal. "Henry deliberately never learns her first name and always calls her Miss O'Shea, so that he will always perceive her as his superior" (Lanters 249). His loyalty to Victor, who remains preserved in the innocence and purity of childhood, causes him to turn on his fellow soldiers who want to shoot Irish looters. He won't allow the ideologues to fire upon the impoverished looters, who represent Victor to Henry, even if the looters mean that "we'll be hanging our heads in shame among the nations of the world" (116) as one of the Volunteer officers claims. Years later, the thought of Victor and Miss O'Shea keep him alive after he's been shot. Finally, the worst part about the revolution, for

Henry, is his loneliness: "I was alone and I had to stay that way. . .But sometimes, usually in the early evening . . .I mourned the living as well as the dead and I ached for Dublin. . .I felt the homesickness like a sudden, slow bit into my heart, because I knew that I was going to have to get up and go away again the next day" (Doyle, *A Star Called Henry* 255). Thus, Victor, Miss O'Shea and Connolly retain a special, unspoiled position in Henry's heart.

Admiration and devotion, however, don't come easily to Henry. For instance, the "heroes" of the Revolution are anything but heroic according to Henry's standards. Pearse was "fat and his arms had no more muscle that his poetry" and prepares himself for "an elegant death" by "hiding his squint" (117). Henry "especially dislikes Padraic Pearse, since he perpetuated the symbols of the nation Henry most fervently dismisses. Pearse's foundational myths of Irish identity were identified with 'the three mothers of our historical memory: the mother church of the Catholic revival; the motherland of the nationalist revival; and the mother-tongue of the Gaelic revival'" (Lanters and Kearney qtd in Lanters 254). Clarke was "as old and frail as Ireland; MacDiarmada, left lopsided by polio, was leaning on his stick; Plunkett had his neck wrapped in bandages and looked like death congealing" (Doyle, *A Star Called Henry* 95). Plunkett, because of tuberculosis, is "a waste of a bullet," but nevertheless has "the energy to beat his breast and drive his knees into the tiles" (117), another aspect for which Henry disparages him. During the executions, Henry remains in a virtual sexual stupor, from which only Connolly's death rouses him.

Henry's cynicism betrays him, however, when he meets Jack Dalton. Seduced by the warmth of a room and a full stomach, he believes Dalton's speeches even when he can see the contradictions in them:

He could deliver sense and shite in the one sentence. And it struck me even then, although I didn't think much about it at the time, that his Ireland was a very small place. Vast chunks of it didn't fit his bill; he had grudges stored up against the inhabitants of most of the counties. His republic was going to be a few blameless pockets, connected to the capital by vast bridges of his own design. But I liked listening to him and loved the idea of knocking down Dublin and starting afresh. (173)

Out of a neediness which he doesn't readily admit, Henry places much of his trust in Jack, and, by extension, the rebellion:

And I believed him. . . .The night before I'd been homeless and alone and now I was warm and full, in the wild and generous company of Jack Dalton, my new friend and old comrade in arms. . . .And by the time he announced that he had the legs walked off his tongue and he needed some sleep for the next day, I was ready to die again for Ireland; me, who had never been further than Lucan, who less than a year before had jumped over the bodies of friends lying dead and destroyed, who would never have given a fuck what de Valera sang in his prison cell. I was ready to die for Ireland. . . .for a version of Ireland that had little or nothing to do with the Ireland I'd gone out to die for the last time. (173)

Henry accepts, adopts, and enjoys this patent fiction and ignores the cognitive dissonance.

Why does Jack's message get past Henry's reality filters? Because it touches his two soft spots, class injustice and the need to belong. Dalton promises autonomy, kinship, and power: "We're the gods here, man" (188). To someone who has never had the luxury of acting but only reacting to circumstances, leadership and legendary status are heady prospects. He is seduced by this image of himself and becomes "one self-important little rebel" (210). Later, a more introspective Henry admits his neediness: "I wondered why I was doing it, far from

Jack and Collins and songs written about me. But some memory of belief would calm me, a feeling of belonging that came when I thought of the people I knew and, always, it was parts of them that came to me. . . . .And I knew why I was there, on the damp floors of those strangers' houses, and I knew that I was right and it gave a point to my loneliness and made a good friend of my anger" (229). To someone who has rarely known love, admiration is a heady prospect as well, and Henry relishes the feeling of belonging. He readily believes Jack's lies about the ballad beginning, "The pride of all Gaels was the young Henry Smart" (172) and sees himself as mythic as Brian O'Linn: "I was a walking saint. . .I quickly loved the silence and adoration that were coming my way" (174).

The song Jack sings cements the deal for Henry. His reaction to the song mirrors his reaction to Jack's speech: "On hearing the song, for the first time in his life Henry Smart feels that he has been given identity and importance—an offer he is unable to refuse" (Jacklein 141). The song "creates a brief moment of harmony but eventually leads to violence. . . . [It is] a negative force that blatantly—and very effectively—simplifies reality and glorifies violence. . . .[The song] proves pivotal, as it leads Henry to replace his apolitical stance with blind loyalty to the rebel cause" (Jacklein 130, 131, 132). Henry, as susceptible to music as his father, loses much of his self-interested, reality-based perspective, after hearing the song. Unlike Henry Sr who creates his idol in Dolly, Henry co-opts Jack's idol simply because it is Jack's. He loses himself and allows himself to believe "It'll be a better one [world] soon. And, the day that was in it, I believed what I'd said" (236). There is little difference in the two male Smarts, and "Henry called his father a gobshite for doing much the same thing, and for similarly believing in his own mythical creations" (Lanters 253).

His desire for freedom and importance almost blind him to reality. Even though he knows the truth, he almost wilfully continues to believe in the myth of Dalton's dream. He knows about the revolution's misrepresentations of the truth: "The vote meant choice, but there was no choice. There was only one right way. Some of us knew the way and it was up to us to lead, not to ask permission of a voting majority, but to lead, to really lead, to show, demonstrate, live, die. To inspire, provoke, and terrify" (Doyle, *A Star Called Henry* 211). He knows the power of flattery and playing to one's ego: "We have to convince them that they have no betters" (220) and "a bit of flattery makes great rebels" (251). When he flatters his "country lads," he says, "I watched them inflating; they were important, singular men, and I'd told them so" (216). He knows the concept of puppeteers and puppets, as "we knew how to make them [Black and Tans] set fire to the right house. We controlled them" (265).

He knows all about lying, flattery and coercion, but he can't recognize when they are used on him. Even though Collins bluntly tells Henry, "You don't exist," he believes him when he promises, "We'll give you your rank when it's all over" (217). When Henry questions Dalton, specifically about Gandon's presence in the GPO, Dalton uses the same, hackneyed yet effective techniques Collins uses. He tells Henry, "You're the real thing. You're the one that'll be remembered, not me" (258). Henry readily accepts Dalton's version, in which he stars, as easily as the country lads accept Henry's flattery. Henry becomes aware that he is a pawn much too late:

> There was no Henry Smart M.P. I was four years short of the voting age, I was never a member of Sinn Fein; I wouldn't have stood for election if I'd been asked, but that was the point, and a point that didn't drill itself into my head until 1922; I hadn't been asked. I was bang in the middle of what was going to become big, big history, I was shaping the fate of my country, I was one of Collins's anointed but, actually, I was excluded from everything. . . .And none of the other men of the slums and hovels ever made it on to the list. We were nameless and expendable, every bit as dead as the squaddies in France. (210)

The narrator Henry is able to see the reality, but the young Henry is almost completely blind to it.

Henry isn't completely devoted to the ideal and the cause however. He retains some of his original self-interest. For instance, he still takes his ten percent from the monies he collects for guns and for the Republic, as well as from the money he appropriates from the GPO for the National Loan. He also uses his status as a war hero to seduce women: With no compunction, he "rides the arse off the mother of one of 1916's executed heroes" and "was just doing what came natural: I was fucking women who wanted to fuck me" (179). Henry's excessive sexuality is a sign that he has not totally surrendered himself to the movement: "Yeats, Synge, and O'Casey had already each in their own way, diagnosed the connection between sexual repression and excessive nationalistic zeal" (Kiberd qtd. in Lanters 236), and it, therefore, comes as no surprise that Doyle's Henry Smart "expresses his exuberant sexuality as an ironic comment on various national sacred cows" (Lanters 255). Notice that in one encounter with Piano Annie, Henry can't stop thinking of the lyrics to "The Rocky Road to Dublin", thus illustrating how his sexuality is undermining his zeal for his country. Miss O'Shea, whose name reminds us of the name of Parnell's mistress, tears her skirt "for Ireland" the first time she and Henry have sex in the GPO, and she becomes noticeably more excited the more patriotic his pillow talk becomes, despite the fact that her behavior becomes less patriotic. She misses part of the fighting, as I mentioned earlier, because she and Henry are having sex. When Henry begins to train the men in the country, he doesn't mind their hostility because "there was some sort of inverse relationship between their animosity and my success with their sisters, wives, and mothers" (Doyle, *A Star Called Henry* 214). Lanters puns that, "given that his daughter's name is Saorirse, one could argue that he is 'riding' to free the nation" (255).

Doyle describes Henry's sexuality in terms of realism and characterization, as well as debunking another predominant myth of Ireland, namely that the "chaste virgin or . . . adoring mother" (Lanters 255). Doyle says that Henry "was actually a very passive character even though he's a man of action. Things happen to him — women discover him. . . . .The official thing was sex was something around that you had to endure. It wasn't to be a recreation. And it never got a reference in public. . . . In my lifetime, things have changed dramatically. A politician said that there was no sex in Ireland. Obviously it's a silly thing to say. . . . If Henry is going to have sex with Miss. O'Shea, then it is going to be in the middle of the GPO" (Doyle, Personal interview 240).

Meeting David Climanis and his wife widens the breech in Henry's loyalty. Henry breaks the IRA's secrecy and confides in Climanis: "And I told him everything. I couldn't understand what was happening to me. It just seemed safe and right. It was in every crease and gesture: he was a good man" (Doyle, *A Star Called Henry* 246). Note that the sense of safety, warmth, and belonging is again what seduces Henry. When Dalton warns Henry to stop seeing Climanis, Henry's two loyalties collide: "Mister Climanis was sound. I knew that much. But so was Jack" (253).

Although he doesn't have the time to tell anyone, participating in the Bloody Sunday murders sours Henry on being an assassin for the revolution: "Henry slowly learns that, just as there's no such thing as abstract math, there's no such thing as abstract death" (Levi 2). He is almost immediately captured and imprisoned after the murders. His silence during the months in prison are more out of self-preservation than loyalty to the republicans: He knows that the British cannot execute him if they do not definitively know his identity. The imprisonment highlights his solitary existence and the fallacy of his beliefs in the Brotherhood. His IRA brothers don't save him; his wife saves him. Denied the spiritual purification an escape via the waters of the sewer would provide him, he instead rides (this time, not meant sexually) the bus to freedom and hibernates in restorative sleep, which removes him further from his past.

The midnight visit from Ivan literally wakes him out of his stupor. Henry realizes that Ivan is not interested in Ireland and only wants Irish rule, or, more aptly, his own rule, when Ivan says:

> I was doing my accounts one night there and I suddenly realized that I already controlled the island, my part of it anyway. The war was over. Nothing moves in this county without my go-ahead. . . Ireland free in some shape or form. It'll happen before the end of the year. There'll be one almighty row about it, holy war, boy, brother against brother and the rest, but I'm in no hurry. I'm ready for it and I have no brothers, only dead ones. I'll be on the right side. I'll be ready to lead my people into the new Ireland.. . .It might well be [very much like the old one] but it'll be ours. . . .And when it's over and the guns are rusty, they'll love me and remember who freed them. But they'll also remember that they were once terrified of me, although they'll never say anything about it. It's only my version that'll get talked about. They'll love me and elect me because I'm the man that freed his country. (515, 516)

The realization that the new Ireland "will be very like the old one" (315) and that "the oppressed have become the oppressors" (Lanters 256) slaps Henry in the face:

> There was no pretending now: I was a complete and utter fool, the biggest in the world. It had been niggling away at me for years but now I knew. Everything I'd done, every bullet and assassination, all the blood and brains, prison, the torture, the last four years and everything in them, everything had been done for Ivan and the other Ivans, the boys whose time had come. That was Irish freedom, since Connolly had been shot-and if the British hadn't shot him one of the Ivans would have; Connolly would have been safely dead long before now, one of the martyrs, dangerous alive,

more useful washed and dead. (Doyle, *A Star Called Henry* 318)

Henry has become the victim of his own creation, just as his father has. "Henry has become his father—a fool and a gobshite, a believer in his own mythical creations, about to be killed by those for whom he used to kill" (Lanters 256). Henry finally becomes aware that

> the brunt of that violence is borne by the poor and the working class. For Henry, the gains of the revolution are seriously qualified, and the new "independence" is full of ironies. He realizes that he has never been free, that revolutionaries as oppressive as the English power structure that they have supplanted have coopted his consciousness. Some hope remains in his little daughter Saoirse ("freedom"), but for Henry and for Ireland freedom remains an elusive abstraction. (Marsh 158)

After Ivan's visit, Henry, although his eyes have been opened, ironically climbs back "through the hole to the kitchen" of the burned-out structure in which he is hiding. Significantly, however, he climbs back into the kitchen, the center of a family and of a home. He quits his blind allegiance to the republican leaders and instead places his own (and his family's safety) over the revolution. He tries to get his wife to leave the movement, using her pregnancy as a reason she should desist from her revolutionary activities. She, a zealot, refuses, but at least she promises to stay away from Ivan's territory, who has threatened to harm her if she continues to ignore his "control" of his territory.

Sensing his change, like a shark senses blood, the revolution's leaders place Henry on the list of those to be killed. They won't countenance any changes in their devotees, just as mythologies cannot exist with alternating viewpoints. Henry's faith in Dalton, while misplaced, is yet well placed: Dalton warns him about the execution order, but he doesn't prevent it.

After a year of hiding from the IRA, Henry knows he must emigrate and leave his newly born daughter and wife. Before leaving, however, he tries to strike out and leave his former passivity. Aware that he is the author of his father's and the Climanises' deaths, as well as the impetus behind many of the men Henry himself executes, Henry confronts the powerful and wealthy Gandon and kills him. Ultimately, this action is futile as Gandon is not responsible for all the destruction and hypocrisy but is merely a pawn in someone else's bigger game. Indeed, like the gurgoyle's spewing rainwater on Fanny Robin's grave, newly dug and decorated by a repentant Sergeant Troy, in Hardy's *Far From the Madding Crowd*, Gandon dies laughing at Henry's meager attempt to right the betrayals of himself, his family, and his class. Indeed, after he leaves his wife at Kilmainham, (thus again imitating his father's actions of leaving his young family) he overhears women speaking of Gandon's death: "He must have been in a state of grace, all the same. Or near enough to it" (342). Gandon's reputation is intact, and Henry is still on the margins.

While Henry shows us the danger of mythologizing, Doyle furthers this theme by employing other characters. For instance, Alfie Gandon personifies the process of mythologizing—the actual change history undergoes as it becomes myth. Henry senses that the secret of Gandon's real identity is important, although he "was lost, but I knew that I was close. Close to what, I didn't know" (165). Henry's feelings towards Gandon mirror his ambivalence toward the revolution, its leaders, and the new Ireland. Notice that he calls Michael Collins "a great man. I loved him. But I wanted to hurt him" (201). Unconsciously, he feels that if he can discover the truth about Gandon/O'Ganduin, he can discover the truth about the revolution and about Ireland. However, the process of mythologizing is subtle: Henry can neither grasp the truth behind the Revolution nor the truth behind Gandon.

Throughout the novel, Henry obsesses over the question of the identity of Alfie Gandon, one of the faces of the revolution but one of the faces of the Dublin underground as well. Gandon is very slippery: Henry Sr "walked past him every night of the week and he never saw him" (165). In this way, he is directly compared to Michael Collins, who "was a plastic man. Everyone knew him but no one could describe him" (193). Gandon is able to be what people want him to be: A bouncer calls him, "a businessman, and one of our own. . . .He was a Home Ruler and a Catholic, not like most of the tail-coated fuckers who robbed the people blind and called it business" (167). Dalton claims he is "one of us. . . .He's a giant in this city, man. Property, transport, banking, Corpo. He's in on them all. He's a powerful man, Henry. And a good one. There's more widows and orphans living off that fella's generosity than the nuns could ever handle. And he doesn't like to boast about it either. . .he's perfect. . . .He's our respectable face" (191). Granny Nash, one of the few who can link him directly to his past, sees him most clearly as "a landlord and a killer. . . .He's still up to his old tricks. . . .The things the wooden fella used to do for him. Except he has other eejits now to do his dirty work for him. He hasn't changed a bit" (167, 241). Dolly Oblong is another who can link Gandon to his past. She says:

> Mister O'Ganduin is a national politician, of a new nation eager to prove itself to the world. The world is watching Mister O'Ganduin and he loves this. . .But he has been slow to give up his old life. He is still Alfie Gandon. He was worried that the new nation would not live. And so, he kept his old business interests. This house. His other interests. But he was wrong. The nation will live and he must kill Alifie Gandon. He must kill the past. (536)

The novel thus indicates that the new Ireland is nothing more than the old Ireland, just with an egalitarian name and a better haircut. The Irish people have unwittingly traded British tyranny for Irish tyranny, although they will be unable to realize this once the past has been killed.

The mythologizing process is a dangerous one, however. Although the myth lives on (in the form of women speaking about his death), Gandon himself is killed by his own creations, Dolly and Henry. He is unable to kill his past, and instead, his past ends up killing him. The same could happen to modern-day Ireland—economically and socially--if it persists in believing the one-dimensional version of its past.

Granny Nash, the voraciously reading crone, not only knows the past but is the past that Gandon wants to kill. Indeed, the present-day Ireland of the novel virtually murders her, as she is almost unable to exist in it and becomes a non-person in the context of the novel. She consciously hides in her imagination—in the form of reading novels--instead of confronting reality, of which she has a pretty firm grasp. Doyle uses fiction to show how fiction has been used to deny the past.

Granny Nash isn't always like this. We first see Henry's maternal grandmother at Melody and Henry Sr's wedding, when she attacks

> a couple of moochers that nobody knew [who] were caught helping themselves to the bottles of stout. . . . Granny Nash jumped onto one of them and bit him on the cheek. . .the sight of her mother hanging on to the poor man's face filled her with fresh terrors. . . The neighbours queued up to have a go at the moochers but Granny Nash wasn't ready to give up and hand over. She was growling and chomping like a scorched bitch from hell; her dirty old thumbs were crawling across the man's face, looking for eyes to gouge. . . .Melody wouldn't kiss her mother; the moocher's blood was still on her chin, her eyes were tiny and mad. (12-13)

Granny Nash, obviously, is a force to be reckoned with. When she sees what she deems to be injustice, she fights back and wins.

At Henry's birth, suddenly the illiterate woman is able to read. She first reads the newspapers on which her daughter gives birth, and she doesn't stop reading. After Henry's family disintegrates, she is his only remaining relative, and she, perhaps because of the newly found knowledge gained from all the newspapers, retreats into reading novels. Books are her refuge and provide stability, something that life in the Dublin slums is sorely lacking. She prefers female authors and is a particular fan of Edith Wharton, whose novels encompass a world diametrically opposed to her own. By reading, she leaves behind the sordid world of hired killings, poverty, disease, and dying family members. She doesn't change, except to hide further and further behind the ever growing stack of books. However, she never makes the mistake of Flaubert's Emma Bovary and believes that reality should mirror fiction; she uses fiction because she believes as Flaubert said, "Life is tolerable only if one can conjure it away" (qtd. in Elkins).

Seemingly untouched by the violence around her and protected by her web of fiction, she is the only one Henry is able to ask for information. She seems to know not only about Henry's parents but also about the power struggles of the Dublin she inhabits. However, she is stingy with the information and will parcel out tidbits in exchange for books—she will return to reality only when an escape into a better world is assured with the advent of new reading material. Albeit unattractive, even repulsive, Granny Nash is a victim of the horrible conditions in Ireland, the Ireland that the nationalists want to kill. Granny Nash's escape into a fictional reality is even more dangerous for the nationalists than it is for her. Firstly, what kind of a country is it, asks the novel, in which all the citizens must escape, literally and figuratively, to survive? Secondly, what kind of a country fears its past, a past from which it cannot escape?

Finally, we have Dolly Oblong, the madam of Alfie Gandon's brothel where Henry Sr is employed as a bouncer. Many of the novel's characters have rightly been called "Dickensian grotesques." Dolly, for one, could nestle quite comfortably amid the pages of *The Old Curiosity Shop* along side of Granny Nash. She is not only a fictional curiosity but also a representation of the Irish myth, its static view of its history.

When we are first introduced to Dolly, seen through Henry Senior's perspective filtered through Henry's narration, she is described as:

> . . . a black mountain. . . . A head that was made huge by hair that would have been plenty for five women. It was a wig, Henry knew. It was one of the things he knew about his employer: she was bald. . .Another thing he knew about her: she was twenty-five. She looked and moved like a monument but she was younger than he was. It had been her brothel since he'd been the bouncer; she couldn't have been far past fifteen when she became the madam. . . .There was a hint of the foreigner in her words, just now and again. . . .She was a grand chunk of a woman. (41)

She has an overpowering "magnificence [with] her eyes made huge by belladonna, by the smell of peppermint that strayed from her mouth to his" (51) and rarely leaves her bed. Even twenty years later, when Henry Jr first meets her, "she was gorgeous. . . .She was hair and lips and eyes that were black, just beyond the power of the lamp. She was wearing a red gown that showed off white shoulders and all of her was massive" (334). Dolly is an early 20th century Dolly Parton, unchanging because she is an illusion of wigs, cosmetics, and perfume (but no surgery): "She was her own invention—like him, but successful—her hair, teeth, her name, everything about her and around her. She'd created her own world and made it happen. She pulled strings from her bed" (45). She is well placed as the madam of a brothel, the job of which is creating false realities and selling self-deception.

Similar is the traditional view of Ireland hawked by some of the novel's self-serving revolutionaries who use the passion inspired by the scent of beauty to wage a revolution. They use Ireland, stagnant, unchanging and unreal, as a prop. Note how

Henry describes Jack Dalton's rousing speech: "His republic was going to be a few blameless pockets, connected to the capital by vast bridges of his own design. But I liked listening to him and loved the idea of knocking down Dublin and starting afresh" (173). The Ireland Henry fights for is smoke and mirrors, wigs and false eyelashes, baldness and fat. Henry doesn't even believe in his own Irishness and admits that the men he is drilling are more Irish than he is: "They spoke English but they knew that they were more Irish than I was; they were nearer to being the pure thing" (214). Conversely, the men he trains are as insulated as he is: "They hated anyone or anything from Dublin. Dublin was too close to England; it was where the orders and cruelty came from. And the homespun bollixes in Sinn Fein and the Gaelic League were to blame too; Ireland was everywhere west of Dublin, the real people were set, west, west, as far west as possible, on the islands, the rocks off the islands, speaking Irish and eating wool" (214). In other words, though "more Irish" than Henry, these men are not "pure" either. Thus, we are left with impure Irish fighting for an ideal we discover is just as impure.

Though Dolly is artificially stagnant—all make-up and false hair—she is able to inspire blind and therefore dangerous loyalty. In the first exchange Dolly has with Henry Sr, she chastises him for an over-zealous job performance (being so careful about admitting Johns that business is declining) and allows him to remain although with a cut in pay. She is so alluring, however, that Henry Sr leaves the conversation madly in love, oblivious to his salary reduction. Though in reality powerless--[Henry Sr thinks she is Alfie Gandon, but we learn in the final chapter that she is merely Alfie Gandon's puppet: "I am his past and he will kill me. One night, like tonight perhaps, he will decide that the time has come and he will kill me. Tonight" (336)]—she is powerful: Henry Sr's family is destroyed by his devotion to Dolly, and by association, to Gandon. Indeed, Henry Sr himself is destroyed by his devotion.

Gandon too is destroyed by Dolly, whom he sees as his creation. He believes that he can destroy her as easily as he has created her. Because he can only see one aspect of her, namely, her subservience to him, he fails to see the threat that she poses to him exactly because she is aware of his view of her. Dolly uses his blindness and helps Henry, whom Gandon has created to be the avenging arm of the ideal republic and who can see through Dolly's façade and is thus not in danger from her, to kill him.

The Ireland Jack Dalton sees - and the Ireland which he perpetuates - is also dangerously false. Ultimately, this single-minded view of Ireland, which won't allow for any disparate conceptions, tears the country apart with escalating violence, a Civil War, and the Troubles. Henry is dispatched to kill a number of former comrades; we learn that Dalton is killed eventually; and Henry even surmises that "Connolly would have been safely dead long before now, one of the martyrs, dangerous alive, more useful washed and dead" (318). Thus, as in Shelley's novel *Frankenstein*, the creation - Dolly, Henry, and the revolution--ultimately survive and are the agents of destruction for their various creators.

A Star Called Henry offers an alternate view of Irish history. Through the experiences of our semi-unreliable narrator, we see the in-fighting, the machinations, and the self-serving interests of the real people involved in the revolution. A static, albeit glorious, version of the revolution helps no one, says the novel, and in fact, is damaging. Only when Henry is able to see past the mythology can he escape and create a life not predicated on the destruction of others.

Chapter 3
Rory & Ita

Rory & Ita (2002), Doyle's first foray into memoir, is a quiet book in which Doyle basically transcribes and organizes his parents' individual remembrances, starting with their early childhoods. The chapters alternate between each of his parents, with his mother's voice bookending the text. The book is "a family memoir that spans much of the twentieth century and, in so doing, provides a uniquely personal insight into the day-to-day existence of a working-class family whose origins are in the Irish countryside and whose lives are, subsequently, passed in Dublin" (Hutchings 82).

Doyle explains part of the impetus for the project in the very brief, three-paragraph forward to the book: "I wanted to ask the questions before it was too late. And they wanted to answer them. The book is about my parents, about the people they were before they became parents. But there's very little about parenting. My sisters and brother are born and named, but I didn't think I had the right to bring them into the book." He began the project because:

> I just thought it would be a good idea. For my kids, I suppose. My father had been very ill. He had a series of heart attacks. Luckily he had a series of successful bypass operations in 1992, I think it was. He's done very well since. He's 87 now. I suppose we can all drop off the planet at any time, and I suppose I knew a fundamental part of [my mother's] life was that her mother died, as you know from the book, when she was three. There's only one photo. She didn't know her. She didn't even know her surname. Nobody spoke about it. . . .I suppose those days are over. If anything, people have too many photographs [today]. If you are at an event with children, parents are climbing over each other to record it. It's ludicrous. I think it's calmed

down in recent years. Capturing everything, everything, and everything. But nevertheless, I thought my kids now are old enough to have very clear memories of my parents. I just thought it would be a shame that, if something happened, there would be a mystery attached. So, as a personal thing, as a family record. And, quite early on, I decided - because I know the way their dynamic works - they are very much a team - to isolate them and talk to them and look at their lives before they were the Rory and Ita you know - because even though, strangely, they were born very very close to one another, they didn't meet until they were in their twenties because of their background. That became Chapter One and Chapter Two, and I thought, "Well, there's a book there." . . . .So it's a good story, and I was more convinced the more I looked. So, it became a book even though it didn't start out that way. It was just a personal thing to keep a record. You know, we just like pictures of them and such. (Doyle, Personal interview 230-31).

The short project ultimately became a twenty-one chapter memoir, almost entirely transcribed, which is, as Doyle calls it, "a social history, a social memoir" (Drewett interview 338).

The fairly apolitical, profanity-free *Rory & Ita* is, oddly, controversial. Although the television series *Family* outraged and polarized much of Ireland, *Rory & Ita* caused a stir with his publishers. "If I was to ask a marketing person what are the mistakes to be made along the way, probably the writing of *Rory and Ita* would be a mistake because it confused things. It should have been the one that came after *Henry* on the list [*Play,* then *Dead*] . . . and then *Rory and Ita* [should have been] the one after that. . . .The book sold in very small numbers as that's the type of book that it was. And then when people . . . go up there to the shop, they just look at how much the last one sold. And *Rory and Ita* sold only a few. These are things that have nothing whatsoever to do with the work. And shouldn't. But they do have consequences" (Doyle, Personal interview 235)

Critics, too, have received the book variously: Although Doyle says that "the bulk of the Irish ones were great (Drewett interview 340), some critics call it a glorified vanity press publication: "More common are remarks that this is a vanity project, that it wouldn't have been published without Doyle's famous name, that family stories are generally interesting only to one's own family" (McGlynn23).

These criticisms have merit. Were an average person to transcribe his parents' stories, he most likely would not even be afforded the luxury of a "thanks but no thanks" reply from an agent or a publisher. Very few ordinary people living ordinary lives warrant the interest of the reading public, hence the incidence of authors whose exciting and inspiring memoirs have later proven to be exaggerated at best, entirely fictional at worst. Doyle writes "about two perfectly ordinary lives that have nothing spectacular, but are full of the moments that all lives are. . . .things that attack or fulfill every family" (Drewett interview 337-38). The book is called "mundane to a fault" (McGlynn 23).

Some critics have been charmed by the very likeable couple and acknowledge that, as every individual is unique, reading even the most common, run-of-the-mill transcription of a life can be fascinating and elucidating. "All personal testimony is of historical interest. . . .It's a pity we can't all have our memoires handled with such dignity and care" (Moore 54). Reading the experiences of people who have lived through civil and world wars is fascinating—especially in light of how unaffected they seem to be. Doyle notes the fascination the book would have for Irishmen:

> It began to dawn on me quite early on that these two people had actually lived, barring the first year, right through the history of the Irish Republic and they had lived through all the changes in Ireland. . . .They went from a rigidly Catholic country into a more, perhaps,

liberal country. They witnessed all these changes and they were both intelligent human beings—and I just thought it would be genuinely interesting in all sorts of ways. I didn't know whether it would be of much appeal beyond Ireland or even beyond a certain age group . . . but I just felt there was the makings of a good book in it, and I still do. (Drewett interview 337)

Rory & Ita is "a portrait of life in Ireland from about 1930 on. . . It is delightfully clear that Doyle has captured the Essence of Irish and bottled it at its source" Rourke (1). While Doyle would perhaps disagree that he has "bottled the essence of Irishness" (the slipperiness of this misapplied concept being one of the major and consistent themes throughout Doyle's recent work), reading about the changes brought about, not only in Ireland but in the world, in 80 years is interesting. Also, as an American, it is fascinating to read about "the Emergency" (World War II) through fairly neutral, Irish eyes. Doyle even comments that "it's interesting, that contradictory thing, not being particularly fond of the Nazis, but not being particularly fond of the Allies either, until the Yanks came in and kind of cleared the air a bit" (Drewett interview 338).

Critics also comment on "Doyle's 'self-suppression'" (McGlynn 23). Doyle is actively absent from this book: Indeed, not even Doyle's birth is described, and he is referred to in only one footnote. Although Doyle does write brief passages going into more detail about his grandparents' lives, providing context for various historical figures mentioned, and offering brief transitions, his characteristic narrative voice is almost entirely absent from this work.

Doyle reacts strongly to suggestions that he didn't author *Rory & Ita* and instead merely transcribed the book:

But it was a hard work, it was really, really hard work. Obviously editing, but also, in a broad sense, fashioning the book—trying to come to a compromise between what I was hearing on tape and what was being transcribed. Then making it roll and flow in a way that was honest, that was, if you like, my parents talking, but at the same time I took the editorial liberties that one is entitled to take to make it flow on paper. . . .It was a bit like they gave me the building blocks and they gave me a hand mixing the cement, but, in a way, I built the house. And then someone comes along and they see the house and they say, 'nah you didn't build that - the guy that made the bricks built that.' (Drewett interview 338).

Although it is true that Doyle intrudes little upon the stories his parents tell, he is still present in the editing and juxtaposing of the narratives. As he says in *Oh, Play That Thing*, stories come "from the people who told them. . . .The teller was part of the story" (359). Thus, his hand is all over this work. "It's Roddy's job to take his parents' oral history of their times and relationship and transform it into something interesting. . . Doyle's art consists in taking these disjointed memories and, through discreet stitching, turning them into a smooth narrative fabric" (Alford 23). With the certain he-said, she-said logic to the book, Doyle has shaped his parents' stories to give them cohesion. He has edited, omitting and including certain passages to give the text shape: "The chronological ordering of the memoir also gives it the impression of an unedited text—Doyle has done as much here to obscure his hand as possible" (McGlynn 23).

This chronological ordering is exactly what shows the reader Doyle's hand, which is acknowledged, although through the words of his mother: "The trouble with reminiscing is that, while events occur in chronological order, memories don't. This applies particularly in old age, when one remembers an incident that happened seventy years ago, and yesterday's dinner is a complete blank. Memories are triggered by sights and smells and sounds, and even certain gestures" (Doyle, *Rory & Ita* 335).

Thus, while the reader feels a certain kinship with both the pragmatic and likable couple, the couple is partially Doyle's creation in that he sets the type. Like any good PR man, he creates an image for his parents. While I am not proposing the Doyles are not the engaging people they appear, nevertheless, their son is the filter through which they speak.

While Doyle seems actively absent, confining himself to dry, transitional prose, he is not, and the book dovetails nicely with Doyle's other work and even highlights commonalities and suggests their origins. *Rory & Ita* allows us to glean a significant amount about Doyle the writer and Doyle the man.

Firstly, many of his works, especially the *Barrytown Trilogy*, have been lauded for their heavy reliance upon fast-pace dialogue and genius at capturing the local Dublin speech patterns and dialect. Certainly, this book is taking his penchant and skill to the next obvious level--having no narrative voice and allowing his characters (this time, very real) to speak for themselves. His books are praised for being extraordinarily oral. *Rory & Ita* is that oral tradition taken to an extreme: "Again, like Doyle's other work, the memoir privileges the spoken word, the inflections of voice and conversation. Like *The Commitments*, the book relies almost entirely on quotation, with any narrative presence submerged, factual, declining to interpret" (McGlynn 23).

Secondly, the book examines the ordinary: "In many ways, *Rory & Ita* is a piece with Doyle's earlier works: it glorifies the mundane, from its cover blurb onward. Doyle's opus neatly captures the beauty of the banal, from Sharon Rabbitte's morning sickness to Paddy Clarke's first cigarette, and in the same fashion, *Rory & Ita* revels in the minutiae that often go unnoticed as we go about the business of living" (McGlynn 23). None of Doyle's early works:

> contained the dramatic plot buildup, exciting climaxes, or cathartic resolutions; rather, they traced the mundane ups and down of the sorts of events that happen in all of our lives. *Rory & Ita* takes this nascent

development to the extreme. Even catastrophic or tragic events—the death of a baby, a triple bypass for Rory—are related as events in a long life, with no melodrama or soul-searching attached to them. What's interesting about the lack of plot is the concurrent absence of interpretation. . . .Doyle offers no framework for making these stories anything more than anecdotes. The absence of analysis almost dares the reader to read something into Rory and Ita's lives, much as Doyle's novels can almost mock an audience's effort to see patterns and meaning beyond the novels' own agendas. And Doyle's writing does have its own agenda: the suggestion of all of these formal features, both in his earlier work and in *Rory & Ita*, is that certain hierarchies of expertise and knowledge are unnecessary, corrupt, or alienating. (McGlynn 23)

McGlynn concludes, however, that the lack of an interpretive narrative voice, though theoretically interesting, proposes serious flaws for the book as a whole.

The humor in *Rory & Ita* is also very familiar to his readers. While Ita occasionally relates a humorous tale, Doyle's father is an extraordinarily charming storyteller, relating tales both about himself and about others. Reviewer Mary Rourke says "Rory Doyle is one of the funniest men on Earth, but who would ever know if his novelist son Roddy hadn't written *Rory & Ita*?". Whether he is talking about how he is named (*Rory and Ita* 17), his first attempt at smoking a pipe (124-5), meeting Ita's stepmother (199), or receiving his war wound by scraping his shin on a liquor barrel (122), he is successful at eliciting at least a chuckle from readers. These wry, often self-deprecating stories remind us of the stories told by Doyle's characters, for instance, Paula Spencer, when she remembers the initial stages of her relationship with Charlo and the distinctive side-to-side waddle the two adopt. She and Rory are both able to look back and recognize the absurdity of their younger selves as well as of others. After all, what is comedy but tragedy plus some time?

Additionally, Rory seems to have a streak of the prankster, smoking up an entire building in order "to make the point that I was fed up with what I was doing" (113) or parodying the cartoon pig, "Count Curly Wee," the discovery of which "had all the trappings of a constitutional crisis" (184), both of which incidents almost get him in severe trouble. While Doyle's characters don't play practical jokes per se, Georgina's very name is Sharon's humorous response to all who have snickered behind her back because of her baby's paternity. Rory and Ita's frequent correcting of each other's stories, found in the footnotes, is another source of humor. Their interplay reminds us of the elderly parents in "Funerals." Indeed, the couple in the short story seems to be dead ringers for the Doyles.

While Ita may not be responsible for much of the humor in the book, she is a representative of one of Doyle's strong, almost stoic female characters. Miss O'Shea, a feared IRA operative who saves her husband from death twice, rarely objects and easily and competently establishes her own life completely separate from Henry's. We see her complain once in three volumes, despite spousal neglect and unfaithfulness, abject poverty, immigration, and abandonment. Paula Spencer, who, although initially resorting to alcohol to survive the tremendous pain in her life, ultimately becomes a strong female character.

Like Doyle's other strong female characters, Ita seems to have few, if any, chinks in her armor. She says of her stepmother's abusive treatment:

> And, I suppose, looking back, there were good times and bad times. . . .She wasn't a good cook but, there again, we didn't die of starvation. We got our meals. And my father seemed content. That was the main thing, really. . . .She was alright, as a rule. . . .I suppose, mentally, she could be cruel, and I don't think she really meant to be; it was just the make of the woman. She was very mean. . . .But I was always resilient and happy by nature. I kind of accepted it; I could have been worse off. . . There were times when it was OK

but, on the whole, it was pretty dull and dreary. And loveless. . . .I always felt a bit in the way. She had her good moments, but they were scarce. I'm glad to say that, at this stage, I never do anything, only laugh about it. It wasn't funny at the time but, looking back, I think it stood to me; when you have things hard early in life it makes you appreciate all the things you have later. . . We just got on with it. You didn't rebel; you just accepted it. That was your life and that was it. But it was an awful shock when it happened. But I suppose, there were a few good times, and we were kept pretty comfortable. There were people who were hungry and cold but we were OK. And the neighbours around us were very nice and I had lots of friends (93-94, 97).

She "didn't look on the War as hardship. I suppose we were insulated against it. I'm sure there were awful shortages, but I have no memory of them; so I can't have been too deprived" (129). When she gets her first job, she doesn't mind being the lowest person in the office: "Every morning it was my job to make the coffee and tea. I was quite happy to do it; I didn't feel in any way servile. . . .The doctors . . . used to come into our office and have tea and coffee with us. It was great. It was nearly like Upstairs Downstairs because they were in no way rude to us but, as far as their conversations were concerned, we just didn't exist" (167). She has a practical view of her engagement ring: "The most important thing was to save the money for the house. The engagement ring was to be worn, but it wasn't going to rob us in the process" (198). Although she loved working, when she got married, she was forced to retire: "I didn't mind leaving work at all. I loved work, but I didn't mind leaving because it was the thing to do in those days. You just accepted that you had to leave work. The marriage bar was up, and you were out on your ear" (210). Although their first house was "pretty sparse, I suppose we had as much as most people" (223). During her first pregnancy, which occurred before a road was built, she had to cross the mud in the development on boards, "planks, across the mud, so I wouldn't slip. It never bothered me" (224). During this same pregnancy, she was afflicted with severe, almost crippling nausea "but I was a funny kind of person, I accepted whatever hit me and just got on with it. . . . I took whatever was coming" (227, 231). Even following the death of her first son after just a day, she says, "I was very upset, but I took everything and got on with it. You couldn't be lamenting in front of the two little girls; they might have thought that he was more important than they were. . . .I always felt, well, these things were meant to happen; they happened, and that was it" (235-6).

Rory agrees that Ita takes things in stride and moves forward. Speaking of the death of his son: "It was traumatic. But we both took it. Certainly, Ita did. She just looked sad but she didn't….she is not that way, the kind that kicks up a fuss. She just took it. We had to live with it. And we did" (253). Most of Doyle's female characters exhibit this type of dogged perseverance in light of hardship: They seem to realize that there is no option but to move forward, and they don't seem to have the luxury of going insane which many of us today do. Even Paula eventually raises herself out of her alcoholic stupor and move forward through the pain of life.

The role of family is also interesting as a reflection upon Doyle's other works. Despite the fact that the Doyles' children are almost never mentioned besides a passing reference to their births, they are the raison d'etre for the concept of the book as well as its publication. Doyle's literary reputation is the very reason this book is published and his parents' voices are heard, even if he himself is only referenced once in the book. Doyle is the medium and perhaps even the censor through which we hear his parents. They are independent of him yet dependent upon him. He has no control over what they say, yet he has total control. Thus, the tension between family helping establish one's identity and inhibiting that process, which is seen in his other work, is exemplified in this here.

As *Rory and Ita* shows, Doyle elevates the individual, with the familial unit being a healthy or unhealthy (sometimes both) backdrop. Paula Spencer, for instance, can relate her problems directly back to her family, most specifically, her husband (although her sister Carmel insists, in *The Woman Who Walked into Doors*, that their father was abusive, something Paula doesn't remember). Paula's sobriety, however, is also related directly back to her family, namely, her children and specifically, her desire to raise her son well, establish a relationship with her adult children, and be a good grandmother. Indeed, she attacks Charlo, thus effecting his permanent disappearance from her life, only after she sees the potential for him to abuse Nicola, her daughter. However, although many of her problems and their solutions can be related to her family, nevertheless, her daily battle with sobriety is her own. Ultimately, her family can neither make her sober or make her drunk. Doyle establishes the primacy of Paula the individual over Paula the mother.

In the Henry trilogy, Henry's family saves him from death: Miss O'Shea rescues him twice, and Saoirse's disappearance at the end of the *Dead Republic* is her attempt to protect him. However, his family almost kills him as well: He loses his leg when saving his son, almost destroys himself trying to reconnect with them, and involves himself deeply with the IRA to protect his daughter. Henry's family, however, does not define him, and he spends most of his life alone. Henry, like Paula, exists as an individual, not as a family man.

The raucous and loving Rabbitte family, is "about a fundamentally emotionally successful family" (Doyle, Personal interview 243). However, this family is also just as certainly comprised of distinct individuals. The fact of their individuality is impressed upon the readers when three family members are featured in three distinct novels which show their three distinct lives. Certainly Jimmy Rabbitte, Sr almost takes over *The Snapper*, but even he is unable to penetrate the individuality of his daughter.

The characters who seem entirely wrapped up in their children and family are the few characters in *Bullfighting: Stories* who are finding the empty-nester life intolerable. The father in "Animals" is almost pathetic in his loneliness, and Donal, in

"Bullfighting," is only able to survive his children's growing older because of an accidental adventure. Thus, being entirely wrapped up in one's family is almost a flaw in Doyle's work.

Ironically, we get a sense that Doyle is, in a sense, praising his parents by not allowing them to talk about their family. We know they are good parents: After all, he rates them "eight out of ten, but . . . 'making good progress'" (Doyle, *Rory & Ita* "Forward"). He also repeatedly mentions his appreciation for their encouraging him "to go to university, for example, if I wanted to go. They were terrific when I came to publish my first book . . . myself. I needed a loan from a bank. I wasn't a home owner. I had no property of my own and my parents went guarantor on the loan" (Sbrockey interview 543). Doyle recognizes his parents' individuality apart from their familial roles (and we can assume they also recognize their children's distinctive personalities instead of viewing them as extensions of themselves). He focuses on his parents' lives before and apart from their family to allow the reader (and his children) to understand and know the individuals Rory and Ita.

However, the memoir as an act of knowing is inconsistent with Doyle's other works. In his novels, Doyle repeatedly explores the concept of history and the inability to know its truth. For instance, Paula searches throughout both her novels to discover what really has happened to her and to her children. She wants to know what is real and what is imagined. Alcohol and physical abuse cloud her memories, and she claims to have forgotten decades, but even before the abuse starts, her memories are not fixed or reliable. She and Carmel can't even remember the same father - is he monstrous or loving?

Henry Smart, too, is looking for some validation of his life. Indeed, *A Star Called Henry*'s primary theme is the demythologizing of history in the search for an elusive truth. In *The Dead Republic*, Henry has nothing but overcrowded, unsubstantiated and often publicly refuted memories of his childhood, and a slippery association with both the IRA and John Ford. Often, when he finally begins to become certain of one aspect of his life, he experiences a Proustian moment of hyper-awareness in which the door to reality suddenly opens and exposes another truth, heretofore unknown and indeed unimagined. For instance, when he suddenly realizes that the IRA has been watching over him since his collaboration with Ford, his impressions of his past as well as his present change. Thus, characters in Doyle's texts are neither certain of the certainty of memory or history, and, if they are, they learn quickly not to be.

Despite Doyle's wanting to dispel "the mystery" of his parents, we find this distrust of history several times in *Rory & Ita*. When one parent asserts a fact, the other parent will sometimes contradict the fact in a footnote. Ita says that a priest used to "take out his handkerchief, a big white handkerchief, and he'd wipe his forehead and blow his nose, quite a loud blow of the nose" (Doyle, *Rory & Ita* 234). The footnote, attributed to Rory, succinctly says, "It was red" (234). Granted, the color of a mucus-filled hankie is inconsequential, but it is important enough for Ita to mention and important enough for Rory to correct.

A more significant instance occurs when they select the engagement ring. Ita remembers having a practical view of her engagement ring:

> I was keen to have one with five stones across, but I have very small hands and they looked ridiculous. But this one suited me better. It didn't take very long to choose. There were a fair number of rings but the prices were on them, and I knew what we could afford. It cost 17.10 pounds. We could have had a cheaper one, but it was what we could afford. The most important thing was to save the money for the house. The engagement ring was to be worn, but it wasn't going to rob us in the process. (198)

Rory, on the other hand, remembers Ita's having a slightly less practical view of the ring, which is explained in two footnotes: "There was an initial difficulty, because I thought this ring was a total waste of money. It wasn't so much a row as Ita being a bit disconcerted and upset, and I didn't realise I was doing that. I just wasn't thinking, that this ring was essential. So off we went and bought the ring in McDowell's; we bought the ring that Ita wanted. . . . .It was 27 pound, a slight difference" (197). Ita responds in yet a third footnote, "It was 17.10s, but we told everyone it was 27 pounds" (198). Thus, as Doyle asserts in his novels, when hard facts like the cost of a ring or the color of a handkerchief can be in disputed, obviously "soft facts," such as someone's mindset, attitude, or inspiration, cannot possibly be accurately documented.

In several instances, neither character can remember important events, such as how and when Rory proposes to Ita: "I just liked Ita more and more. Not long after I'd met her, actually, I made up my mind that I'd like to make it a permanent arrangement. I was standing at her door, saying goodnight to her, and I decided that I wanted to make my intentions clear. I think I said something or other, but, for the life of me, I can't remember" (189). Ita can't remember much about the wedding: "I can't remember the ceremony; I just can't pin it down. I can't remember saying, 'I do.' I must have said it, but I can't remember" (211). However, interestingly, she can remember the lavender soap she buys with her first paycheck.

Thus, the truth of memory - how much can we trust undocumented "facts;" the nature of memory; why we remember what we do remember; and the cause of memory and how we make ourselves memorable - are all questions posed by this couple's simple trip down memory lane.

The origins of Doyle's use of detail can presumably be traced in this book, as he melds both of his parents' styles. Ita's narrative is full of the Balzacian type of detail - a plethora of intimate descriptions of people, places, and events. Doyle recognizes this trait: "My mother's memory was so particular that she could recall furniture, the colour of lino, and every item that seemed to be in the kitchen" (Drewett interview 327). Her narrative, for instance, opens with a deeply detailed description of a gramophone:

The first thing I remember is the gramophone arriving. .
. .It was a lovely thing. I can still smell the wood of it. It
was dark wood, with a press below the turntable for the
records. Slats behind the turntable, six or eight of them,
each the width of my hand, opened when a handle was
turned, and released the sound. It was a good sound. It
was beautiful. I can still remember it, and the little
needles and the little box, the dog of His Master's Voice
on the lid. And the needle had to be fitted in. (Doyle,
Rory & Ita 1)

She goes into even more detail about her house, and describes
her father first in terms of wearing "a felt hat and he always
wore black boots with toecaps, which he polished himself. 'He
wore brown suits with a very fine white line; you'd hardly see
the line'" (13). Ita's chapters talk about her home, her family,
and her friends: "Ita. . . marks time according to the people
closest to her at a given time" (Rourke 2). Ita describes major
events in terms of how they affect her.

Rory's narrative, on the other hand, leaves out personal
details and descriptions, instead focusing on how events
affected not only him but the country. Doyle says, "My father
brushed that type of question aside and started reminiscing
about great historical events that he couldn't possibly have
witnessed" (Drewett interview 327). Look at the difference in
their memories of the Eucharistic Congress, a celebration in 1932
celebrating the 1500th anniversary of St. Patrick's return to
Ireland, a celebration which neither was allowed to attend. Rory
says,

It was decided to have this great display of faith, a
coming together, after ten years of statehood, a big
celebration of what was the Catholic Church and
Ireland. There were men's nights, and women's nights,
and the children's. It lasted the best part of a week but
it seemed to go on forever. There were banners put
across the street, all the way down the town. Some of

them were supposed to have been blessed by the Pope and one of them, I remember, said, 'Cod Save The Pope'. (Doyle, *Rory & Ita* 70-10)

He finishes by telling a humorous story about an old tramp. Ita remembers being "very annoyed because I wasn't let go....I remember going out to the back garden and kicking the wall...I remember my patent leather shoes; the wall was very solid, not very good for patent leather" (88).

The discussion of brown bread is another good example of their narrative distinctions: Rory explains:

Again, towards the end of 1940, I think, the German U-boat campaign increased, and all the wheat that we used to get from Canada and the US became very scarce. So it was decided, in the milling of the Irish grain, not to separate the husks. The result was a new kind of brown bread--they called it brown bread but it wasn't wheaten bread, just a dreadful imitation. It tasted appalling. (119)

Ita says:

And I remember this awful thing that people still talk about, this brown bread; I remember when it came in - maybe I'm a bit peculiar, but I thought it was alright. Denis Hingerty was working up in Belfast, and he'd come home every now and again, and bring white bread. And Mrs. Hingerty always gave us some of this white bread, and it was absolutely beautiful - it was better than cake. But the famous brown bread - people complained that they'd had problems with diarrhoea, but I can't remember anything bad about it. (130)

Ita gives details, in a sense, that better explain how the world moves about her - not egotistically but domestically. She looks at and describes her world instead of the world. Rory focuses more on the world, which may or may not change because he is involved in it. The difference perhaps can be attributed to his involvement in politics and work in journalism, although perhaps his worldview sparked both.

Doyle is a mix between the two. His characters, certainly, see situations in terms of how the situations affect their lives. For instance, Paula's life revolves around the effects she has wrought upon her children. Henry tells us nothing about the 1916 executions because he is in bed for the duration of them. Thus, Doyle must have an ability to see the world in this way. However, Doyle, as a novelist, must and, obviously, can see the larger view of political and social discourse, for instance, how immigration and racism are affecting Ireland. (Interestingly, while Doyle obviously has a firm grasp and opinion of the Irish and world political picture, he doesn't explain this picture in detail, as his father does, which dearth of explanation has sent more than one non-Irish reader scrambling to the Internet in order to connect the dots). Doyle's storytelling is a mixture of both his parents.

Finally, Doyle's atheism can also be seen in this narrative. As I talked about in the Prologue, despite his parents' regular church attendance and relatively normal Catholic experiences, neither character mentions faith or God. The only time in the entire book that we get a glimpse into their belief system is when Rory talks about the autobiography of Clemenceau, a French politician, entitled *In the Evening of My Thoughts*. Rory comments, "At the end of his days, he had nothing to offer or to look forward to. The book was so devoid of any hope or feeling for the future, or any sense of belonging to human fraternity, that it quite cured me of a budding agnosticism" (182).

The Church is a strong presence in both childhoods. "Their earliest memories breathe in their Catholic tradition as naturally as air" (Rourke 1). Both were taught by religious, nuns for Ita and Christian Brothers for Rory. However, their church involvement went further than that. Rory says, "We attended the Rosary, anything that was going" (50). Ita's family, "every night, they used to say the Rosary" (66). As a good Catholic, the young and adult Rory "firmly believed that if you looked in one of the window of the Protestant church you were likely to see the devil looking back out at you. I believed it. I was a grown man—in fact, it was just a few years ago—before I saw the inside of that church" (49). Rory was taught and appreciated "the Papal Encyclicals, *Rarum Novarum, Quadrogessimo Anno*, and one of the gospels. . . .*Rarum Novarum* was about the rights of the worker; it's a very great social document" (78). Thus, both were indoctrinated in the Catholic Church as youth.

As adults, their faith continued. They had a Catholic marriage, christened their children, and continued to attend Mass despite the imposition of their growing family: Ita tells us, "We went to Mass in Baldoyle, which was our parish at that time. And very awkward it was; it was like a country parish. There was a bus, but we couldn't go together because of the babies. One of us went first, and then there'd be a second bus for the second Mass. I'd go to the first Mass, and it was a Father Dillon who said that Mass" (233). Ita names her son, who dies after only a day, after Saint Anthony: "I was told that Saint Anthony was great; if I prayed to Saint Anthony, the baby would be grand. I gave somebody half-a-crown to put into Saint Anthony's box in the church, and to light a candle. I thought, well, call the child after him and give him half-a-crown, the least he can do is take care of the baby" (235). As an older woman, Ita "and some other women cleaned our local church after ten o'clock Mass, every Monday morning. As we cleaned, we chatted quietly and, as we were cleaning His house voluntarily and free gratis, we decided He wouldn't object" (319). Finally, while they socialize with people of all religions, Ita describes her neighbors in terms of their religion.

Their church is integral to their lives, and they have a realistic and often humorous (if not always reverent) tone towards it. "And then he'd begin talking [in the homily]. If the TD was good at talking, he wasn't a patch on his brother. He went on and on, and on and on, and all I'd be thinking about was getting home and seeing if the girls were alright and getting the mean into the oven for dinner" (234). The couple tried to keep the Sabbath, except in the case of dirty diapers: "We broke the Sabbath, and out went the nappies" (232). After the death of Roderick Anthony, Ita says about Saint Anthony: "But he didn't [take care of the baby]; he let me down. I don't pray to Saint Anthony any more. I decided he was a dead loss" (235).

Despite their faith, the narrative joins Rory and Ita, as we have seen, as two separate individuals, not made "one under God," but as two separate and joined individuals. The choices Doyle makes in editing and grouping the narratives lend to this effect. There isn't a sense of their being "fated to be together;" their meeting and subsequent relationship seems almost happenstance. We can't know how much the atheist Doyle unconsciously edits sections regarding their faith, but it, at least, is interesting that so little is said about God in the narrative of two apparently faithful people.

Rory & Ita - the words of his parents - is an interesting reflection on Doyle's writing. We are left with the ages-old chicken and egg question in that we do not know which is the true reflection of the other. How much did Doyle's already intact style mold his parents' narratives, and how much did his parents mold Doyle's style? "Certain inflections that could be styled 'Doylesque' do recur, raising an interesting question about whose voice has shaped whose. Is the Roddy Doyle we read a product of the linguistic rhythms of his parents, or are their speech patterns as rendered here influenced by Doyle's own sense of voice" (McGlynn 23). We don't know if Doyle, for instance, is inspired to create stoic female characters because his mother is so brave, if he fashions her into a stoic female, or if his mother and his heroines are totally unrelated. We don't know how much of his sense of humor - the way he tells stories and allows his characters to interact and comment upon each other - is learned from his parents or how much their humor is fashioned by his own.

Although I am not a psychologist, I can't help but give armchair psychology a try and attempt to discern pieces of Doyle the man from pieces of Rory and Ita, the parents. Doyle admits, "Obviously, because I lived with them for so long I'm fashioned to a big extent by them" (Drewett interview 338). While we are all unique individuals, some qualities just don't fall far from the proverbial tree. Identifying these qualities and positing a guess about from which tree they fell is perhaps a fruitless task, but nevertheless, a fun one.

Obviously, Doyle's love of reading was encouraged when he was a child, and he is a product of both parents who were avid readers, Rory reading instead of playing in sports, and Ita receiving literary tomes as Christmas presents. Doyle says, "The house was always full of books" (Sbrockey interview 543).

However, less obvious traits can also be seen in the pages of this memoir. For instance, any follower of Doyle is aware of his dislike of publicity and any type of fuss. While he is not Howard Hughes-esque, after winning the Booker Prize he refused to remain for the expected interviews. An official complained, "But you're a Booker Prize winner. The Prize brings its responsibilities." Doyle shot back, "Do you want it back?"(qtd. in White 25). Indeed, he continued to live in the same house he had lived in as a schoolteacher for years after becoming the Irish literary star.

Neither does Doyle seem to experience an existential angst as he writes all night long in a booze-filled garret. Instead, as I've already mentioned, he's "quite happy to work office hours" (BookLounge) and calls his writing "pretty mundane really" (Doyle, Personal interview 246).

Thus, Doyle is no fuss and no maintenance, like his mother, who says, "In all my life I have lived in two houses, had two jobs, and one husband. I'm a very interesting person" (Doyle, Forward, *Rory & Ita*). As she says several times, "I took whatever was coming. . . .I took everything and got on with it" (231,235).

Doyle also has the confidence to stand up for himself. For instance, after one impertinent journalist attempted to rearrange the furniture in his house, he stopped all interviews from his home. Doyle's quiet confidence can be seen when he had enough faith in *The Commitments* to finance an expensive self-publishing endeavor. Doyle's father shows similar chutzpah throughout the narrative, from smoking up his workplace because he was being mistreated as an apprentice, to leaving his secure apprenticeship for a job in the uncertain world of journalism. In all of these stories, there is a sense that both Doyles know their relative worths and are not afraid to bank on them.

I've called Doyle the writer of the underdog. In the *Barrytown Trilogy*, he allows the voiceless working-class to "fuck this" and "shite that" their way into an adoring public's hearts. He empowers an unwed teenaged Sharon and an abused, alcoholic Paula by allowing them to tell their own stories. After Jimmy Rabbitte, Sr. has been made redundant, he is allowed a novel, as is the young child of a broken marriage and a poor orphan from the Dublin slums, (who is allowed three novels.) He has written short stories about immigrants and middle-aged men, all of whom feel displaced in some way. Thus, Doyle lets the voiceless speak and speak well. He is passionate about people's rights and is offended by the Catholic Church when it refuses to allow these rights, for instance, the right to receive a divorce. He is passionate about people being able to live their lives unencumbered by institutionalized moral dictates.

This compassion for others can also be seen in his mother. Numerous times in her narrative, she makes a remark about someone that shows the depth of her discernment and concern. She remembers her maid named Lillie:

> a strange thing about Lillie; it was very sad really. . .
> Lillie had her half-day on a Thursday, and Lillie got a
> new outfit one year and it was as near to a school
> uniform as you could possibly buy. Black shoes, and
> she had the navy beret. . . .So, I met her one day going
> off on her half-day and she was carrying a school case
> and wearing the outfit and I remember, I thought it was
> odd but looking back on it now, I think it was sad. (36)

Ita sees Lily's obvious desire to seem educated and of a higher social class, and this realization disturbs the young girl. She sees her father as "a very, very quiet man but, sure, he must have been dead lonely" (43), an insightful comment from a daughter who can look past the pain he inflicted by his questionable choice of a second wife and see the despairing man. The irascibility of an elderly woman who lived in a room at Ita's summer refuge she sees as "a form of depression" (62). At her Confirmation, she notes two inappropriately dressed girls, and even as a teenager, feels compassion instead of disdain: "There were these twins. . . and they were dressed up as if for their First Communion. They had white dresses and white veils. I felt so sorry for them" (89). Finally, Miss O'Toole, her office manager, "was a highly organized, highly intelligent woman. . . .she dressed beautifully and she had a lovely figure; she was rather plain because she had rather big teeth, but she dressed so well and held herself so well and she was so slim that she still looked kind of attractive. She was, I always thought, a very lonely lady" (169). Ita can see past the professional exterior and see the hurting woman. Ita's remembrances always show sympathy for others in a way that most people's memories don't.

Doyle's novels, too, show sympathy and empathy, whether for young children, displaced immigrants, recovering alcoholics, redundant and middle-aged men, teenagers with little hope for a bright future—he is always able to look past the stereotype and see the person, just like his mother does. "I suppose [the idea of] writing the book was to drive [characters] back into the center. So I never actually see the characters as marginalized" (Personal interview 225). "An acceptance of people as they are" (Rourke 2) is one of Ita's legacies to her son.

Thus *Rory & Ita*, although not a riveting account of nail-biting events, is an interesting biography on several fronts. First, both of the elder Doyles come across as charming in their own rights, both people we would want to spend time with and get to know - the interesting neighbors across the hedge that we always want to visit with but can't ever seem to find the time to do so. Next, despite the fact that they lived through a world war and were raised by parents who lived through and participated in the War of Independence and the Civil War, their lives seem relatively untouched by violence and unaffected by the "History" around them. "The political tumult of twentieth-century Irish history is surprisingly marginal in their lives" (Hutchings 83). For non-Irish and Irish readers alike, it is an interesting reminder that life, for the majority of us, continues in its banal fashion, no matter how many bombs are thrown. (Indeed, after reading *Rory & Ita*, the Henry novels seem wildly more fanciful and exaggerated than they do on an initial reading.) Finally, exploring *Rory & Ita* to find traces of both their son the novelist and his novels is an entertaining way to spend an afternoon. For some reason, seeing hints of Doyle and his works in the transcribed words of his parents seems much more rewarding than merely tracing themes across his oeuvre of fiction. In the final analysis, were Roddy Doyle not Roddy Doyle, national hero, this book may never have been published. But since Roddy Doyle is Roddy Doyle, national hero, we are glad that it was.

CHAPTER 4
OH, PLAY THAT THING

Oh, Play That Thing, published in 2005, is the second instalment in the *Last Roundup* trilogy with carry-over characters, but not countries, as our hero Henry Smart has emigrated to America to escape the IRA. Despite his heretofore extraordinary life - surviving a childhood in the slums of Dublin, murdering for the IRA, enduring torture and imprisonment - the twenty-two-year-old Henry still has a lot of living and learning to do.

Reviews are mixed. Some critics praise the "prose that echoes the syncopated beat of the Jazz Age itself, [in which] Doyle brings Henry as well as Armstrong and his music to vibrant life" (Boughton qtd. in *Contemporary Authors* 5). They even say that "Doyle displays his trademark sensitivity and wit in a tale full of adventure, passion and prose as punchy as a Satchmo riff" (Block qtd. in "Roddy Doyle," *Contemporary Authors* 4).

Others disagree. As is the stereotypical middle child, namely, neurotic and without a strong identity (being flanked by two sisters, I am able to testify to this), so some critics see this novel. It struggles to find a true narrative strain, hurling Henry from bizarre situation to bizarre situation, from bizarre mentor to bizarre mentor. Without the narrative backbone of the Irish Revolution, Doyle is forced to create his own timeline, encompassing the Roaring Twenties and the Great Depression (the latter almost as an afterthought, similar to the treatment of the Irish Civil War in *A Star Called Henry*), stirring in racial injustice and the Mafia, the cumulative effect of which doesn't seem to work. Some say that the novel is confusing at times and call it "frantic, ill-conceived. . . .Doyle's headlong style . . .has become so compressed and elliptical that at times it's difficult to know what's going on. The American street vernacular feels like a put on. . . .And in the long, staccato exchanges between characters, within which an occasional flashback adds extra complications, it's sometimes not clear just who is speaking to whom" (Quinn 1). It was "a baffling mess—seeming not so much picaresque as entirely arbitrary" (Walton 39). The magical realism feel continues in this novel, although more strained and less magical: ". . .Now Doyle appeared to confuse magic realism with wild coincidence, the absence of recognisable human motivation and the right to throw in any bits of social history he fancied: from the hobo jungles of the Depression to jazz-age Chicago" (Quinn 1). Additionally, "although nothing extraordinary happens to defy the laws of realism, there is a certain amount of mental magic which underpins the story. The coincidences are too strong; the characters at times are stereotypical caricature, and the language and happenings almost too poetic and idiomatic" (Ball 2). While it seems extreme to me, at least one critic found it to be "an uncharacteristic misstep in a brilliant writer's estimable career" (qtd. in "Roddy Doyle," *Contemporary Authors* 4).

Despite these misgivings, the novel is still interesting, and the reader is still invested in Henry as a character. Although Henry has experienced a number of painful situations and learned a number of painful lessons, he still has much to learn, particularly about identity. Henry, although a memorable character in *Star*, adapts too well to his surroundings in this novel and becomes lost in the scenery, seeming to be more of a one-dimensional conduit showcasing the other characters than a character in his own right: Indeed, at times he seems to have regressed and has almost entirely lost his sense of self. This, he is ripe for the several characters who serve as mentors to him and try to teach him a sense of personal identity.

Plot Summary

This novel, divided into four parts as are its sister novels, begins after Henry's hasty departure from Ireland for England, where he spends two years trying to and failing at hiding from the IRA.

We first see Henry as he enters America, full of dreams and ambition, hoping to lose himself in the mélange of immigrants and to start afresh with a blank slate--but keeping an eye out for fellow Irishmen in case the eraser is dirty. Doyle sends Henry to America because of its vastness and its freshness, although he admits that the decision made writing difficult: "Trying to continue the story written by the same person but in a very, very different environment. Trying to create a book which continues the story, but also has its own shape. The chaos and the adventure that was the 1920s is in the book, the music, and the contradictions—the village nature of New York, and the hugeness of the place as well. But, so much work" (Drewett interview 348). With this novel, he tried not "to overstep. It's an older man, but still a very young man. He's in a very different exciting place that's inventing itself every day" (Personal interview 15).

Henry quickly lands a job in advertising—he wears sandwich boards touting local merchants' wares while he distributes illegal liquor on the side. After Henry sees the possibility of expansion, imagining a fleet of good-looking sandwich carriers using their allure and savoir faire to push cigars, meatloaf, and funeral services, he breaks with the local gangster for whom he works, ignorantly believing he and his newly hired crew can hide in the busy streets of New York. Not only can he not hide, but after his crew is repeatedly ambushed, Henry himself is almost killed by the local mobsters. He escapes in the company of his first mentor, "Fast Olaf's half-sister," a manipulative and far-seeing con woman/philosopher, who not only has an insatiable appetite for sex but also has the unique ability to discern people's needs and fill them. Henry and she, supported primarily with the earnings from her unique brand of fortune telling, leave New York City and settle temporarily in Sweet Afton, a small town outside of New York, until, his enemies hot on his trail, Henry is forced again to leave suddenly.

Part 2 finds Henry in Chicago, a city which offers even more possibilities than New York for the runaway. Because he is no longer confined to an island (Manhattan or Ireland), Henry feels safe and even safer when he begins a relationship with Dora, a light-skinned African American who becomes another one of Henry's teachers, showing the naively color blind Henry the limits race imposes.

Through Dora, Henry meets the irresistible Louis Armstrong and is quickly hired to be Armstrong's "white man" (170). "You my white skin, O'Pops. You beside me, I manage myself. I can cross the line. Any time I want. . . " (212-213). Henry becomes a member of his entourage, bodyguard, part consultant, and part companion. Since Armstrong won't allow white men to manage his career and must navigate the uncertain waters of the music industry alone, his paying gigs are sporadic, and he is frequently "black broke" (182). Henry introduces him to robbery as a way to finance his career.

During one of these illegal forays, the next stage of Henry's life emerges in the form of a reunion with his wife, Miss O'Shea, who is working as a maid in one of the homes he burgles. This odd turn of events is called "one of the most egregious plot twists in recent fiction. . . .I'm not sure even Dickens, with his love of coincidence, would have risked such a stunt" (Quinn 2). After Miss O'Shea's expected recriminations, the two reconcile and, for a short time, raise their daughter together.

Soon, however, Henry begins to be restless and, in Part 3, he leaves Miss O'Shea and his daughter and returns with Armstrong to New York, Harlem this time, to jump start Armstrong's career. In New York, Armstrong's career blossoms, and Henry senses a growing distance between them. During this period, Henry reconnects with his former lover, Fast Olaf's half-sister, who has reincarnated herself as the mystical sensation Sister Florence Grattan McKendrick, high priestess of the Divine Church of the Here and Now, which espouses doing "whatsoever you want. Don't put it off. . . .Spend that dollar, scratch that itch, eat that donut. Because the Lord wants you to. He insists on it. . . .He put us here to live it to the hilt" (282-83). Henry decides to scratch that itch and joins her entourage, advising her and expediting her appearances, which ultimately causes a rift with Armstrong. Before Armstrong and Henry completely separate, however, both Henry's former gangster enemies and the IRA find him; Armstrong and the half-sister join forces in helping him escape to Chicago, where the IRA finds him again and Miss O'Shea rescues him from execution.

Part 4 finds Henry, Miss O'Shea and their daughter and on the run. The family, which soon includes a son, live through the Great Depression stealing, begging, and slowly starving their way across the country: "The novel turns into a baggy picaresque through Depression-era America. . . " (Quinn 2). After more than five years of eking out an existence, the family is separated when Henry slips as he and his son Rifle are hopping on a train. Rifle survives, but Henry goes under the train, losing his leg and all contact with his family. He hears tales of Miss O'Shea, "Our Lady of the Working Man" (358), a Depression-era Robin Hood, but after years of searching, Henry loses hope of ever finding his family. He crawls into the desert to die, only to be rescued by Hollywood legends Henry Fonda and John Ford, who are shooting a movie nearby. Ford recognizes Henry, or, at least, his type, and is intrigued: "We both know what you were. And that's what our next picture is going to be about. . . . It's your story. How'd an Irish rebel end up here? That's the real Irish story. We both know that. And that's the story we're going to tell" (376). Thus, we are primed to read the third and final installment of the man who ends the novel with "I was alive. I was forty-five. I was Henry Smart" (376).

Argument

The Henry of *Oh, Play That Thing* is not in control of his life: Just as he is swept through the twists and turns of the Dublin sewers as a youth and adolescent, the *Oh, Play That Thing* Henry co-opts the beliefs and ideals of those he is around, namely, the half-sister, Dora, Armstrong, and Miss O'Shea. Although *A Star Called Henry's* Henry follows Connolly, Dalton, and Collins, he nevertheless retains his ten percent, fiscally and emotionally. The *Oh, Play That Thing* Henry rarely keeps his ten percent, which is perhaps why one critic says, "The volume is staccato; the backdrop is great, the story imaginative, a potentially powerful vehicle, but . . the heart of the story, the believable core, was hard to find" (Howard 49). There is no Henry Smart - no believable core - in the novel, only his shadow, overshadowed by whomever he is accompanying.

After the beginning pages, he doesn't concern himself with money at all, a raison d'etre for the young Henry. He doesn't skim from either Armstrong or the half-sister, signifying his diminishing sense of self and eroding our belief in him as a character. Still on the margins—Louis Armstrong's white man, Sister Flow's "brother," the unidentified voice on and uncredited author of several of Armstrong's hits—this Henry affects nothing and influences nothing.

Henry, when first in America, is still naïve, blinded by America's endless promises of boundless prosperity. Though he says, "I don't believe in anything. . . .I can hope and wish. . . .But I never believe" (84), he believes fully in America's "do-over" mentality. He believes he can achieve a fresh start because of his energy, youth, and good looks. In one sense, he has re-set the machine and re-started his life. However, in starting over, he unfortunately forgets the lessons he has learned and consistently misreads his surroundings, particularly in the beginning of the novel. Despite the fact that he is an IRA assassin, almost paranoid in his concern for the apparently extraordinarily long arm of the IRA smiting him on the streets of New York, he readily believes he will remain unnoticed by the local mob boss from whom he steals merely because he sets up his sandwich-board operations several blocks away: A hired gun for the mob boss berates him: "Everybody knows where Louis Lepke is king and isn't king. Except fucking you. . . .You decide to skim off the top. . . . Are you that stooped. . . ..And all this time you think you are the fucking smart guy" (93). He underestimates his acquaintance Mildred, who betrays him. He begins to believe that the half-sister has a psychic gift, even though she frankly admits she doesn't; and yet he fails to heed her warning and sense the danger from Norris, the Sweet Afton merchant whose attention forces Henry's precipitous departure.

The Henry of *A Star Called Henry* would not have been so naïve: Having lived his entire life outside of the law, stealing and murdering his way through childhood and adolescence, living his life on the run and surviving by reading people and anticipating consequences, he is street savvy and understands what a slight nod or out-of-place wink means. Although he places too much trust in his comrades in the IRA and doesn't realize when he is being used, nevertheless, he certainly can read a situation. Indeed, almost all of the IRA members that he knows have been killed, yet Henry escapes early enough to survive, a testament to this ability.

Other characters adopt him and afford him more respect than he seems to deserve. They each try to teach him how to preserve his self. Henry, who has lived a lifetime in his scant twenty years, seems to need a lot more "larnin'" than a reader of *A Star Called Henry* would expect. Although it takes the entire novel, in *Oh, Play That Thing*, Henry recaptures himself through his contact with powerless minorities: "Things happen to him—women discover him. And he is found in women, so to speak" (Doyle qtd. in Personal interview 240).

Henry's first mentor, a master at understanding, blending in, and benefiting, is Fast Olaf's half-sister who disappears early in the novel and reappears as Sister Florence Grattan McKendrick. Doyle says about the character:

> Sister Flow . . . I came across the name and even Woody Guthrie had a song about her and she was this outrageous evangelist who disappeared and reappeared. She was a great communicator who had a great sexual allure even though she wasn't traditionally what you would call attractive or a beautiful woman but she had something going for her because people were battering each other to get into the doors of her church every Sunday and she had, as far as I remember, a big neon cross on top of the church that you could see

for miles and miles. And a radio station and shop.
(Personal interview 224)

The half-sister, a successful con artist even outside her incarnation as Sister Flow, is the ultimate chameleon and therefore extremely successful, always ending up on the good end of a con, even when it goes awry.

This ability is perhaps the result of being, as a woman, relatively powerless. Despite her being Henry's lover and mentor, Henry never learns Sister Flow's real name and refers to her as "the half-sister." Thus, not only is she not important enough to have a name, she isn't even a full sister. Even though she fires the gun which saves them both from gangsters, she realizes, "They won't be looking for me. Not for long, anyways. You now. You're a different story, I guess. . . .But you're the guy. They'll remember you. . . .So, I'm going to drift back into Dodge one of these days and no one'll notice except what I want them to notice. You, though, daddy, are a different little story. They'll be looking everywhere for you" (Doyle, *Oh, Play That Thing* 101). She is correct in that, because she is female and easily dismissed, when she does return to New York, no one recognizes her. Just like the unnamed prostitute in *A Star Called Henry* that Henry decides not to kill on Bloody Sunday, society deems the half-sister not important enough to matter.

However, the half-sister is adept at capitalizing on her unimportance, something Henry isn't. From the beginning, she insinuates herself into situations. She accentuates her buxomness because "the market wants it. . . .The flappers are the thing, see. All the girls out there want to be flappers. No tits, no hips. That's what the girls want. But that's not what the boys want, you know. And the boys are the market right now. Always and forever. The boys want tits, tits I can give them" (28). Thus, she reads the needs and fulfills them, effacing herself and becoming immersed the background du jour.

Henry begins to learn marketing from her. He understands, "Sell the words, sell the goods and the life. Sell the need, and the salvation. Smile with the consumer, suffer with her. . .Terrify the man. . . then save him. . . . Create the whole, then offer to fill it"

(35). He hires sexy women to tout the effectiveness of his boards, sells ordinary soap as a miraculous method of recapturing one's youth and innocence, and uses other tricks to create a need in people that the products his boards will fulfill.

However, when the half-sister uses him to test her autosuggestion, an "early form of Neuro-Linguistic Programming" (Ball 3), instead of learning how to use it, he buys into it, to his detriment. He believes her mantra, "Day by day, in every way, I am getting better and better," and he makes the same mistake in American that he makes in Ireland: He beings to believe in his own schtick. In Ireland, he believes that cabbage and fresh air are worth killing for and that he is the invaluable player his superiors flatter him to be; in America, he believes he can overcome class (and the mob): "Lugging another man's boards, I was another stiff, a mick fresh off the boat. Lugging my own boards, I was a man of business, a young man on the go. And not lugging them either; presenting them" (Doyle, *Oh, Play That Thing* 21). Thus, Henry is trying to fulfill his own needs as well as those of others. However, he isn't subsuming his own personality as the half-sister does, but instead he tries to be unique and noticeable. Perhaps because he has been marginalized so greatly throughout his life, he finds deliberately playing the chameleon anathema and can't do it.

In Sweet Afton, the half-sister reads the needs of the community spectacularly and fulfills them. After only two days, she is already making money on those "desperate for her magic:"

> She was the barker. She announced their need, told them what they lacked and wanted. She worked on the women; the men came natural. They gawked as she passed. Loving her, hating her, wanting her, and more and more because they knew it wasn't going to happen. . . . They sat and watched, and raised no Cain when the missis passed the seed money to the cute little carpetbagger. There wasn't a bark or objection from

those men; they were happily robbed. . . .She made an industry of it. (106)

The half-sister drops her blatant sexuality for a subdued, more marketable sensuality, along with her hope-filled prophesies and joie de vivre, all of which she senses are missing from these rural lives.

Although she has already taught Henry this lesson, she must remind him how to sell himself, in this case, as a diviner, despite his naive protestation that "they don't need new wells" (105). The half sister reminds Henry, "They want the show, daddio. It's a long winter and we're miles from Broadway" (105). Henry finally re-learns what he has already been taught in New York and starts finding well water: "But they knew what they were paying for now, and it wasn't new water. It was the elegant, wandering man they were paying for, and they had him for the day" (105).

Henry, alas, is a naïve, too eager, pupil. Even more so than when he meets Jack Dalton, he neglects to keep his ten percent emotionally. Desperate for a savior, he believes in the half-sister more readily than he believes in Jack, despite being intellectually aware of the falseness of both their words:

And I began to wonder if there wasn't real magic there. It wasn't the palms or coffee grounds, but I wondered if she could really read, without the usual props of the con. She could feel those knots of unhappiness; and it was easy enough, then, to untie them. And I wondered if some of that magic didn't come from me, from rubbing up to me. It was coming back, the feeling—the glow. I was, remember, the miracle baby. I'd made women feel special, not that long ago, as they gazed down at me in my padded zinc crib. . . .Fast Olaf's half-sister was doing the same thing now, glowing for Sweet Afton. (111)

Though Henry is consciously aware of her con, he believes in it. She is releasing his knots of unhappiness in the same way she is for the rest of the town, only he can't see it.

For instance, Henry believes that she cares for him because he never has to pay for sex, mere semantics because she demands a cut of the bootlegging profits. She gives Henry snatches of her philosophy, testing it on him, and he is too naïve to realize it, even though she is frank with him: "Know why I'm doing it? For me [said Henry]. She laughed. She threw her head back and laughed at the ceiling, and stopped. The market wants it, she said" (27). Henry, albeit temporarily, believes she is creating herself for him. Henry never understands that she is preaching her own self-interest, even though she tells him explicitly what she is doing: "You know me better than that. You wanted education, and you got it. In spades. Better than the book. You want me, it's a different proposition. You knew that. I know you did. I prey on weakness. You know that. I'm being straight with you. Always" (43-46). Henry incomprehensibly trusts that she cares for him, even loves him, despite her saying their partnership is based on the fact that "we're stuck here together, until it's safe to toodle back. We got here together. We're in the sack here together. I got things you want, you got things I can use. Sounds as near to partnership as I'll ever need or want. Till it's safe to go back. Till it's safe for *me* to go back" (101). When Henry has to leave, she answers his frantic query, "Where'll we go?" with "Not *we* this time, daddy" (125). Henry is left alone because he has refused to learn what she is trying to teach him. Despite her apparent honesty, Henry unwittingly falls under her spell.

Perhaps the real need that she fulfils for Henry is for a feeling of importance. He yearns to feel special. Because Henry believes he is an afterthought, a distant second to his dead brother Henry, the star, he too readily believes and follows. He plays the dentist after she tells the town he is a dentist. He finds water after she tells the town he is a diviner. Notice that when they meet in her incarnation as Sister Flow, his first suggestion is that she spell her name "f-l-o-w," to which she responds, "I already do spell it f-l-o, fucking, w. Have done since 1927 and I thought of it all by myself" (286), illustrating Henry's inability to be a real, creative force. He can make suggestions - for instance including Louis Armstrong as back up to her recorded sermons - but he isn't able to create anything: Just as he steals the sandwich boards from Johnny No, just as he steals others' belongings to finance himself and Armstrong, he steals Armstrong's talent to further Sister Flow's recording career. In this novel, Henry's inability to act on his own is blatantly apparent, which is perhaps why even his elbow is cropped out of the famous photo of De Valera and why only a few lines exist of the ballad of Henry Smart.

This innate feeling of inferiority and marginality is ultimately why Henry can not fully learn half of the half-sister's real lesson. While Henry clings to his meager sense of importance, her extraordinary confidence, paradoxically, allows the negation of herself for gain:

> [Her] strength was her unshakeability. She believed, absolutely, in nothing. But herself. Her head, her body. Her temple. Her tits, her face, her mind, breath, cunt, eyes, future, legs, her teeth, her choices, her wrists. The world was what she saw and came to her, and what she could make come to her. *Every day, in eve-ery way.* She believed in the power of her arse. She slapped it and got me to slap it. She loved the smack and sting, the proof that it was hers. She knew what it could do. One well-aimed swing could bring you fortune, fame, a bed for the night. She believed. She believed in the thing, the now, what she saw and felt, now, no putting off or waiting. The future would be better, only if you had the now. It applied to everything, nipples, money, health, but only if you had them. Nipples got you bigger nipples, money made you more, health gave you everything, now. She believed this, and she was making a religion of it. All other faiths dangled transcendence, the transcendence of the dirty world as probably,

possible, or sure-fire certainty; transcendence as a promise or a threat. (120)

Henry doesn't want to transcend the here and now. He is trying to create his place in it. He feels no compunction about eating, having sex, or any of the other polite evils which plague the average person, but instead he constantly tries to leave his mark - through sex, music, or the single-minded ideal of freedom. Henry has no problems scratching his worldly itches, none of which take away the feeling of always being second. Indeed, the half-sister even says, "[You were] never happy. You were always restless" (281). Henry, who has always had a problem with establishing his importance as an individual, cannot negate it for other people. Thus, his failure to adopt fully her rhetoric is the ultimate reason he is forced to leave Sweet Afton and the half sister is able to stay.

Henry is taught again importance of establishing a fixed identity and asserting it, this time, by his second mentor, Dora, a beautiful, light-skinned African American whom he meets in a nightclub. Dora, another her powerless minority, quickly begins to teach Henry, and he calls her, "My latest teacher, presenting me with nothing but the facts" (141).

Although just as self-confident, Dora is the antithesis of the half-sister. Dora refuses to compromise, to blend, to mix in, no matter the personal cost. Firstly, Dora works as a poorly paid maid, giving up a lucrative job in the white sector because she refuses to pass as white:

I don't want to pass for white. . . .I spent all my life being less than white. Thinking I was better than most because I had some white man's blood, and knowing all the time that I was just a nigger bitch. Get my hair straighted, put bleach on my face, I was still a nigger bitch. And not enough of a nigger neither. Not white enough, not black enough. Just a jaundice-coloured bitch, didn't matter a goddam how many men was after my tail. I hated my own self and walked through those nigger bitches thinking I was better than them because my ass wasn't as black as their black asses. . . .Took a long time to get out of that white man's trap. . . .I just be Dora. (142, 145)

Thus, Dora is fighting to be Dora, whereas the half sister is fighting to be whomever the market needs her to be. Henry is fighting, although he doesn't know for what.

Dora, however, cannot "just be Dora." She doesn't exist in a bubble, and she fully understands this. The African-American Dora must live "inside the rules" (143) of a white society. She teaches Henry some of these rules, including the morays of the black and tan clubs, which he learns readily: "There were no written rules, nothing to point at; they had to be learnt and remembered" (151).

Henry can learn "rules," although he cannot learn to understand the big picture and thus idealizes and projects upon Dora, as he does with the half sister. He sees only one aspect of African American society, which has become his new idealization. From his view, the distinctly African American appreciation of music "was living like I'd never seen it. This wasn't drowning the sorrow, the great escape, happy or unhappy. It was life itself, the thing and the point of it. No excuses: it was why these men and women lived" (148). He admires the impromptu excitement of her impoverished neighborhood, while ignoring its alleys and rickets-ridden children.

Henry, true to form, is being willfully ignorant. He still believes in the lies that he creates: He thinks that he and Dora are "made for each other" because "I'd come out of hiding. And here was a woman who'd got there before me; she'd stopped hiding too" (148). He says, "She was new too, invented seconds before and plonked down in front of me. Just for me, the new American" (136). Notice Henry's egocentrism here - he imagines that Dora is created just for him. Unfortunately, although Henry intellectually understands, he doesn't fully understand that Dora's reality as an African American is, in fact, hiding to a certain degree. He doesn't understand how humiliating it is when Dora hides her identity when she agrees to pose as white to gain admittance into a club where Armstrong is playing. Later, when he leaves her alone, he again doesn't realize the position in which he places her, and she must reluctantly dance with a mobster in a black and tan club because "a coloured girl couldn't sit by herself and wouldn't be let stand alone for long" (152).

Henry not only willfully ignores Dora's reality, but he also is hiding in a fictional world he creates: Whereas Dora can afford only one dress to wear out at night and thus only has one dress, Henry squanders the money he earns as a day laborer on tips: "I worked all day for the dollars and nickels I handed around as I moved through this new world and made myself memorable, a man to know, a man to step aside for. But I was handing out far more than I earned lugging beef and hog-meat. I was spending more boodle than I'd ever had before" (152). Henry also suddenly believes, "I wasn't Irish anymore. . . .I was a Yank" (135). Henry doesn't know who he is. He is acting at being someone. Henry tries to emulate Dora's self-awareness, but he isn't able to do so. His inability to understand himself and her position places her in dangerous positions, which he fails to appreciate.

Whereas the con woman seems to take Henry's "failure" to learn her lesson in stride, Dora has little patience for Henry's ignorance: "You Irish and you telling me you don't know the difference between black and white? You don't know the rules? You people wrote most of the goddam rules" (141). To Dora, Henry's viewpoint comes across as willfully ignorant and even potentially dangerous: "Her anger made the rabbits swing. . . There's a line, Henry, and you don't see it cos you don't have to. But we do" (145). Indeed, Henry's ignorance is dangerous, which Dora says: "You a white man on a coloured street that ain't your street. That the problem? No, sir. A coloured lady on her own coloured street. She the problem" (148). Though Henry gives lip service to the unwritten behavioral and racial rules, he flouts them and purposefully draws attention to them as a couple, "dragging it to her, just to prove her wrong. To prove that we could stand here and talk, that we could do it as long as we wanted" (146). On their last night together, in a scene reminiscent of his last encounter with the half-sister, Henry endangers them both when he refuses to "obey the rules" and Dora must rescue him: "We safe, I think. If we sensible. He made his point. . . .You being stupid again. The point ain't me. It you. So, when Dipper finish this number, we finish dancing and you go. . .No more. Get out. It me too, you know. You in trouble, I in trouble. Go on. She was angry and scared" (159). Henry knows her advice is sound: "But Dora was right. She knew the rules, the do's and all the don'ts. . . .I was safe, as long as I did what was expected. There was no messing here; I saw that in her face. I was choosing life or death" (159). Henry, however, does not leave. Instead, he selfishly stays and endangers Dora because he has already moved on to a new dream: "I'd been called" by Louis Armstrong (160).

As with the half-sister, he can't compromise himself to fit into societal norms or others' expectations only because he has no real sense of the "he" he would be compromising. Thus, although Dora introduces Henry to Armstrong, she has little effect on him otherwise. He doesn't understand her example of "being Dora" within the confines of societal rules. Instead, he tries to "be Henry" outside of the rules because his version of Henry is too fragile to withstand the pressure of those rules. His Henry isn't well defined enough to live outside of the rules, as the half-sister shows him, nor is it strong enough to exist inside the rules, as Dora shows.

The next notable personage in Henry's life is "Dipper, Gate, Gatemouth, Dippermouth. Daddy, Pops, Little Louie, Laughing Louie, Louis Armstrong" (136), for whom Henry works as a combination bodyguard and companion. Doyle says he included Armstrong in the novel because:

> I was still writing about Henry and still thinking I had to...I was in New York. I can tell you it was around Halloween 1997, and I was there with my family, and we were at the Sunday reception of the *New York Times*

Book Review section. And there was a book about Louis Armstrong. I can't remember which one it was. And it seemed like a good book. I'd never been interested in him particularly. I remember when he was on TV and that he said he was on *The Andy Williams Show* or something like that. Everybody loved him. Looked like Muhammad Ali, really. Everybody loved him. And I like the little stories and incidents about his childhood. Particularly reading about it. So, I decided I would read the book. And I did. And it was there that I saw interesting coincidences between his own life and Henry's - self-defined, mythological, he created his own mythology, really. Telling lies as well. It just got interesting. There was a story in there around when Armstrong was about 19 or 20 and was leaving New Orleans for Chicago to become the world famous Louis Armstrong and he knew a bouncer, a night club bouncer from New Orleans. And he told Louis that when he got up there to make sure and get yourself a white man to put his hand on your shoulder and say, "This here is my nigger," you know. And there is a lot in that story. It's kind of funny, but it's shocking and kind of sad. And I thought, "That's interesting." So Armstrong was going up to Chicago with that advice in his ears, between his ears. So I wanted Henry to meet him off of the train, so to speak. I put that kind of behind my ear like a cigarette or something for future use to see if it worked out. And then gradually he became part of the story. (Doyle, Personal interview 236-37)

Armstrong is indeed similar to Henry in many ways. Unlike Henry, however, he has a plan to achieve greatness and a conception of himself and what he is up against.

Armstrong is trying to find himself and his way, as an African American in a segregated America. A minority but a male, he is creating his persona and the rules by which he can live simultaneously. His identity is fixed enough that he can dissemble and act "the eejit" (188), like the half-sister. However, he won't completely change or humiliate himself to pacify the masses, as the half-sister does. Armstrong is in the process of walking the delicate balance between being himself while being what others want, of following the rules while making up his own. Henry has never done this. He has certainly disregarded some rules—the British imposed ones, for instance—but only substituted others for them, the IRA's. He has never actively tried to create his own rules for others to follow. During their partnership, Armstrong models this. Henry, however, again doesn't learn.

Both men are able to temporarily transcend worldly divisions and lose themselves in music. Armstrong's music is able to make Henry overcome his "Irishness:" "At last. I wasn't Irish any more. The first time I heard it, before I was properly listening, I knew for absolute sure. It took me by the ears and spat on my forehead, baptized me. . . .I was a Yank. At last. . . .It was furious, happy and lethal; it killed all other music. It was new, like me" (136). Armstrong's music makes Henry feel bigger than a nationality—not Irish or American but both and neither. Armstrong is a minority but a force—bigger than the law but subject to the law—priceless but penniless. His music makes Henry feel this way, although he isn't.

Paradoxically, Armstrong also makes Henry find his past. In his first meeting with the musician, Henry believes, "He'd seen the man I used to be. A man who carried a good suit through checkpoints and locked doors. Louis Armstrong had looked at me and seen someone he wanted, a man he needed to know, a man who'd stroll right on with him" (144). Armstrong's lyric lament for his mother makes Henry grieve for his own childhood, lost in his mother's alcoholic stupors:

> It was the blues, his grief crying out of the bell. But it was no lament. It was the cry of a terrified child, left all alone, forever. No notes, no breaks, but all one howl that rushed at her dead body; it was angry and lost

and—What about meee!—it turned and turned, and returned to the body, and washed, and dressed her. His mother, mine—she skips and she laughs, her black eyes shine happy—he sent his mother home. . . .It didn't soften; there was no fond look back, no shared prayer. (156)

The music mirrors Henry's own aching and shattered feelings from the first novel. Armstrong, via music, is able to articulate this loss, a luxury that the young Henry never is afforded until this moment. Thus, Armstrong allows Henry to connect with his past but transcend it.

Despite his time with Dora, Henry equates his own experiences of being Irish with those of being African American. Henry sees little difference between the oppression he faces and African Amerians': "I could have told them: I'm Irish, lads, one of the Empire's niggers, and I *know*" (254). He feels at home with Dora and Louis: in Harlem, he says, "I'd be safe here too, but alive again. I didn't know what I'd do, but I knew I'd be doing it here. I didn't know why—it was stupid, sentimental" (148).

Armstrong, however, won't whitewash the differences. Besides his needing to use Henry's race in order to be autonomous himself, he notes that being Irish is not the same as being African American: "That the Irish in you, Henry. Always the bad news. . . .You got to start thinking like a Negro. We not heading into a whupping. We just got away from one" (224).

Henry also mistakenly believes that Armstrong is "restless" as the half-sister calls Henry (281). He says that life with Armstrong "was fuckin' chaotic. . . .There was no such thing as rest. . . . He was running, to get away, to catch up, to grab control of himself and his life and his genius. . ." (188). Henry sees himself in this version of Armstrong and projects himself onto Armstrong: "He needed control, but he hadn't worked it out. I was the start but he wasn't sure how" (183). However, Armstrong is not running and is not restless. He is simultaneously moving purposefully and standing his ground, which Henry eventually learns. "He wasn't running at all. The man was standing firm. He wouldn't work for the mob. He wanted the freedom of his sound. And, all around, they were closing in, ready to cage him" (211).

Henry's misperception of their situations leads to his misperceiving Armstrong and not learning Armstrong's lessons. Henry mistakenly thinks Armstrong's desire is to "be black and not let it matter. Overcome it." But this is Henry's dream—to overcome being Irish. Armstrong's dream is simply, "No, man, nay, nay. Sick of having to be proud or ashamed. Just want to blow my fucking cornet" (319).

Henry learns little from Armstrong. In fact, he regresses somewhat during their association. Henry becomes "Louis Armstrong's white man" (170) and is content to be "watching him, listening to him invent the best music yet" (168). His former lover Hettie says he has changed in that he "dressed like an African dresses when he ain't going to work. Sundays. . . You walk like an African. . . .You move loose. . . .like an African" (256). Henry, who thoroughly enjoys his status as Irish war hero, now doesn't want to be "the only man on stage." Henry says he is afraid he is becoming "too new, too defiant and bright" (256). He has lost the feeling (imagined or not) of being the glowing baby. He claims that life with Armstrong is "the first time in my life [that] I was ordinary" (259). Additionally, Henry abandons his family for no reason to accompany Armstrong to Harlem, despite the fact that he knows how much Miss O'Shea and his daughter need him (229). And, we are still forced to sit through the (almost by now obligatory) instances of being on the margins of greatness, like when he forces the studio into allowing Armstrong a fourth take, "the most famous trumpet solo in jazz history was played by Louis Armstrong but it was brought to you by Henry Smart" (169); as well as the unattributed voice over in *Tight Like This*.

Henry eventually does regain some sense of self. He begins to feel uncomfortable and self-conscious in Harlem and often must force himself to "keep forgetting that I was the white man, strolling with the black man; stopping to talk with other black men, entering the barber shop with the black man, bringing my white man's hair in with me" (253).

> I was tired of being the white boy. It was only starting to seep in: my purpose was my whiteness, and my willingness to walk it beside Louis. It was often a pleasure, but it was none of my doing. It was the age of ballyhoo but I was saying nothing. I knew what I was doing, and I'd known it from the start—*You're the white man puts his hand on that white man's shoulder*—but maybe I wanted my own trumpet (247).

He finally wearies of being an also-ran, the "not-a-star" Henry, just as he does with the revolution.

As with his friendship with Dalton, he realizes, that, although his friendship with Armstrong is real, his usefulness has an expiration date. "Louis didn't need me. He had Rockwell; he knew how to use him. I was just hanging around. . . .the distance was there now, and we both knew it. But I couldn't say goodbye, and neither could he" (266, 285). However, he distinguishes Armstrong from the Revolution:

> Louis hadn't fooled me, or promised me anything. He'd sung to me, like Jack had. . .but the song had been real, not just a couple of words and notes. He'd sung the song from start to end. . . .And I had decided to join. But I hadn't joined anything. I was in because of what I wasn't. I wasn't black, I wasn't a player or an agent or a manger or a shark or a friend of Al Capone's. I wasn't the things that the dangerous white men were. So I was useful—just as long as I wasn't anything. Just Louis Armstrong's white man (247).

Although we think Henry has finally learned the importance of individual autonomy, he hasn't. He betrays his friendship with Armstrong by persuading him to provide the background music on the half-sister's recording, despite the fact that she vehemently dislikes Armstrong and is overtly condescending and racist. His inability to learn from Armstrong makes it no surprise for the reader when Henry must be saved again, this time by the joint forces of the half-sister and Armstrong.

His last teacher is literally his teacher. Miss O'Shea teaches Henry for two days before he is bounced from the parochial school. Although *A Star Called Henry's* epigraph, lyrics from Irving Berlin's "Cheek to Cheek," points to a romance so overwhelming that it supersedes both worldly cares and intoxications, she, as his wife, is relatively insignificant in his life, more a series of episodes than a unifying force. Henry would do well to learn from her, although he does not.

Doyle had very little difficulty creating the character of Miss O'Shea. She is the result of the vast amount of research he did for the Trilogy.

> I began to read about Cumann na mBan and these women, these extraordinary women—some of them quite eccentric women. They found their voice in Cumann na mBan, this organization for women, and then it was stifled somewhat. So she'd be one of these people who'd be very, very disappointed by what was going on. There was a lovely little book that accompanied an exhibition in Kilmainham Jail; great text, and lovely images of various women looking extraordinarily impressive and very elegant in their various uniforms. I think it was called *Guns and Chiffon*. That got me thinking about this particular woman, Miss O'Shea, and this enthusiasm for the Irish language which I have always found quite funny. . . .And the sheer innocence of her thinking that at least we'll have the Irish language—that type of thing. I enjoyed her casual brutality as well. I think there's a dark humour to that. She's the teacher quite early on, I seem to remember now. Very quickly she became very clear to me, and I enjoyed the few days that he [Henry] had at school—the joking within that. (Drewett interview 346).

Her character changes somewhat in *Oh, Play That Thing* when she gives up fighting to follow Henry to America. However, the Cumann na mBan is still in her, and she becomes the rebel again during the Great Depression period.

The primary reason for Henry's inability to learn from Miss O'Shea is that she exists more in his imagination than in reality—she is a fantasy for him. He thinks of her as parts of a whole, never as a whole: "brown boots that had a woman's toes neatly packed into their points" (Doyle, *A Star Called Henry* 73); a "bun . . . a mass of the finest brown hair;" and "brown-black eyes" (110). Henry's last sight of her in Ireland is only an image of hair in a distant window. When they meet six years later in Chicago, it is dark and Henry "still couldn't see her properly" (192), although he could make out "brown eyes and some slivers of hair that had escaped from a bun" (194).

Their relationship is culled directly from Schoolboy Fantasy 101. Even though he is only eight years old, filthy and lice-infested, he believes she is enchanted with him, sexually rather than maternally or even pityingly: "But I had a smile that made women wonder and I used it now. I smiled up at her and watched the results. She blinked, and coughed. She reached out, then stopped herself. But she had to touch me; I could see that. And she reached out again; she braved the filth and rested her hand on my hair" (73). And with the 14-year-old Henry, she is supposedly just as lascivious: "My eyes were blue and fascinating whirlpools. . . .And Miss O'Shea hadn't even got to them yet. She was still feeding on my britches. I stood at ease and let her. She was mesmerized" (110). Shortly thereafter, in their first sexual encounter, Miss O'Shea literally and figuratively shakes loose her schoolmarm hair, takes off her librarian spectacles and turns temptress.

Their marriage does little to bring reality into their relationship. He calls her, "My teacher, my wife, my absolute ride" (205). They see each other only in hurried sexual encounters punctuated by dangerous revolutionary expeditions. Henry takes particular pains to be forever ignorant of her first name to perpetuate the fantasy. He wants to stop time and for her to be "his Miss O'Shea" forever. Not only a sexual receptacle, she is also the container for all of Henry's projections: She is both the warm and comforting virgin, the insatiable and sexually demanding whore, and the fearlessly devoted warrior. Miss O'Shea ultimately realizes the fantasy aspect to his ignorance: "[It] used to be exciting. And now I think, it just makes me very sad. That you never knew my name" (Doyle, *Oh, Play That Thing* 204). For Henry, who continually defiantly yells, "I am Henry Smart" in order to validate his existence, purposefully remaining ignorant of someone's name is, in a sense, invalidating their own existence in favor of his own (still) schoolboy projections and longings.

We discover, in *The Dead Republic*, that her name is Nuala. Interestingly, the collection in which "The Quiet Man" is published is bookended by two stories about Nuala Kierley, a "passionate and committed patriot whose love for Ireland is such that 'no man that ever drew breath would oust Ireland from its pride of place in her heart'" (Walsh qtd. in Moynihan 59) and who eventually discovers that her husband is an informer.

Because she is more or less a fantasy for Henry, he never fully commits to her. In his relationship with her, he keeps his emotional ten percent (which he doesn't do with his other mentors.) Thus, the reader does not find it entirely peculiar that Henry makes no effort to contact or find her when he gets to America. True, Henry claims to miss her viscerally:

> And, Christ, I missed Miss O'Shea. I turned every corner expecting to see her, even though there were thousands of miles between us, as far as I could know, and it was five years, more since I'd seen her and longer still since I'd been able to hold her. I'd heard nothing of her; I didn't know if she was free or still in jail, fighting her war or rearing our growing daughter, missing me or doing what I'd been doing for years, running away. (141)

However, his actions belie these sentiments. Henry hasn't heard anything of her primarily because he hasn't tried. Even Miss O'Shea berates him: "You never even wrote a blessed letter. . Have you never heard of the telephone, Henry. . . .A great invention altogether. Even in Ireland. Or telegrams?" (201).

When he confesses to his marital indiscretions, he withholds his customary 10 percent: "I told her. But not everything. I was honest, not stupid" (203). Henry is shocked that she not only has kept her wedding ring but also her wedding vows, which makes him initially treat their bloody fight as a joke, hoping "she'd soon have enough and she'd get down here on the floor and fuck me, fuck me, fuck and forgive" (206). Indeed, his primary concern is that none of his blood "got into the jacket" (206). When he decides "it wasn't funny any more, it was time to stop" (206), his first thought is to escape—to leave—and he runs to the door, which is locked. He doesn't remain out of any loyalty to Miss O'Shea or his daughter but only because he is forced to do so. Henry is not interested in a relationship with a real wife, and he prefers to think of her, despite her physical presence, as being "still in Ireland and I was far away" (199).

After their reconciliation, he considers himself "fat on happiness. . . .A father again—for the first time. . . .I was a family man, now and bring home good bacon" (215). However, Henry is physically and emotionally rarely home, being "away for days with Louis, in the Okeh studio. . . .The place was still in my feet" (215). Thus, Henry is still living a fantasy, seeing fatherhood and matrimony as a temporary gig.

Henry's inability to commit to Miss O'Shea makes betraying her and accompanying Louis to New York much easier. Henry's excuse is that Armstrong isn't safe in Chicago and that his job is "looking after him" (229), a lie which Miss O'Shea immediately challenges: "Looking after a black man, instead of your own family" (229). Henry tries to deflect his guilt by saying that she doesn't need looking after, which he knows is false as he can see her exhaustion: "She was tired; I could see it. And the day was only starting; the coffee was still in the air. It had caught up with her. It was in her face, on her shoulders" (229-230). Nevertheless, Henry's restlessness is more powerful than any feeling of responsibility. He further betrays her in New York as his thoughts center on other women—having sex with Armstrong's women and persuading Armstrong to record a song about Piano Annie—rather than on his family in Chicago. Finally, after he realizes Armstrong doesn't need him, he deliberately chooses to stay with Sister Flow instead of returning to Chicago.

As an aside, Henry's tendency to betray isn't unique with Miss O'Shea: It is just most obvious with Miss O'Shea. Henry betrays almost every character he meets in the novel, from skimming off the top with his sandwich boards and bootlegging operations, to scamming both Mildred and Hettie with the "magical" soap, to endangering then dropping Dora. This tendency to betray his friends escalates during the novel, and his betrayal of Armstrong is as shocking to the reader as his betrayal of his family. After reuniting with Sister Flow, he asks Armstrong to play background on her recording, even though he senses that Armstrong must act the "nigger minstrel" (291) to the antagonistic Sister Flow, who wants to get him "whupped or killed. Lynched" (315). He betrays his mentor and friend, as well as his wife and daughter, not out of a sense of self-preservation, but instead, as a favor for a manipulative con woman. Indeed, the half-sister is about the only person Henry does not betray, perhaps because she, a con artist, is savvier than the other characters. This tendency to betray others—while failing to acknowledge the betrayal—is only an indication that he has no unwavering sense of self with which to remain unwaveringly loyal.

Henry's near death at the hands of Ned Kellet and the IRA finally jars him into learning something. All the lessons of his mentors eventually coalesce when his and his family's lives turn nomadic during the Great Depression, and Henry is a changed character. No longer losing himself to transcend himself, he lives day to day with his family, hopping on trains, living in

Hoovervilles, and stealing to survive. Henry finally seems content, living meal to meal with his family.

His separation from his family occurs, not because he chooses someone else, but because he sacrifices himself to save his son. He loses his leg but has found himself. For the first time, he actively and doggedly searches for his family. For the first time, he misses them as much as he says he does. He is not sidetracked by other women, glamour, or intrigue. He is finally truly consumed by thoughts of his family.

The final scene in the novel is significant. Henry crawls into the desert to die but is discovered by Henry Fonda, acting on a nearby movie set. Interestingly, Henry's life is saved many times, and only by those without power. The novels use the powerless—women and minorities—to save the powerful, white men. In *A Star Called Henry*, Piano Annie saves him after he escapes from Kilmainham. She clothes him, houses him, and finds him work. Sister Flow saves him several times, as we have seen, in Sweet Afton and in New York. Miss O'Shea literally carries a wounded Henry to safety in *A Star Called Henry* and again saves him from a near execution. Armstrong twice distracts men intent upon harming Henry with his music and drives Henry to Chicago, thus effecting his final escape from New York.

Henry Fonda's discovery of Henry is significant in that for the first time Henry is saved by someone with power and wealth. Henry, although having lost his leg, has become empowered and does not need to rely on the oppressed for survival. Despite his circumstances, he has returned to himself. The power of the wooden leg, the talisman of *A Star Called Henry*, has returned. Note the parody of Christ's resurrection: Henry "lay down. He waited. He died. He waited. Died. . . An actor called Fonda went out for a piss and found me" (374), a Doylian baptism for the newly resurrected Henry with his apostle John (Ford) eager to proclaim his Gospel . . . in the final instalment of the trilogy.

Certainly the picaresque tradition allows the hero to experience disparate adventures and encounter a wide variety of personalities. While a picaresque hero must be a type of chameleon to encounter so many different situations, Henry blends in so well that he, the main character, is more the background of this novel. He is such the blank slate that we wonder what such intense characters, like Armstrong, Sister Flow, and Miss O'Shea, see in him. The novel's end leaves us hope, however, for a transfiguration to a more interesting Henry.

CHAPTER 5
PAULA SPENCER

Paula Spencer (2006) is the follow up to Doyle's 1996 novel *The Woman Who Walked Into Doors*, which deals with a thirty-nine-year old woman who has been beaten by her husband for seventeen years and has since turned to alcohol to dull the pain of her existence. In the first novel, we see Paula Spencer kick out her husband, struggle to give up drinking, and attempt to minimize the damage her alcoholism and abusive marriage have done to her four children. Despite the grim summary of events, the novel is not tragic. Indeed, Doyle says, "There is room for hope, however. This woman has gone through a brutal marriage for seventeen years and the husband is gone. She actively threw him out. . . .she's going to make a stab at it" (qtd. in White 140). *Paula Spencer*, published ten years later, shows this "stab at it."

In *The Woman Who Walked Into Doors*, Doyle plays with time. The structure of the novel is spiral instead of strictly chronological, and we see Paula's attempt to re-create her past and understand it. She can't comprehend how her life has become so horrific and tries to discover the answer in her memories. However, because of the numerous beatings and even more numerous alcohol-induced blackouts, she doesn't trust her memory. She seeks validation for them from her sisters, which rarely comes. Indeed, at times, their remembrances differ from hers radically. "What she does in the book is she's looking back as far back as she can go. She's trying to separate what actually happened from what she thinks might have happened. She's trying to get her sisters' memories to tally with hers" (Sbrockey interview 547). She doesn't understand how she could have become what she has become. The novel, written in first person, is her exploration of her life: "By understanding what happened to her, she hopes to start to make changes in her life and in herself" (White 117).

Paula Spencer shows Paula eight years later and four months sober. Doyle uncharacteristically decided to return to the character Paula because

> she seemed to be a good guide through the changes that had occurred in the ten years between the two books. And I think I was right. Kind of a wise, interesting character who may not be gaining overtly from the boom but who wouldn't be feeling bitter either—and who would actually bring me back to street level. So the decision to write a book from her point of view was a good thing. I may well have said after that I will never go back to that character again, but I probably will go back to that character again, if there is an interesting story to be told. (Doyle, Personal interview 228)

Although the narrative is third person, we still see events from Paula's perspective: Doyle is "a fluke inside the intestine of his characters, a man who writes like a recording machine of the heart and voice" (Callil 1). Doyle says that his decision to write in the third person was to make the books distinctive:

> I didn't want it to be about those first ten years. I didn't want it to be in sequence. And also I wanted it to be fresh. If I was to go first person to first person, then inevitably you're going to be falling back into the character. But, if I wrote it in third person second tense—that was a bit of an experiment. I could distance myself from the first book also. I could stay close to it but I could write alongside it. In first person I use the analogy of she's holding the camera. In the third person, it's somebody else holding the camera. It helped with a different perspective and a different vocabulary. It helped me stay close but not be her. (Personal interview 15)

When she kicks out her husband, she is "abandoning the happy the happy narrative, false though it seems to us, and admitting that the unhappy one is the real story of her life" (Jay 59). *Paula Spencer* examines how Paula continues to write her narrative, trying to make it happy, while dealing with an often unhappy, daily existence without alcohol and with four, very scarred children. She has grown tremendously in eight years and continues to grow - as a recovering alcoholic, as a mother, and as a woman - during the year covered in the novel. We see a protagonist who has explored her past and seldom questions the truth of her memories any longer.

We also see a protagonist who is struggling with the question of "What do I do now?" Now that she has her past, how does she move forward with its burdens? "More than anyone, she knows. You can't leave things behind. They come with you" (Doyle, *Paula Spencer* 12). Paula's painful past constantly threatens to derail her sobriety. She can't escape the physical pain of repeated beatings: "The pain [in her back] lights up every other pain. Every wound and break she's had, going on and off. Reminding her. Catching up. . . .But the back is there, the twinge. I can do this. I can bring you down" (248). Nor can she escape the emotional pain. Just as physical injuries often remain or leave scars, so too do emotional injuries, which we carry with us. We continue to circle the same wagons our entire lives. Our actions never exist in a vacuum, and we feel their consequences throughout our lives.

In *Paula Spencer*, we see a protagonist who vows to accept the past and all its ramifications—"no running away" (45). We see our protagonist's transformation from being someone who is looking for an escape from her past and its accompanying guilt into someone who embraces her past and her mistakes as a part of who she is. In the novel, we see Paula learn to accept herself as a mother, as a woman, and as an Irishman.

We meet Paula when she is four months, five days sober. Although she works hard at her two jobs as part of an office janitorial staff and a household cleaning woman, alcohol and motherhood are the two most powerful forces in Paula's life, both warring to control her. She defines herself in terms of drink and its effects, primarily on her children. Notice how she is introduced: "It's more than four months since she had a drink. Four months and five days. . . .A third of a year. Half a pregnancy, nearly" (1). She links motherhood to her sobriety and thus, to her alcoholism, showing her guilt over her failure as a mother because her alcoholism has "thicken[ed] a family atmosphere with mistrust and guilt" (Hall 1).

Paula is ambivalent about being a mother. Her four children are the most important part of her life, and most of the novel concerns her feelings toward and relationships with them. She loves her children deeply: "Paula gave birth to Nicola. She's her mother's daughter. It's thrilling. Despite the circumstances, the drink, the beatings, a big part of Paula survived—there, every time she sees Nicola. And Jack. It's not just love. It is love. She loves them; she loves herself. She made them. . . .Pride and joy. . . .It was exactly what she felt when she saw Jack or Nicola" (Doyle, *Paula Spencer* 167). Indeed, her maternal instinct is what drives her to hit Charlo with the frying pan and kick him out of the house and of her life and her children's lives: "But when I saw him looking that way at Nicola, when I saw his eyes. I don't know what happened to me—the Bionic Woman—he was gone. . . .My finest hour. I was there. I was something. I loved. Down on his head. I was killing him. The evil. He'd killed me and now it was Nicola. But no. No fuckin' way" (Doyle, *Woman* 213).

Because of her overwhelming love for her children, however, she feels tremendous guilt about the way she has neglected her children: "Alcoholics can stop drinking but what is there for the children of alcoholics? Is it always too late? Probably" (Doyle, *Paula Spencer* 253). She knows that her children were "forced to grow up. Teenagers shouldn't have to wash their mother's face and hair. They shouldn't have to peel their own potatoes. They shouldn't get their first alcohol at home. They shouldn't be homeless on their sixteenth birthday" (49). Mothers "can't have problems" (132), and obviously Paula has, the knowledge of which is "always there but sometimes—

now—the shame is enough to kill her" (179). At times this guilt and shame-inspired self-loathing makes her "want to run. She wants to hide and die. She wants to free him, and Leanne and Nicola and Jack" (227).

She hates the guilt and, sometimes, her children for causing it: She has heard that "all mothers feel guilt" (46), but her family has "made her feel useless and so guilty she's wanted to maim herself, to push the guilt in under her skin so no one can see it or smell it. But she knows" (137). At times her children, though they have taken care of her, exhaust her because she has to face them and their problems caused by her alcoholism: "It's about being careful. For the rest of her life. It's killing her. She can feel it. Every word, every little decision. Chipping away. She wants to just give up. Not give up, but take a break. Not to have to ignore Leanne. Not have to worry about Jack. To sit down and feel comfortable" (86). She sometimes wishes to be free of the burden of having "to hide from children" (91): not having the burden of having to prove herself sober and responsible.

Paula, despite her tremendous feelings of guilt, recognizes that not everything is her fault: "It's not fair at all. Leanne's in trouble—Paula's fault. But that's not fair either. She's doing her best. . . .She's always blamed herself, for everything. It goes without saying now; it gets her nowhere" (23). Paula wants a reprieve from the feeling that her children believe their lives are her "fault." She wants them, and herself, to acknowledge "the impossibility of knowing what chain of consequence we loosen in a moment: tossing away a date stone, firing a crossbow, or, as Paula did, stepping onto the dance floor with a sexually attractive man" (Hall 2).

She has four children, each one evoking both pleasure and pain in different ways. 15-year-old Jack, the youngest, is also the "easiest" one. Jack, who is only three or so when Paula is able to extricate herself from her abusive marriage and about ten when Paula first starts making serious attempts at sobriety, hasn't had to endure as much abusive neglect as his older siblings. "He's self-aware. He's bright. He's gorgeous. She looks at Jack. She doesn't feel guilt. She'll never have to beg forgiveness" (Doyle,

Paula Spencer 159). Jack causes few problems for Paula and is primarily a source of pride for her: "She doesn't worry too much about Jack. She doesn't need to, and she doesn't know why not. A dead father, an alcoholic mother—it's not a great start in life. But he's grand. He seems to be" (9). Jack is "never obnoxious. In a chat with other women about their impossible teenagers, she'd have nothing to say. She'd have to make up something. He's lovely. He organizes his own pocket money; he works. He's good in school. He's had nothing pierced. He's made no young one pregnant. She should be very proud of him. She is. . . " (49). Finally, she knows that "she still has Jack. . . .He's still her baby" (2). She doesn't "have" any of the older children.

However, loving Jack is not problem-free. She worries: "He's too like a fuckin' saint. She thinks that sometimes. She wants to shake him. She wants him to throw things and hate her. She'd understand. She'd cope. She doesn't really know his friends. She's not sure if he has any. . . .But she doesn't know his life" (49). Although he doesn't scream or act out, he has lived with Paula long enough to still be "looking at the floor, under the couch, for the bottle, the glass" (7). Ironically, because she hasn't let him down as much or as often as her other children, she is the most terrified of disappointing him. She doesn't want to mar her almost clean slate with him. Paula constantly feels the need to prove her sobriety to him: "She stands up. That's for him. I'm fine - look. I'm awake and alert" (8). When she, desperate for a drink, violently and sloppily tries to find alcohol under Leanne's bed, she is most concerned that Jack has witnessed her degradation. She knows she has gotten lucky in that Jack is relatively unscathed by her past, and she is terrified that she will do something to negate his apparent normalcy.

In a similar vein, Paula enjoys her role as grandmother more than that of mother precisely because it is uncomplicated. Paula is "a good granny. She loves it. She felt nothing but joy when Nicola told her the news that she was expecting. That was the first time she seriously gave up the drink"(35). With her grandchildren, as with Jack, she doesn't have to apologize. She can start fresh and judgment-free. She can play the part of the munificent grandmother and doesn't have to be a "beggar" (231) as she is with her own children. Any concerns or worries her grandchildren may have are easily assuaged with a present, for instance, socks, which we see in an exchange with her five-year-old granddaughter Vanessa, who is upset that Paula drinks some of her younger sister's soda. Her own children's reactions to her "drinking" cannot be handled so easily.

With her other three "lost children" (51) come overwhelmingly crushing guilt and shame. John Paul, the oldest, becomes a heroin addict and disappears from home when he is fourteen and "was gone months from the house before she really lost him" (109). He re-enters Paula's life several years before the novel's beginning merely by showing up on her doorstep. He is sober, working, and married with two children. John Paul has become "good. A good man. He's been through a lot. There was no fatted calf. He didn't expect one. It wasn't why he rang the bell. She'll never forget it. Nine years, four months and thirteen days. She opened the door. And he was there. And she didn't know him" (52).

Despite the "happy ending," her relationship with her son causes Paula tremendous anxiety. She loves him but she knows she has no right to do so. She understands why he has not contacted her earlier, but she is still angry and hurt: "Two more grand-children. They're gas kids. They're lovely. God though, they scare her. . . .Paula wasn't there when they were born. That's the problem—one of the problems. They were there years before she found out. That kills her. She deserves it. She's no right to anything, no natural right—she gave that one away. But no one deserves it. It's savage, ridiculous—they lived four miles away" (52).

She remembers John Paul intimately as a child: "He was a jumpy kid, always flying. Looking everywhere but taking nothing in. Adorable, because he was heading the wrong way. People patted John Paul, when they could catch him. He was a stupid kind of kid and she'd loved him more for that. She'd laughed. She'd shaken her head" (109). However, she doesn't know the man he has become and how he becomes him: "John

Paul's not a talker. He doesn't chat. He's in control; he can never let go. It's a powerful thing. But it's frightening. He manages every part of himself, like a sheepdog at the sheep. A loose hand on the table gets pulled back in. His lips never curl. He doesn't sigh. Every word is examined before it's let out. He's worked very hard" (109). She regrets the loss of the carefree child and blames herself. She desperately wants to be his mother—to know him intimately again--but she can't. She doesn't even feel comfortable with him. "All she wants is to know him. Even a bit. He came to her. He rang her doorbell, nearly two years ago. But he's still the same stiff stranger. . . .But this man will never say I love you. Not to Paula. She'll never be able to say it to him. It'll always hang there. She'll always be the beggar" (226-231). He isn't dependent upon her like Jack and has no stake in her sobriety. His shell is so impenetrable that Paula wants to lash out: "What is it she has against him? It's there, the urge to sneer. She doesn't know why. She really doesn't" (114). His wariness and disinterest are reminders to Paula of her inadequacies, of her destructive past and the precarious nature of her future.

Her relationship with John Paul is also problematic because, as a former addict, he understands her alcoholism. She can't lie to him. "He knew. She knows that now. But she didn't. He knew she was an addict. She didn't. She drank too much. She'd have admitted that. She was an alcoholic. She knew that too. But she didn't know what it meant. . . .John Paul looked straight at her. And she realized. It made her want to die or kill him. . . ." (55). She knows that he understands the dangers inherent in her recovery. Paula can't fool him, which scares her. Thus, he pressures her, in a way different from Jack, to stay sober.

Her relationship with Nicola is a mother-daughter one, except that Nicola plays the role of the responsible mother, not Paula: "Nicola looks after Paula. She checks on her—that's what tonight is really about. . . . Nicola reared the younger ones as much as Paula ever did. She picked up Paula and washed her. She fed Leanne and Jack. And after she left she still looked after Paula" (35, 252). Nicola, a successful sporting goods representative, cannot relinquish her codependent role as Paula's mother and gives her expensive gifts - a television, a refrigerator, a cell phone - which Paula accepts with mixed feelings: "She's showing off a bit. But that's fine with Paula. She's proud to have a daughter who can fling a bit of money around. The pride takes care of the humiliation, every time. Kills it stone dead" (4). Obviously, the pride doesn't kill it everytime.

Paula is amazed at the success of her oldest daughter, who has, in her way, become as controlled as John Paul, seen again in the hands: "[Nicola's] fingers are long and her nails are always perfect, never a scratch or a cracked nail. Nicola has never let work or age get into her hands. That's the most amazing thing about Nicola, Paula thinks. Or what it stands for - they stand for, her hands. Nicola is in control. Nicola can manage. Nicola is much, much more than she's supposed to be. Paula adores her. . . .Nicola knows all about taking care. She's been looking after them all for years" (132).

Despite Paula's admiration and Nicola's attentiveness, the two are not close. Nicola's constant mothering and invulnerability are annoying, even insulting, to Paula and to the rest of the family: "They hate her for it. They hate her and they hold her beautiful hand. She's had her problems and they haven't cared. They don't want to know. She's been their mother, and mothers can't have problems. Paula wants to be Nicola's mother" (132). Her previous dependence upon her and the gifts bring back the guilt and ambivalence: "Carmel and Nicola were there. They were coming to the rescue. Paula loves them for that, and resents and sometimes hates them for it. . . She's never hated Nicola. . . .They've annoyed her and they've made her feel useless and so guilty she's wanted to maim herself, to push the guilt in under her skin so no one can see it or smell it. But she knows. Without them, she'd be dead" (137).

Paula most resents Nicola's inability to recognize her change and her growth:

She has that voice—you're going to disappoint me. Paula could do without it. . . .[Paula] is not to be trusted. Nicola looks after Paula, not the other way round. . . .She tries not to let Nicola annoy her. But it's been happening. Nicola's the one who's furthest from her. It didn't feel like that before, but now it does. . . . She feels bad about Nicola. But it's hard. Nicola sees no difference between Paula now and Paula the way she was ten years ago, five years, last year. Nicola was never a child; she never could be. Paula's fault—she knows, she feels it. . . .Nicola will never trust her. She'll always be checking. Paula doesn't drink. She's nearly ready to make that claim. But she can't say that to Nicola. Because she'll see Nicola's face. Not disbelief, or sarcasm. Just sadness. . .It's hard to take. (176-77, 252-3).

Having been hurt so often, Nicola cannot dare to hope for Paula's permanent sobriety. Her co-dependency allows precious little room for Paula's change, which, ultimately, could prove to be crippling to both characters.

The most problematic relationship is with the 22-year-old Leanne, who lives at home. Leanne isn't a "happy ending" (135) as her other children appear to be because Paula believes that she "gave her away years ago. She threw Leanne away" (74).

Leanne, herself an alcoholic, struggles the most with the remnants of her abusive childhood—or, at least, her struggles are the most apparent to Paula because they manifest themselves so apparently. "Leanne scares Paula. The guilt. It's always there. Leanne is twenty-two. Leanne wets her bed. Leanne deals with it. It's terrible. Her fault. Paula's fault. The whole mess. Most of Leanne's life" (6). Confronting Leanne's diseased behavior reinforces the guilt that is Paula's constant companion: "Leanne's in trouble—Paula's fault. . . .Leanne didn't lick it off a stone. She grew up with nothing else. And a few good months aren't going to change that. There have been good months before. Paula could count them. They won't add up to much more than a year" (23-4).

Leanne openly wears the psychological scars of her childhood as opposed to the others, who, no less affected, at least hide them behind a mask of normalcy and calm. Unlike Nicola and John Paul, even Leanne's body—seen again in a description of her hands--shows the ravages of her past : "Leanne's hands are desperate. Scratched raw, especially the wrists. Paula hates to see those scratches, self-inflicted—all her life. They remind her of the little girl, holding onto Paula, clinging, getting between Paula and Charlo. Protecting her. Leave my mammy alone. The skinny little wrist, the little red fingers, the nails bitten to blood and nothing" (150). Almost every description of Leanne is negative: "Her face is blotched. Her eyes are dirty. She was never beautiful. Paula can't help thinking that" (70). Paula sees that "Leanne is skin and bone. Paula sees that, out of the house, out in the open. Leanne is dying" (87). When Leanne breaks her foot and has to remain home for several weeks, Paula resents her helplessness: "Smashed-Ankle Barbie herself. Leanne on the couch, in a dirty tracksuit, firing bullets at the telly with the remote control. . . It's no wonder Paula's going mad" (82).

However, Leanne is a hard worker with a scathing wit, a determined personality, and plenty of intelligence - in other words, just like her mother - which is one reason Paula is so ambivalent towards her. Paula sees herself in the hungover Leanne: "It wasn't just the early-morning mess. The mad hair and last night's mascara. It was the colour of her skin. The veins on each side of her nose. The look in the eyes that came straight at Paula, the anger and panic, the terror, the whole lot coming at her. It was Paula looking straight back at Paula" (21). When she sees cigarette butts near Leanne's bed, Paula thinks, "Drunk and tired, out of her face. Paula thinks it - Jesus Christ, she's as stupid as me" (91).

The two mirror each other in several scenes. For instance, they have several physical fights over alcohol, once when Leanne is trying to get alcohol and later when Paula is. The two almost literally switch places in these scenes. In another juxtaposition, Paula tries to mother Leanne by making up her bed, taking away the sheets wet with urine; later, when Paula is sick, Leanne does the same thing, discarding the sheets, wet this time, from sweat. Both have drunken nights at the hospital, and both carry physical and emotional scars from an abusive past and an alcoholic adulthood. Paula sees the good and the bad—more often the bad—in Leanne, which only reminds Paula of the bad in herself and the years she is trying to ignore. Paula sees herself in the unattractive, psychological mess that is her daughter—and it scares her: "Can she point at Leanne and say [with pride], That's my daughter. . . .Who'd want to point at Paula and shout, That's my mother. There's no reason why any of her kids would do that. She has no right to expect it" (169). We see that Paula needs to accept Leanne, and ultimately herself, in whatever manifestation Leanne - or Paula - appears: "It's herself she has to fight against, not Leanne or John Paul. They're innocent. Leanne doesn't have to pass any tests. She doesn't have to do anything. Leanne is Leanne. That's what Paula has to accept and love. The Leanne she'll meet later today. Or the Leanne who might not come home. Leanne tomorrow morning. That's my daughter" (169).

Interestingly, this mirroring is also why she dislikes John Paul's wife Star: "Star doesn't look like a mother you'd run to. She doesn't look like a mother at all. Maybe that's it. Paula looks at Star and sees herself. She's not good enough. . . .Star looks like a junkie. That's it. Paula doesn't trust her" (112-13). Paula knows she too hasn't been the type of mother children run to, nor does Paula trust herself.

Their relationship is further complicated because Leanne is in the middle of alcoholism herself and therefore a threat to Paula's sobriety. On one hand, Paula's sobriety is an insult to Leanne's alcoholism. Paula's well meaning attempts at helping Leanne stop drinking are violently rebuffed. A drunk Paula makes it easier for a drunk Leanne to exist. A recovering mother pressures Leanne into recovery. On the other hand, having Paula sober is contradictorily keeping Leanne drunk. Were Paula to slip back into an alcoholic fog, Leanne would feel compelled to stop drinking and take care of her mother: "Leanne will stop drinking now. She won't touch another drop, so she can look after her mammy. She has Paula where she wants her.

Where she knows her. The house isn't big enough for two alcoholic women. One needs to look at the other, from a height, from a depth. They both need the love that's given to those who hate themselves" (181). Either way, Paula's sobriety seems, to her, to be harming Leanne. And so, Paula feels again as if she were sacrificing her child, ironically, this time by being sober.

Because of the enormity of Leanne's problems, trying to repair the damage to Leanne is much more difficult than it is with her other children. Even though coffee with John Paul is hardly enjoyable, it isn't violent. Even though she can't stop Nicola's sometimes intrusive visits and phone calls, she can postpone the visits and fail to answer the phone. Also, because neither of her adult children live with her, the reality of their daily challenges remain a mystery to Paula. Even with Jack, Paula is ignorant of much of his life outside the home. Leanne, however, cannot be ignored, no matter how hard Paula tries.

Paula's relationships with her children define her yet restrict her. These relationships buoy her yet threaten to sink her. While addicts initially believe that sobriety will make their problems disappear, Paula is far enough into her recovery to realize the fallacy of this belief. Her past has consequences and she must handle them.

Paula also must learn to cope with herself as a woman. Charlo's beatings drive out of her much of her sexuality, and she currently relates to her body in terms of what is aching and what is not aching yet. She sees her body as functional—something to be managed—never as something beautiful or pleasurable. Despite her remaining good looks, we learn early on in the novel that "she hasn't had sex since her husband died. A year before he died; more. She doesn't remember it. She didn't know it would be the last time. Twelve years—thirteen years ago. It's pathetic. No it isn't. . . .You don't measure you life in sex. She knows that now. . . .The more you fuck, the happier you are. That's rubbish. She knows that" (6).

As a girl, Paula defines herself and is defined in terms of men. Sexuality is a form of power, something she learns in grade school. She "wanks" a boy in the back of their religion class, which makes her proud: "I did it to him; he didn't do it to me. I did it. My First Wank. . .I'd survived. I was someone" (Doyle, *The Woman Who Walked Into Doors* 41). Women of Paula's generation are labeled as young girls in sexual terms: "Where I grew up - and probably everywhere else - you were a slut or a tight bitch, one or the other, if you were a girl - and usually before you were thirteen. You didn't have to do anything to be a slut. . . .Anything could get you called a slut. My father called me a slut the first time I put on mascara" (45-6). However, when she is accompanied by a powerful man, she becomes powerful by association: "I stopped being a slut the minute Charlo Spencer started dancing with me. . . .I was Charlo's girl now and that made me respectable. Men kept their mouths shut when I went by. They were all scared of Charlo and I loved that. It was like revenge" (45, 49). The temporary power she achieves as Charlo's proxy is transformed into abject powerlessness when he begins to beat her. Thus, since her sexuality garners her a type of power, her feelings of powerlessness reflect a lack of sexuality. She realizes that "she used to be good at looking at men. She could look straight back at any age, height, shoe size. Charlo knocked it out of her. That must be it. The confidence, the guts—gone" (Doyle, *Paula Spencer* 32).

She has ambivalent feelings toward her body, which we see in her thoughts about Carmel's breast cancer: "Carmel's being killed by her own breasts" (235). Her body gets her involved with Charlo, and her body gets him out of the house and saves her. Her body gets her to work, but her body can prevent her from working as well. It is something that enables her to earn money as a housekeeper, but it also carries in it the seeds of her destruction. "[The pain in her back has] happened before. It goes away. Like a threat, something that'll come back when it wants to. A nerve, just gently trapped. It's horrible. It's playing with her. She feels like a cripple already. . .The pain lights up every other pain. Every wound and break she's had, going on and off. Reminding her. Catching her" (248).

She is also able to be somewhat proud of her appearance. Although, Paula has had an extraordinarily hard life, she is nevertheless attractive. The men outside the bookie's office look at her as she passes by: "They're still looking. She can't see them, but she knows. Looking at her arse. Looking at each other. Not bad for forty-eight" (29). Her sisters wonder "Where d'you hide your fat, Paula" (221). She honestly appraises herself and thinks, "This distance, this light. She's a good-looking woman. . . .She's a good-looking woman" (10). She can still see traces of the "girl who wanked Martin Kavanagh [who] was five foot three inches tall. . . . She had brown hair, long and straight. . . .She had good skin; She had women's legs. . . .Her mother said she was nice enough looking to be a model but she had a crooked tooth so she knew she couldn't be one" (Doyle, *The Woman Who Walked Into Doors* 42). She can appraise herself critically and disinterestedly, but nevertheless she cannot see herself as a woman.

Part of the destruction caused by Charlo makes her view her own body, as well as those of others, as parts of a whole, Prufrock-like. Notice her attraction to the chef in the Italian restaurant: "There's a fella that does the bread and pizzas. She's seen him in the window. A dark guy, not that handsome—something about his hands. She doesn't stop to watch. She can't. She can't be gawking in windows at middle-aged young fellas" (Doyle, *Paula Spencer* 12). The man on Big Brother has a "nice arse on him" whereas the "the blondey one with the boobs" doesn't impress her much. She is going to vote for a political candidate because "his eyes are gorgeous" (14). The driver of the van taking her to the White Snake concert has "ears [that] are Irish." Her mother's "hands are twisted and savage. . . .She smacks the huge, red knuckle of her wrist" (186). Her daughter's "wrists are desperate. Scratched raw, especially the wrists" (150). John Paul is so controlled that "a loose hand on the table gets pulled back in. His lips never curl" (109). The focus of the novel's end is Carmels breast, which has been removed in a mastectomy. Carmel attempts to cope with breast cancer by reducing the entire experience to the text message, "1 tit" (279). Paula initially defines her body in similar terms.

Finally, Paula has to accept herself as an Irishman in the Ireland of the Celtic Tiger. Paula "wakes up," almost Rip Van Winkle-like, in 2004. Although she has been sober before, the cumulative time of her sobriety is negligible. Thus, she is experiencing the new Ireland for almost the first time and with varying degrees of acceptance. Her "refreshing take on the world, at once innocent and street-smart . . . . [is] the device of a returned local, someone both bemused and in the know. We observe her as she observes the changes. Her tone conveys a wry awareness that she is late to join the race" (Hall 1). Paula sees that:

> The whole area has changed. She's been here since the beginning. It was a farm a few months before they moved in. It was all young families, kids all over the place. Out in the middle of nowhere. No bus of its own. Near the tracks, but no train station. No proper shops, no pub, no church or schools. Nothing but the houses and the people. It had been great back then. It had been so simple. But that's just rubbish. She knows. It hadn't been great. It had never been great. It's all changed now, anyway, the area—the estate. Or it's changing. It used to be settled. It isn't any more. The cafe is a start. And the new name on the pub. There's two groups of people living here now. Those who call it the old name and still go in, and those who call it Finnegan's Wake and don't go in. (17-18)

As her neighborhood is changing, so is the world, and Paula must learn to exist in the technological world of cell phones, DVD players, and computers. When she gets her first cell phone, she doesn't know how to turn it on or off. She is dumbstruck by Jack's computer and is unable to navigate Dublin's new transportation system.

Another aspect of the new Ireland is the influx of immigrants. She feels like a relic from an early time: "It's changing, the whole place. One of the old shops is a café now, opened a few weeks ago. An Italian place, real Italians in it" (12). Although her world is full of emigrees, Paula is often so consumed with her own world that she is relatively untroubled by this new presence: "There's an African woman on the check-out. Nigerian, or one of the others. What other African countries do they come from? Paula doesn't know. There are wars everywhere; you could never keep up" (25).

Other times, she is curious, sometimes admiring and sometimes fearful, of them. She wants to ask African women: "What's it like for them? Are yis not freezing? . . . What made you come here? But questions like that must piss them off. . . They're blacker [than American black women]; their bodies are a different shape. They're rounder women, bursting with strength. They like wigs, some of them, or bits of wigs—extensions. Going to work with purple hair. These girls have style" (59). Paula "likes looking at all the foreigners. Some of them scare a bit. The Romanians, the women. They're a bit frightening—wild, like they've come straight out of a war. But most of them are grand" (25-6). Her workplace is where she notices the largest impact:

> That's another big change, maybe the biggest. The men doing the cleaning work. Nigerians and Romanians. She's not sure if they're legal. She doesn't have to know. She's not paying them. They come and go. They're grand. They're polite. She feels sorry for them. It's not work for a man; she'll never think different. The African lads come dressed to kill, like businessmen and doctors. They change in to their work clothes and back into their suits before they go home. Ashamed. God love them. Handsome lads. They deserve better. (40)

She identifies with these handsome lads who deserve better. She deserves better too, she thinks, on some level. However, she isn't blinded either by this identification or by some type of liberal guilt to the flaws of the individual immigrants. For instance, she dislikes the Romanian man in her cleaning crew because of "he was full of himself" (198), which isn't solely a foreign trait (and is even shared by an Irishman in Leanne's job) and ultimately fires him because of poor work performance.

However, the slightly egocentric Paula is disturbed by immigrants primarily for one reason: Their presence makes her reflect upon her own failures. On the way to clean during a rock concert, she finds herself the only white woman in the van:

> She doesn't feel uncomfortable but it's weird. She's the only white woman. And the only Irish woman—she supposes. The only one born here. . .She's a failure. She shouldn't be in this van. She should be outside looking at it going by. On her way home from work. Already home—on her way out again. Irishwomen don't do this work. Only Paula. . . .Ten years ago there wouldn't have been one black woman on this bus—less than ten years. It would have been Paula and women like Paula. Same age, from the same area, same kids. Where are those women now? Carmel used to do cleaning and now she's buying flats in Bulgaria. . . .She's been left behind. She knows that (56-7).

Her musings not only show Paula's state of mind but also show the extraordinarily low status of the African immigrant population. Paula, the alcoholic widow of a murderer, is socially equal to them.

Paula's commentary on immigration highlights conflicting attitudes in Ireland about racism. Paula thinks, "They're all over the place, the foreigners, the black people. Is that racist? They're all over the place. She doesn't know" (25). Paula, like much of Ireland, isn't quite sure what racism is and what it is not. "The dominant belief in Ireland now seems to be that racism, perhaps even race itself, arrived with the wave of immigrants from the African continent in the 1990s. An alternative, almost equally popular belief appears to be that there is no racism as such in Ireland" (Reddy 374). The novel indicates that Doyle seems to believe that racism is part of the immigration packet. For instance, Paula wonders about Charlo: "It's funny, she doesn't know if he was a racist or not. She hasn't a clue. She'd know these days quickly enough" (Doyle, *Paula Spencer* 25). The reader knows, if Paula doesn't, that Charlo, an uneducated, cruel, abusive victimizer, would have been racist and would have taken advantage of the questionable status of the refugees. Certainly, his wife would have discerned his predisposition for this attitude. Thus, her question is, in effect, Doyle's denial, or at least, uncertainty, that racism can exist systematically in an all white country.

Paula is not the only Irishman who comments on the changing face of the population. Her friend Rita is suspicious of the immigrants: "And I'll tell you another nice thing about up there. The girls in all the shops and cafes and that. They're Irish. It's great. They know what you're talking about" (79). Rita is the only character that espouse these thoughts, though, and she is portrayed negatively: Paula thinks, "Those girls must be great if they know what Rita Kavanagh is talking about. Five minutes in the car with Rita would drive Paula fuckin' demented" (80). Thus, the novel subtly implies that racism and xenophobia exists in isolated, eccentric individuals, like Rita, and is not a "systemic injustice" (Reddy 374). More discussion of Doyle's attitudes towards race is found in the chapter concerning *The Deportees*.

Paula's progress throughout the novel is shown in how she learns to accept each of her changing roles. As a mother, Paula has made substantial progress with each child: "They're knitting together, her children; they're coming back to her. That's what it feels like" (128). Her relationships are not guilt or trouble-free, but they are better.

First, Paula finally becomes involved in Jack's life in a parental role. When he is suspended from school, Paula acts like his mother for the first time in the novel. She uses a stricter tone of voice when Jack speaks back to her: "That's not an answer. She's never spoken to Jack like that" (203). She has ideas about handling his suspension and is pleased with her ingenuity: "She's a tactical genius" (212). However, her parenting instincts are faulty, as her plan includes lying to the teachers, and are ultimately ineffectual, as Jack is suspended anyway. However, Paula at least has begun acting like an authority figure for her teenage son.

Her relationship with John Paul also shows signs of promise. Finally, John Paul cracks his stoic demeanor long enough to compliment Paula and express a semblance of concern for her: "You're doing alright. You're facing it. . .If you were running away you wouldn't actually be running. You'd have stopped. You wouldn't be bothered. You wouldn't be here. . .He's said nothing new but she had to hear it. He should hate her; he shouldn't be here. But he is. That's why she believes him. That's why, maybe, she believes herself" (229). Their final interaction shows John Paul inviting Paula to his new house and volunteering to pick her up in his van, something he neglects to do earlier in the novel and which Paula notes as a sign of his latent anger. Progress has been made.

Nicola, so tightly controlled she is almost static, is harder to move than John Paul. She is so entrenched in her role as mother that she seems unable to change. Paula does try, however, to assert some independence and free Nicola from her codependency: "They're both trying. They're trying to meet. And they know it. - You're not to come running every time you think there's something wrong, says Paula. Nicola fights back the objection; Paula can see it. . . .I'm grand, says Paula.—D'you believe me. . . .She doesn't, but Paula won't say it" (258). Nicola is too damaged to give up control easily, but, at the very least, Paula has begun the dialogue with Nicola, and Nicola is listening.

Finally, Leanne is making progress with her alcoholism (we learn from John Paul), and her relationship with her mother is changing. Paula is trying hard not to judge Leanne and not to expect her to to binge drink. However, Paula fails in their last interaction of the novel. Despite herself, she pries intrusively and implies that Leanne is hungover, which causes an immediate backlash from Leanne. On the positive side, Paula immediately recognizes her mistake and apologizes. Leanne doesn't accept the apology, but neither does she slam the door as she leaves, and the reader is left with a feeling that their relationship is healing.

As a woman, too, Paula has grown by the end of the novel. She has her first date in more than twelve years. When she meets Joe, she doesn't objectify him. Although she notices his nice shoes, she describes him in terms of his family, his occupation, and his age--normal ways to describe a new acquaintance. The confidence that Charlo has knocked out of her is returning. She is a much different woman than the forty-eight-year-old who is afraid to glance at the baker with the nice hands. She knows, "He likes her, though. He listened to her. He laughed. He looked at her once, and she could tell; he wanted to hold her, probably grab her. He wanted to fuck her—ta-dah. That's kind of nice, although it's weird as well" (271). She is regaining some of her former confidence.

While Joe does not seem like a perfect match for Paula, what is significant is that she is having a relationship with a man on her own terms. When she first dates Charlo, she changes even her walk for him: "His side-to-side walk. . .they all walked like that then, the fellas. . .walking like they're afraid they'll topple over because their balls are so heavy. . . .I began to walk like him so we wouldn't keep bashing into each other. . . .We must have looked ridiculous, the pair of us, strolling. . .like two hard penguins" (Doyle, *The Woman Who Walked Into Doors* 54). However, she asserts herself with Joe and tells him she doesn't want to take a walk: "I work hard, Joe. A walk is too like more work" (Doyle, *Paula Spencer* 278). She refuses to hide her past from Joe in that she tells him immediately about Charlo and his ignominious death. She also tells Joe that she is a recovering alcoholic. She isn't allowing a man to define her—she is defining herself proudly. Paula is refusing to be changed or to hide because of a man. She won't allow the ugly parts of her life to be ignored anymore because she has finally realized what her five-year old granddaughter already knows: She is who she is, and that is enough. [When Paula questions Vanessa's choice of socks as a present - "They're only socks" (173)—Vanessa responds, "They're brilliant. . .Socks aren't supposed to be anything [except socks]" (173-4).] Paula isn't supposed to be anything but Paula, and when she meets new people, she is learning that being Paula is enough.

Finally, Paula is also waking up to the new Ireland. While she hardly has the Celtic Tiger by the tail, nevertheless, she isn't living paycheck to paycheck any more. Her new refrigerator has food in it. She has mastered her cell phone and can text with ease, as well as surf the net to find information about breast cancer: "Paula's small victories are connected to becoming a consumer, a user of technology" (Hall 1). She gets a new stereo and starts listening to contemporary music: Indeed, Carmel says Paula's music collection contains "no good stuff [like in] the 70s," to which Paula responds, "That's thirty years ago" (240), thus showing how contemporary Paula has become and how much of her missing time she has regained. We see that what goes on Paula's list eventually gets crossed off her list. And if it hasn't been crossed off by the end of the novel, we know it will be, which is confirmed by her sisters: "Yet, says Carmel. - You see, that's it. You said Yet. You're going to get one. We know you are. You're fuckin' amazing, by the way" (246).

Paula has made great progress in her roles as mother, woman, and Irishman. With a year of sobriety under her belt and a full carton of milk in the refrigerator, prospects look good for Paula. However, we know that Paula's struggles are not over and that she will not live happily ever after, much like Siobhan in *Her Mother's Face*. In the final scene, she finds an old packet of Empress of India seeds that she earlier has postponed planting, thinking "she might plant them next year, in the spring" (62). Now, however, she examines the packet and notes that, "the flowers look gorgeous. Vibrant flowers on deeply coloured foliage" (275). Then, she throws the packet away. There will be no lush flowers in Paula's immediate future, at least, not from that packet - although the reader believes that Paula is fully capable of buying a new, fresher, more fruitful packet.

CHAPTER 6
THE DEPORTEES AND OTHER STORIES

Doyle's collection of short stories, *The Deportees and Other Stories*, is unique in that it is his only work dealing primarily with non-Irish characters living in Ireland - their reactions and others' reactions to them. Of the eight short stories, three feature immigrants as main characters and four show how Irish characters must readjust and reconfigure their lives in light of the insurgence of a large immigrant population, or, as Doyle says, "Someone born in Ireland meets someone who has come to live here. The love, and the horror; excitement, and exploitation; friendship, and misunderstanding" (Doyle, *Deportees* xiii). The collection is also unique in that for once, Doyle, the champion of the Irish working-class underdog, depicts his Irish characters as powerful and the immigrant characters as the put-upon, down-trodden, marginalized group. The Irish, in these stories, are no longer "the niggers of Europe," as the colorful Jimmy Rabbit so politically incorrectly puts it in *The Commitments*.

Published in 2006, the project began in 2000 when Doyle began writing for *Metro Eireann*, a newspaper catering to a multicultural audience. At the time, the Celtic Tiger had all its teeth: From 1995 to 2000, Ireland experienced an unprecedented economic boom which catapulted this once impoverished country into becoming, as Doyle acknowledges, "one of the wealthiest countries in Europe" (xii). The boom continued, although at a slower rate, until 2008, when the country fell into a recession. During the Celtic Tiger years, Ireland became a favored destination for immigrant populations, particularly those from Central Europe, who were also attracted to the country being both English-speaking and primarily Catholic, factors which made assimilation easier. By 2007, 10% of the population was from other countries.

As is typical with any influx of immigrant populations, the natives grew restless, and they were not particularly welcoming or accepting: "This land of cead mile failte ('a thousand welcomes'), which has sent its children abroad for centuries, is now asking indelicate questions about foreigners" (Deignan 48). Disliking the xenophobic tendencies of his countrymen, Doyle contacted Abel Ugba, one of the publishers for *Metro Eireann*, and volunteered to write serialized stories for it.

Metro Eireann, which calls itself "Ireland's Only Multicultural Newspaper" with the slogan "Many voices, one Ireland," was started in 2000 by Abel Ubga and Chinedu Onyejelem, both Nigerian immigrants. Its purpose is stated in its first issue: "Though from different backgrounds, immigrants and other persons who make up an ethnic minority in Ireland are united by one vital factor: the majority want to contribute to the development of Ireland, the country they now regard as their new home, and they want a free hand to do so. Our main job is to articulate this desire and help it become a reality" (qtd. in Reddy 377). According to Onyejelem, the monthly publication is geared towards "anyone interested in diversity" with a tolerant attitude of "live and let live" (qtd. in Reddy 378).

> From the start, then, Metro Eireann has positioned itself firmly within an integrationist, celebrate-difference racial discourse that is centrist and reformist, not radical or revolutionary. . . .In appealing to readers' better natures—the sense of fairness shared by 'good-minded people'—the editors implicitly stake a claim for sameness despite apparent difference: immigrants are just like everyone else in wanting to help 'develop' Ireland and all they're asking is a 'free hand' to do so. (Reddy 378)

Judging from the advertizing, the audience is mostly comprised of immigrants rather than liberal-leaning native Irish.

Doyle's fictional stories began running in the second edition (May 2000) in 800-word serialized installments, which lend them "the feel of a sharp sitcom or short film screenplay" (Deignan 47). The stories were collected and published six years later, and the collection is thought "generally [to be] stronger than the sum of its parts". These are some of Doyle's first forays into short-story land, something of which he earlier had not thought himself capable. "I'd love to be able to write short stories, but I just don't think they're there, or they're not in me" (Sbrockey 542). This fact, coupled with the serialized nature of the stories, prompted Doyle to include a "disclaimer" in the book's "Forward:"

> I once read about a character in a U.S. TV daytime soap who went upstairs for his tennis racket, and never came back down. No one missed or asked about him; daytime life went on. The stories in this book have their tennis-racket moments. Characters disappear, because I forgot about them. Questions are asked and, sometimes, not quite answered. The stories have never been carefully planned. I send off a chapter . . . and, often, I haven't a clue what's going to happen next. And I don't have to care too much, until the next deadline begins to tap me on the shoulder. (Doyle, *Deportees* xiii)

As previously stated, Doyle began writing the stories because he wanted to counter the negativity facing the new population, and thus became the champion of the immigrant, working-class underdog:

> Three or four years into our new national prosperity, I was already reading and hearing elegies to the simpler times, before we became so materialistic—the happy days when more people left Ireland than were born here; when we were afraid to ask anyone what they did for a living, because the answer might be 'Nothing'; when we sent our pennies and our second-hand clothes to Africa but never saw a flesh-and-blood African. The words 'racist' and 'racism' were being flung around the

place, and the stories were doing the rounds. An African woman got a brand new buggy from the Social Welfare and left it at the bus stop because she couldn't be bothered carrying it onto the bus, and she knew she could get a new one. A man looked over his garden wall and found a gang of Muslims next door on the patio, slaughtering an Irish sheep. A Polish woman rented a flat and, before the landlord had time to bank the deposit, she'd turned it into a brothel, herself and her seven sisters and their cousin, the pimp. I heard those three, and more, from taxi drivers. I thought I'd like to make up a few of my own. (xii)

He rhetorically asks the Irish population, "What's the threat? Do we need to be white? No! Do we need to be Catholic? Jesus Christ, no! What is it that we'd be trying to protect?" (Drewett interview 347).

Doyle's stories attempt to put the new population in a favorable light, but at times they go overboard. Most of the immigrants in the story are far superior to the Irish, which is problematic "for a book concerned with debunking the kind of prejudice that holds immigrants to higher standards than members of the host society [because] the Africans of Doyle's early stories are generally more educated, physically attractive, moral, cooler, socially polished, or eloquent than the working-class white Irish who would judge them" (Burke 14).

Many of the stories use humor liberally and are not dark and heavy. Doyle says his choice to simplify the stories and use humor was deliberate:

It's not that I refuse to see it as a problem, but it seems to me that if you do decide that an influx of people from different cultures is a problem, then any challenge is already defeated. If you decide, particularly, 'this is a problem that must be solved'—how do you solve the problem—you send them back to where they came from, or you don't let them in in the first place, which is sadly the case here. So I suppose the stories are fighting the notion of it as a problem. . . .So there would be a tendency for me to think, 'I'll do a sort of a *Family* treatment to it'—and people will feel guilty watching it or they'll feel uncomfortable watching it, but why not counter by making people laugh. (qtd. Drewett 347)

Although not all the stories furnish a "happily-ever-after" ending, most of them do end positively, the lone exception being an uncharacteristic ghost story. Again, we must keep in mind his *Metro Eireann* audience, "those who are already converted" (qtd. in Reddy 384), meaning the immigrant population or the more liberal Irish who would not need to be pelted with story after story of the horrors of prejudice.

At times in the collection, xenophobia and racism seem conflated: Indeed, six out of the eight stories deal with prejudice faced by African immigrants, but Doyle does not specifically address racism in each of them. Although "a cynical witticism of pre-Celtic Tiger Ireland held that 'there is no racism in Ireland. . . because there are no blacks in Ireland'" (Burke 14), because the Irish often discuss the émigrés in terms of nationality, "Discussion of race thus gets displaced onto discussion of Irishness/not-Irishness, with the racial dimension that determines this discourse neatly hidden" (Reddy 376). Three camps have emerged regarding issues surrounding racism in Ireland: Some believe it "arrived with the wave of immigrants from the African continent in the 1990s . . . thereby subtly blaming racism on its targets" (Reddy 374,379); others deny its existence altogether; while others believe it exists in rarified pockets and "is unusual and always takes easily identifiable forms" (Reddy 374-5). Doyle, which we could predict based on these stories, seems to be of the third mindset, believing that "there's no ideological racism in Ireland. It's just lazy. . .Stupid, lazy, knee-jerk reaction. . . .Contact is the key [to eradicating it]" (qtd. in Reddy 382). The stories do, at times, express the simplistic message, "to know me is to love me," and too easily resolve issues surrounding racism, which may be a problem inherent in "Doyle's own positionality—white, Irish, settled, male, economically secure. . . . he is the one ventriloquizing blackness. . . .an African speaks for himself but only through the good offices of a white Irishman" (Reddy 386).

 The stories can be divided into three groups. First, in several stories, he uses individual characters as metaphors for Ireland, ultimately alerting his readership to and exposing the dangers of extreme nationalism and xenophobia. In the second grouping, he reminds the Irish that "there but for the grace of God go I(reland)" and that it has not been long since and may not be long until (and indeed, as of this writing, it has already occurred) a crippled Irish economy. He does so by putting his immigrant characters in situations very similar to those of his early, working-class characters. In the final division, he ridicules *in toto* the notion of "us" and "them," which the proximity of so many different nationalities has raised, by examining the notion of "Irishness," one of Doyle's recurring themes, seen also in *The Last Roundup Trilogy* and in *Bullfighting: Stories*.
  In "Guess Who's Coming to Dinner," Doyle recasts the iconic Sidney Poitier movie, examining how liberal and open-minded people react to being forced to live out their heretofore unchallenged ideas about race. In this story, 45-year-old Larry Linnane, his wife Mona, his son and four daughters live together. Larry is "the new Irishman" and likes it: "Their [his daughters'] voices reminded Larry of the Artane roundabout—mad, roaring traffic coming at him from all directions. And he loved it, just like he loved the Artane roundabaout. Every time Larry drove onto and off that roundabout he felt modern, successful, Irish. And that was exactly how he felt when he listened to his daughters" (Doyle, *Deportees* 3). Like Ireland at the beginning of the Celtic Tiger, Larry's prosperity, both financial and social, makes him secure. This prosperity insulates him from the immigrant population. He is able to ignore them and the abuses they are fleeing while he is snuggles with and suckles from the Celtic Tiger's teat.

However, he isn't allowed to remain insulated because his girls "brought the world home to him" (3). The pro-feminist, progressive Larry has raised his daughters to be independent and strong: "'Stand up for your rights.' That was what he'd roared after them every morning, on their way out to school. 'Get up, stand up. Don't give up the fight'" (6). Notice, however, that despite his admiration of his daughters' strength, he revels in their attention and service, as when they iron his shirts and bring him cakes. Larry has had the best of both worlds thus far: independent daughters who are subservient only to him. Thus, he has been able to maintain the illusion of being progressive: "Larry was an honest man, but it was a long time since he'd had to prove it" (9).

When one of his daughters meets and befriends Ben, a Nigerian accountant living in Ireland as a refugee, Larry reacts badly. He doesn't want to confront his deeply held and long ignored prejudices:

> So it wasn't that Stephanie actually brought home the black fella. It was the idea of him, the fact of his existence out there somewhere, the fact that she'd met him and danced with him and God-knows-what-elsed with him. But, if it had been an actual black man that she'd plonked on the table in front of Larry, he couldn't have been more surprised, and angry, and hurt, and confused. . . .He never thought he'd be a man who'd nod: yes I object to another man's colour. (5-6)

Larry's progressive attitudes have never been tested, and he fails the initial exam.

Similarly, the immigrants flooding Ireland's shores are literally bringing the world to the Irish. The change in the population is testing Ireland, as well, in terms of social programs and relief. Doyle says, "The inequality is still quite striking and just unacceptable. The level of services is, from a socialist point of view, again unacceptable" (qtd. in Drewett 346). Ireland is being forced, as is Larry, to confront its own deeply held prejudices. The Irish believe themselves to be, as Larry thinks, "warm, friendly people. . . .in 1985 when Live Aid was on, the Irish people gave more money than any other country in the world. A small, little country" (15). However, Ben's experiences prove differently: "He can't walk down the street without someone shouting something at him. . . .And not just eejits. . . Respectable-looking people. . . .In suits. And women with their kids" (15). Thus, Doyle is admitting that racism exists in Ireland.

When Larry does examine his feelings, however, he unearths xenophobia, not racism, thus implying the racism isn't endemic. "He wasn't a racist. He was sure about that now, positive. . . .Why didn't he want a refugee in the family? Well, there was AIDS for a start. Africa was riddled with it. And then there was—it wasn't the poverty, exactly—it was the hugeness of it. . . .It was too different; that was it. Too unknowable, and too frightening for his daughter" (9). Unconsciously, Larry, and hence, Ireland, is upset by the thought of his daughter—his feudal property—being ravaged by the outsider, thus potentially diluting the precious, fully-Irish, white, Catholic bloodline. If we are to believe Larry, race isn't the issue. Otherness is the issue. Obviously, race is a part of otherness, but it isn't its only component. Somehow, however, this conclusion seems disingenuous. The reader does not believe Larry's reaction would be the same were Ben born Polish, Catholic, and white.

Instead of creating a feel good situation at dinner in which Larry and Ben share the same opinions and become fast friends, Doyle turns the (dinner) tables. As an immigrant, Ben is Larry's social and economic inferior as his questionable status in the country prevents him from working as an accountant. However, Larry initially develops a "man crush" on the striking, handsomely dressed young man who is obviously his intellectual superior: "He just wanted them all to love him. Especially the black lad in the suit" (11).

However, the situation doesn't remain as such. Extending noblesse oblige to the worthy homeless feels good to Larry. Larry finds it easy to admire Ben as long as Ben is pleasant, agreeable, well groomed, and deferential. This last is the most important aspect for Larry: The immigrant must know his place and show proper gratitude. When Ben asserts himself, however, by chastising Larry's use of profanity, a furious Larry erupts and orders him out of the house.

Doyle is pointing out the perhaps unwitting hypocrisy of people who are put off by the influx of culture that accompanies the influx of immigrants, while accepting of the immigrants themselves. Minorities who conform to the dominant culture's morays are thus acknowledging their second-class status—and easier for the Irish to accept. By refusing to give up their own culture and traditions, the immigrant population is, in effect, asserting their equality.

After Ben's disgust at Larry's verbal vulgarity, the situation changes. Prompted, Ben begins to talk about his family in Nigeria—his brother's arrest, his sister's "disappearance" and his desire for his "children to live as children do here. I want them to take comfort for granted. I want money in my pocket" (23-24). Larry's feelings for him change when he starts to understand him: "Larry knew what had happened. He knew what 'disappeared' meant. He'd seen a programme, years ago; women going to a dump in the outskirts of a city, in South America somewhere, searching every morning for the bodies of their husbands and sons. He'd missed the start of the programme; he'd just been flicking through the channels. But he'd watched, mesmerized. . . ." (19).

Larry, who is by now pacified, wants to forget and ignore Ben's, and by extension, Africa's, pain. He wants to insulate himself in economic and social prosperity: "He just wanted to talk, and talk and talk. To hear his kids talking and laughing. To fill the room with their noise. To prove that they were all alive and solid" (21). Larry wants to ignore the evil in the world because acknowledging it is uncomfortable and frightening. Unable to imagine the devastation he would feel if his own children were killed, he finds masking evil with ignorance or noise much more palatable. Indeed, notice how the family changes topics by introducing the subject of dessert. Ben allows the topic to be changed only after he connects dessert to his sister, thus refusing to be diverted from his loss. He won't let the tragedy of his and his countrymen's existence to be swept away by dessert, noise, or pleasantries.

The horrors of Ben's tale shames Larry and makes him accept Ben into the fold, thus ending the story a little too easily and a little too happily. The story implies that, as already said, "racism is an easily remedied matter of unintentional ignorance in the otherwise fundamentally decent individual rather than the result of systematic inequality" (Burke 14). Larry, in a humorous scene, gives his blessing to the union of his daughter and Ben, only to learn that the two aren't dating. Larry is comically devastated: He is ready to give his imprimatur on a mixed-race union to prove his sincerity. However, after admitting mea culpa, Larry is absolved, without even having to beat his breast or say a Hail Mary. He can keep himself surrounded by his precious daughters a little longer. He has let the enemy in and realizes that he isn't an enemy. "The story is reassuring: African immigrants do not want to marry your daughters; they just want to work and lie in peace in Ireland (Reddy 381). Would his response have continued to be so gracious were the ebony stranger romantically interested in his daughter, thus becoming the real catalyst for the disintegration of Larry's kingdom, nay, harem? A radical change in someone's psyche surely takes longer than the course of a meal, and the resolution seems simplistic at best. "Larry's racism, then, is like a weed: likely to spread if not eradicated but easily uprooted and disposed of. Doyle surely knows on some level that this view of racism is fantastical and grossly oversimplified" (Reddy 381).

While the story admits the presence of racism, it seems naïve in the solution it proposes: Familiarity breeds respect and not contempt, with the solution to racism being an individual connection established by the recognition of a common humanity. What happens, however, when Larry is jostled in the street by another African or finds his favorite pub being replaced by a shop selling African foods? Will he be so quick to remember the disappearances and Ben?

The final scene has Larry asking for the name of Ben's cologne, "Towering Ebony," a reference to a population that obviously will not and cannot be ignored. The cologne is sold in shops "that sell all the African stuff. Will I be welcome in one of them places?" asks Larry. Ben answers without hesitation, "Yes, of course" (Doyle, *Deportees* 26). Larry, venturing into a new, all African environment, will be accepted, unlike the Africans, who have ventured into the all Irish environment. Doyle gives the reader a happy ending with both characters smiling in mutual understanding over a commercial matter. Immigration won't change Irish life and the economy; it will enhance it, the story says. Were Ireland to understand and respect the immigrant population, perhaps a happy ending could be effected as well.

"The Deportees" is a gift from Doyle to his readers, most of whom can't help but wonder what happens to Jimmy Rabbitte, Jr after the demise of the ill-fated soul band in Doyle's first novel *The Commitments*. After all, knowing that "it all works out" for the 36-year-old Jimmy gives Doyle's fans one less thing to worry about. In the story, Doyle exploits the plot of the wildly successful 1987 novel—indeed, he begins both works with the same lines: "Jimmy Rabbitte knew his music. He knew his stuff alright" (Doyle, *Commitments* 1, *Deportees* 27). Then comes the formation of a band, a crew of disparate strangers, the inevitable disastrous first gig, followed by the more successful but still comedic forays into the musical scene. At times the story of the band seems "already done:" We don't get to know the characters well, and how many different disastrous-gig situations can one devise, after all? "The trajectory of the ensuing narrative is far too similar to *The Commitments* in arc, humor, dialogue, and white Irish perspective to provide any real sense of the motley collection of immigrants who make up the band" (Burke 14). Nevertheless, the change in Jimmy's socio-economic situation from his 1987 foray into the music world to its 2007 incarnation, as well as the use of deportees instead of northside Dubliners, both reflect the significant economic upturn and give the familiar story a freshness: The story "provides one gauge of the transformation that occurred in the country during the Tiger's two-decade flourishing" (O'Grady 1).

At the beginning of *The Commitments*, Jimmy is working in a shop, living at home, and frequenting pubs. He wants more of his life, which is apparent in the questions he asks of Outspan and Derek, band-member wannabes: "Why exactly—d'yis want to be in a group. . . .Yis want to be different, isn't tha' it? Yis want to do somethin' with yourselves, isn't tha'it. . . .Yis don't want to end up like (he nodded his head back [towards others in the pub]) these tossers here. Amn't I right?" (*Commitments* 6). Jimmy's ideas are bigger than those of "the tossers" surrounding him. He has a deep sense of identity as an "other"—of his precarious place in Ireland and in the world:

> Yeah, politics.—Not songs about' Fianna fuckin' Fail or annythin' like tha'. Real politics. (They weren't with him.)—Where are yis from? (He answered the question himself.)—Dublin. (He asked another one.)—Wha' part o' Dublin? Barrytown. Wha' class are yis? Workin' class. Are yis proud of it? Yeah, yis are. . . Your music should be abou' where you're from an' the sort o' people yeh come from. –Say it once, say it loud, I'm black an' I'm proud". (*Commitments* 9)

Jimmy, solidly working class himself, equates the band to the civil rights movement:

> The Irish are the niggers of Europe, lads. . . .An' Dubliners are the niggers of Ireland. The culchies have fuckin' everythin'. An' the northside Dubliners are the niggers o' Dublin.—Say it loud, I'm black an' I'm proud. (*Commitments* 9)

Although Doyle himself says that "the line would make no sense" today, when Jimmy says it in the late 1980s, it inspires his fellow characters to embrace their powerlessness in order to become powerful.

Thus, this inspirer of the uninspired is the perfect organizer for a band comprised of the current group of underdogs. However, the middle-class Jimmy begins the band, not out of any sense of righting a social wrong, but because he is a little bored of suburban life, a little scared of having another baby, and a little tired of being a father. We find out he is considering starting a band just as his wife does:

> Married nine years, and they still slagged each other. He got into the bed and slid up to her back, and wondered which she'd noticed first, the gut or the erection. He'd been putting on the pounds; he didn't know how. He never ate and it was ages since he'd had a pint, weeks, months—fuck. . . .He waited for the baby's next kick. He was suddenly exhausted. The kids would be coming in soon, climbing in on top of them. . . He tried to stay awake. Kick, for fuck sake, kick. He was gone, and awake again. Did it kick? Did it? Stay awake, stay awake. –I'm thinking of forming a group, said Jimmy (Doyle, *Deportees* 30).

He announces the new project directly after thinking about his middle-age body, bemoaning the sleep deprivation that comes with small children, and feeling his new child kick. He wants to turn the clock back fifteen years.

He just as suddenly decides what type of group to form. When he is knocked down by a careless Romanian, his hand is subsequently crushed by an Italian on a bicycle, and he is helped to his feet by an African, he realizes he can recreate the Commitments, and perhaps their success, with the immigrant population. Note the advertisement he uses, which has much of the same wording the one he writes to find the Commitments: "Do you want the Celtic Tiger to dance to your music? If yes, The World's Hardest-Working Band is looking for you. . . .White Irish need not apply" (36). While the "hardest working band" phrase is the same, the more recent notice alludes to the immigrants' "other" status by offering them a type of power over the Celtic Tiger. Although he eventually deletes the last line (the older Jimmy is considerably more politically correct than the younger), we still see that he is equating contemporary white Irishmen with the undesirable rednecks and privileged southsiders of the Commitments advertisement.

While *The Commitments* romps through the band's rise and fall, "The Deportees," although fun, nevertheless shows the darker side of Ireland. In *The Commitments*, Jimmy only has to worry about managing personalities and finding gigs. The only hint of "real world" issues is the anti-heroin banner at their first gig, and even that is made humorous by the misspelling of heroin: "Jimmy grabbed Darren's shoulder.—Come here, you bollox. There's only one E in heroin. . . .—The syringe is very good though, isn't it? said Dean.—It'll do, said Derek.—It's grand.—None o' those cunts ou' there knows how to spell an' anyway" (Doyle, *The Commitments* 95-96). Drug abuse and addiction have not yet become the problem that we glimpse in *The Van*.

In the short story, however, the real world encroaches frighteningly upon Jimmy's bubble. First are the threatening anonymous phone calls, made as Jimmy is forming and promoting The Deportees, the new group.

> He recognized the absence of voice, remembered it too late. –Nigger lover. And Jimmy dropped, he actually fell to the path, and cried. He couldn't stop. He was exhausted, angry, hopeless. He cried. He couldn't explain it, not really. Just some sick bollix, getting his life from his late-night calls, a sad bastard with nothing and no one else, but Jimmy couldn't help it, he couldn't stop. That evil out there, on a night like this. (*The Deportees* 48).

Additionally, Gilbert, who plays the djembe drum and screams, is about to be deported, and Kenny, an Irishman is prejudiced against Paddy, a Traveller. Thus, Jimmy, and the reader, glimpse the oppression the disenfranchised face on a daily basis.

However, The Deportees, despite their immigrant status, still share in the Celtic Tiger's munificence: "They were older, foreign, the country was too prosperous, they weren't hungry—something. Kenny [an Irishman] from Roscommon was the only one to dive at the plate [of cakes]" (51). Likewise, Jimmy is not as hungry, although he is not so settled that he can't be inspired by his own words and by the music. Nevertheless, they still embrace the music Jimmy presents because "it rolled and growled; it was angry and confident, knocking shite out of the enemy" (52). The word "enemy," a term well known to those from war-torn or impoverished native countries, reinforces their tenuous status in the country by implying an enemy,

Just as the Commitments play music that reflects their situation, the Deportees also can be identified by their music, but in a much more poignant way. For instance, they perform the music of Woody Guthrie, "the so-called 'dustbowl troubadour' whose songs both record and represent a substantial swatch of the historical fabric of depression-era American life" (O'Grady 1). They change Guthrie's "Blowing Down That Dusty Old Road" and "they'd hop on the possibilities and make the song theirs. WE-ELL, YOUR TWO EURO SHOES HURT MY FEET. . . AND I AIN'T GOING TO BE TREATED THIS WAY. . . .YE-ES, I'M LOOKING FOR A JOB WITH HHH-HONEST PAY. . . .AND I AIN'T GOING TO BE TREATED THIS WAY" (55). The Commitments's song list is comprised primarily of songs about relationships, and thus the limited possibilities for the futures of most of the band members can sometimes be forgotten. The music of the Deportees, on the other hand, highlights the injustices endured by them.

The Deportees, despite their differences, are quite successful, another of Doyle's gifts to his readership. The story concludes with a thumbnail sketch of the happy lives of each character. We are even privileged to see "what happens" when the story ends, and all the characters and the band are successful. (Even the anonymous caller shares in the warmth as

Jimmy laughs at his last call and holds up the phone, allowing the caller to hear the band's magic.) The multinational co-operative works: "The story reads as a sort of a parable of multicultural co-existence in latter-day Dublin. . .the makeup of the band is fraught with tensions, suspicions, and the potential for profound intercultural misunderstandings. But with Guthrie's music of social conscience, and of social consequence, as their common denominator, The Deportees transcend their differences to emblematize clearly Roddy Doyle's vision for a harmonious new Dublin" (O'Grady 2). Economic success reigns when people can just co-exist, which isn't all that hard, implies the story. The story is "feel-good. . . conveying a hopefulness . . . that multiracial cooperation and even love are possible despite the machinations of government agencies (the threatened deportation of Gilbert) and the racist hatred of what Doyle depicts as a tiny minority of Irish" (Reddy 383).

Thus, "The Deportees" sets up a situation very similar to that of *The Commitments*, although Doyle contemporizes the players and the issues. Both works show the oppressed class being forced (by Jimmy) to confront, accept, and transfigure their powerlessness. Just as we can still recognize Jimmy Rabbitte through the fog of prosperity and surrounded by different people, we can still recognize Ireland, Doyle is saying. Ireland, though no longer the insulated and isolated island, is still filled with the humor, optimism, and good cheer that it was in *The Commitments*. The world and its problems have encroached and have changed it, but for the better.

"Black Hoodie" offers a warning as to the potential dangers of stereotyping. The unnamed narrator forms "Black Hoodie Solutions" with Nigerian and Irish classmates for a school project "to advise retail outlets on stereotyping of young people, and best practice towards its elimination" (Doyle, *Deportees* 135). In practice, as "Ms. Nigeria," ironically nicknamed by the narrator to highlight stereotypes, explains to the teacher, she and the narrator wear suspicious-looking black, hooded sweatshirts and browse through various local shops. The store's security invariably stereotypes the couple as potential shoplifters and focuses attention on them, while their partner, ensconced in a borrowed wheelchair, steals as much merchandise as he can. The three leave the store, only to return immediately to show the shop owner how much they have been able to steal because of security's misplaced attention. The project works very well until the trio gets caught in a department store, ironically while waiting to return the merchandise they have just stolen and make their sales pitch. They are hauled to the police station to wait for their parents, where a police officer makes racist comments to Ms. Nigeria. However, after the narrator stands up for Ms. Nigeria, which coincides with the arrival of her impressive looking parents, the police officer backs down. The happy ending shows the narrator and Ms. Nigeria holding hands as their parents walk ahead, talking congenially.

Obviously, the story depicts the financial drawbacks to stereotyping. If a people focuses negative attention on a new population of immigrants, it both closes itself to opportunities and blinds itself to real dangers. The children's research proves this on a small scale; Doyle's readers can extrapolate the financial losses onto a national scale. The story again, almost predictably, typecasts the Irish policeman as a racist bully whose posturing deflates as Ms. Nigeria's father enters. Ms. Nigeria's father:

> looks the business. His suit is blue and serious looking. But the really serious thing about him is his face. He's the most serious-looking man I've even seen. I'd say Ireland's overall seriousness went up at least 25 per cent the day he got here from Nigeria. . . .He's like a whole African country, Uganda or somewhere, that just stood up one day and put on a suit. Like, he's massive and so is his voice. And so is his wife—you should see her. If he's the country, she's the country's biggest lake or something. (151)

The policeman seems to shrink when faced with this powerful force. "The Fed is trying to make himself taller. He's up on his toes" (151). He also loses his verbal acuity, of which he is so proud when he uses it to make fun of Ms. Nigeria: "You can tell. He's trying to talk like her da. But it's not working. 'Perspective' comes out like he's not all that certain what it means" (152). When confronted by real power, the policeman is almost comically ineffectual.

The story offers another predictably easy and happy ending. The narrator gets to hold hands with Ms. Nigeria, his new girlfriend. The parents also seem to get along, and the one racist bully is effectively handled. The Nigerian parents are much more impressive and effective than the narrator's father. Indeed, the narrator's successful step into assertive manhood is made possible by the presence of her parents, not his. Ms. Nigeria is holding his hand not because "it's pretty windy. Maybe she's afraid it'll pick her up and throw her in the Liffey, so she's hanging onto me" (153). Instead, she is holding his hand because "I think I'm her fella" (153). The new population isn't needy. It isn't using Ireland merely to save itself, the story implies, but it can actually contribute to Ireland, if it is allowed to do so.

In the next group of stories, Doyle places immigrant characters in situations reminiscent of those of his earlier, working-class characters to show that, although the nationality of the underdogs is different, their treatment is the same. The Irish citizens, who only ten years before Doyle portrays as socially, economically and physically oppressed, have now become the social, economic, and physical oppressors. Additionally, the response of this new group of underdogs mimics that of Doyle's earlier maltreated characters. Some embrace their otherness with pride; others remain silent about the abuse, either pretending it doesn't exist, reconfiguring it or redirecting it; others resist, sometimes verbally, sometimes violently.

Economically, this new breed of Irishmen is far superior to the likes of the Rabbittes, the Spencers, or the Smarts. In Doyle's pre-Celtic Tiger novels, almost all of his characters are solidly working-class, the exception being Paddy Clarke's parents, who appear to be middle-class. Indeed, look at the difference between Jimmy Rabbitte, Jr, in *The Commitments*—living at home, working in a shop, and throwing up in the kitchen sink-- and Jimmy Rabbitte, Jr, in "The Deportees," living in his own middle-class home (bought not rented) with a front garden, and possessing all the toys a 36-year old man should have: a car, laptop, cell phone, and massive collection of CDs.

Indeed, besides the Clarkes (whom we don't really get to know because we only see them through young Paddy's eyes), the only characters from Doyle's earlier work who have enough money to be influenced by it are Jimmy Rabbitte, Sr, and his friend Bimbo, and this is only after their chipper van begins to become successful. Jimmy Rabbitte, Sr, remember, is laid off from his job as a plasterer in *The Van* and is forced onto the dole, thus becoming emasculated, redundant, and depressed. When his friend Bimbo asks him to join him in a business venture, he leaps at the chance. However, Bimbo and his wife Maggie, because of the leverage gained by Bimbo's initial investment and the money that the van generates, begin to dominate the van's operations, and therefore Jimmy Sr's operations. Initially, Jimmy Sr ignores the change in Bimbo: "Thanks [for letting me drive], said Jimmy Sr, although he didn't really know why; the engine was his as much as Bimbo's" (Doyle, *Van* 185). Although hardly catapulting him to wealth, the monies generated by the van are sufficient to change Bimbo from being someone "soft" and "one of the nicest, soundest people ever born" into a "mean, conniving, tight-arsed little cunt" (294). Eventually, things turn violent. Their two physical encounters, while not deathly, are nevertheless hurtful and do irreparable emotional damage. Their friendship is perhaps ruined because of the shift in power that financial success brings.

In the short story collection, money has lost its ability to change the Irish because the characters we see already have it: Any change financial success would wrought has already occurred. The ghost story, "The Pram," shows us the most financially successful Irish characters. O'Reilly, such a high-powered business woman that she doesn't have time for a first name, lives in a home with a "piano [that] was in a tiled hall, close to the stained-glass windows of the large front door" (Doyle, *Deportees* 155). Her daughters take tennis and piano lessons and are looked after by Alina, a live-in, Polish nanny. The O'Reillys drive BMWs, and the titular antique pram is introduced to us almost immediately as being "very valuable" (155). O'Reilly works so she can "pay you [Alina] to keep him awake. . . .In this country, the babies sleep at night. Because the mummies have to get up in the morning to work, to pay the bloody childminders" (167). This is a new Ireland indeed.

With money comes Big-Brother-like power. O'Reilly has control over Alina's entire life "Nothing is your private affair. Not while you're working here. Are you fucking this guy? . . . . Fuck away, girl. But with three provisos. Not while you're working. Not here, on the property. And not with Mister O'Reilly" (160). Thus, money allows O'Reilly to dictate Alina's sex life - when, where, and with whom. By proxy, the daughters also share in this control. They berate her for making them wait after school; they ruin her blossoming relationship with the Lithuanian biochemist with their tattling. Her economic class makes her totally helpless and impotent, even against two young girls. Alina not only begins to feel imaginary eyes watching her, but eventually, she even "felt their [the O'Reillys'] presence all round her" (170).

So, how does Alina react to and retaliate against the abuse? Much like Jimmy Sr, she initially ignores it and follows O'Reilly's dicta. As instructed, she doesn't scrape the pram's sides; she doesn't speak to the baby in Polish; she doesn't withhold the news of the baby's first laugh. She is perfectly programmed. Eventually, Alina, despite the sinister feeling of imaginary eyes at her back, reasserts her own autonomy by beginning the relationship with the biochemist in the park. She is using the oppressive system for her own ends by meeting her would-be lover on the proscribed two-hour walks. She fails to retain control of herself, however, when the twins, whose real, not imaginary, eyes watch Alina's movements, guess correctly at the relationship. The fact that two children have such power over their adult nanny is more frightening than Alina's mysterious feeling of being watched. In this case, the evil Alina knows is not more manageable than the evil she doesn't know.

Alina tries to deal with the further loss of control with fantasies of graphic violence: "Alina was going to murder the little girls. . . . She would poison them. She would drown them. She would put pillows on their faces, a pillow in each of her hands. She would lean down on the pillows until their struggles and kicking ceased" (160). Violence is a normal reaction to oppression: Jimmy, remember, reacts violently against his best friend twice. Alina, of course, does not initially realize her daydreams. Nevertheless, she does want to control the girls' lives as her own is being controlled and decides on a nonviolent means. Since she has no economic power, she attempts to gain control by telling a scary story about an evil, child-stealing woman with a horrible pram: "She would terrify them. She would plant nightmares that would lurk, prowl, rub their evil backs against the soft walls of their minds, all their lives, until they were two old ladies, lying side by side on their one big deathbed" (160). In Doyle's novels, most storytellers, i.e., *The Snapper*'s Sharon and the Henry trilogy's characters, are, surprisingly, weak. They tell stories because that is all they have. No one believes Sharon's Spanish sailor story; and Henry even admits that "stories were the only things the poor owned" (Doyle, *A Star Called Henry* 9).

Alina's story is similarly unsuccessful. Initially, the young girls deflate it with their questions and comments, and Alina has to stop: "Alina said nothing until she felt control of the story return to her. She could feel it" (Doyle, *The Deportees* 163). Then, after the girls again thwart Alina's grab at power by tattling, O'Reilly not only forbids her to continue the story but shames her in the process: "My my, said O'Reilly.—And look at the fair Alina's skin. How red can red get. . . .We'd better call a halt to the story, Alina. . . .It's getting under your skin. The little girls laughed again" (170).

Alina doesn't stop, however, and she continues the story the next day. We sense that she is beginning to lose control of it as it causes her a sleepless, terrified night and she begins to believes that the pram indeed is haunted. Perhaps she has lost control of her story because she discovers it originally is O'Reilly's invention. O'Reilly has already told "the girls the bloody thing was haunted, to keep them away from the baby when he was born" (174). Thus, Alina is not the true storyteller, and the story becomes yet another vehicle through which O'Reilly can control her. Even the focus of the horror changes from the Alina's invention of the old woman to O'Reilly's haunted pram.

Ultimately, the story terrifies the girls, who are so scared that they scream and urinate on O'Reilly's expensive rug. Alina, herself terrified, almost vomits from fear. Her self-control has eroded so greatly that she is barely able to control her own bodily functions, nor can she keep herself from painfully squeezing the girls' chins. She ultimately loses all control of herself, goes mad, beats O'Reilly to death with the decorative, heavy fireplace poker, and kidnaps the baby in order to drown him in the pram. In a sense, she is attempting to break free of her overwhelming economic oppression by using the very symbols of it, an expensive, useless ornament which "had never been used, until now" (176) and a large, cumbersome but pricey pram.

According to Gilbert and Gubar's mad woman in the attic theory, insanity is one of the few tools which women like Alina can use to break free from others' control. Paula Spencer does the same thing: When she strikes Charlo with the frying pan, she loses all sense of herself: "I don't know what happened to me— the Bionic Woman—he was gone. It was so easy. Just bang— gone. The evil in the kitchen; his eyes. Gone. The frying pan had no weight" (Doyle, *The Woman Who Walked Into Doors* 213). Temporary insanity works for Paula in banishing her abusive husband from her life. She uses the symbol of her oppression, a weighty kitchen object foisted on her by her mother-in-law (not only the symbol but the creator of her oppressor) to free herself.

Unlike Paula, however, Alina is unsuccessful. The symbol of Alina's oppression, namely, the expensive the pram, prevents her escape by getting stuck in marsh: "They found her in the sludge. She was standing up to her thighs in the ooze and seaweed. She was trying to push the pram still deeper into the mud. . . .They lifted the baby and the struggling woman onto the bridge" (Doyle, *The Deportees*, 178). Like Bertha Rochester, madness does not allow her to escape and the last image we have of her is of confinement. Alina does not ultimately break free, although she is successful at breaking free specifically from Reilly's oppression.

Burke calls this the "collection's most successful story" because Alina is not drawn as a paragon of virtue, intelligence, or savoir faire: "Doyle is most successful in his project to humanize the immigrant when he resists the temptation to make him or her a paragon of virtue, achievement, or coolness or to make immigrant status the determining factor of a character's inner life: the fact that Alina is a mistreated worker in a foreign country doubtlessly contributes to her disaffection, but she is subtly enough drawn for the reader to realize that she'd likely have been unstable in any setting" (14). Nevertheless, the economic disparity and powerlessness that she feels in her situation only hastens her disintegration.

In "New Boy," Joseph, the titular character, encounters social oppression instead of economic oppression. The Irish characters attempt to dominate him not because he is poor, uneducated, or physically weak, but merely because of his situation - he is an immigrant. Here, money doesn't give the Irish characters the ability to target him; their social status does.

In the story, Joseph is similarly positioned to Paddy Clarke at the end of Doyle's Booker-prize winning novel. Paddy, who previously has had the friends and experiences of the average ten-year-old-boy, is suddenly relegated to the fringes of society and subject to ridicule because of his parents' separation. Indeed, he begins to separate himself from his friend Kevin because of the pained maturity earned from watching his parents fight and his family disintegrate. He and his best friend Kevin get in a bloody fight because Paddy, self-destructive because of his extreme emotional pain, lashes out at his schoolmates: "I didn't care. If he hurt me I'd hurt him. It didn't matter who won. I didn't try to get around him, pretend he wasn't there or I'd forgotten. I walked right up to him. I knew what was going to happen" (Doyle, *Paddy Clarke* 272). After the fight, which Paddy wins, he says, "There was a hole inside me for a bit; getting used to it. . . . I wanted to be left alone. . . " (276). The novel's penultimate scene involves children chanting, "Paddy Clarke - Paddy Clarke - Has no da. Ha ha ha! I didn't listen to them. They were only kids" (281). Thus, Paddy has grown up, and in so doing, has lost his place in society. His hardened exterior of unconcern masks a deeply anguished little boy.

Joseph's situation at the beginning of the story mirrors Paddy's at the end of the novel. Joseph, as are most of the other immigrants in the collection, is not only intellectually superior but also more mature than the Irish around him. His experiences with genocide in his native country have made him very aware of situations involving power struggles and have left him detached from others. Most likely, he appears hard to others. The class bully Christian (interestingly named by the atheist Doyle), immediately begins to taunt Joseph. Joseph, however, having witnessed the slaughter of his townspeople and family by soldiers, is not scared of a ten-year-old's tough talk. Like Paddy, he refuses to be intimidated by Christian or his cohort Seth. "Joseph has to learn how to interpret and to negotiate the social codes that operate in this microscosm of Dublin itself. Carrying . . . the emotional baggage of earlier childhood trauma in his war-torn native country . . . Joseph proves altogether capable of handling both the verbal and the physical bullying inflicted on him" (O'Grady 2). He is what Paddy wishes to be - unaffected by the taunts of other little boys. Joseph, because of his past, knows that violence ultimately will not solve his problems, which Paddy, alas, does not realize. Joseph tries to avoid fighting but is forced to defend himself when the schoolyard children gather around him: "All the children in the school, it seems, are watching. They stand behind Joseph, pressing. . . .Joseph knows: something must happen, even if the bell rings and announces the conclusion to this thing called break. . . .Joseph does not respond. He knows: anything he says will be a provocation" (Doyle, *The Deportees* 93-4). The fight is more or less of a stand-off, with Joseph grabbing and bending Christian's finger until they are separated by the teacher.

The teacher, trying to discover the reason for and the initiator of the altercation, reprimands all three boys. In a scene similar to one in *Paddy Clarke*, Joseph refuses to implicate the other boys and responds to the teacher, "Nothing happened" (97). Although Christian and his sidekick Seth are clearly the aggressors, when the ineffectual teacher is called away, the three boys unite when they start making jokes at "their joint recognition of their teacher's incessant repetition of the word 'now'" (O'Grady 2), which she says almost thirty times in the short story, emphasizing for us the fact that Doyle is writing about Ireland as it is "now."

Paddy observes, "If you were going to be best friends with anyone . . . you had to hate a lot of other people, the two of you, together. It made you better friends" (Doyle, *Paddy Clarke* 182). Christian, Seth, and now Joseph "become united. . . .They are united in their silence. They do not like one another but this does not matter. They stand there together, against Miss" (Doyle, *The Deportees* 97). The boys realize that "they can instead focus their collective energy on the bumbling woman in the front of the room. In this sense, the differences arising from national origin seem less significant when compared to the much more profound sense of alienation that springs from the human condition - even when you are a meek (or snotty) 11-year-old boy" (Deignan 48).

Thus, Joseph's situation becomes the opposite of Paddy's: Joseph becomes one of the pack - an equal, brought together by humor and a common enemy - whereas Paddy becomes the other, alienated, alone. We leave Joseph and his comrades laughing just as hard at Miss, who, not quite as inane as previously thought, recognizes what has happened and seems almost pleased at the outcome.

"I Understand," the last story of the collection, is also the most brutal and, paradoxically, the most hopeful. Doyle "decentralizes white Irish perspectives and consciousnesses, requiring his white Irish audience to imaginatively inhabit an African self. . . .we have a fully-realized Other who refuses to be Other" (Reddy 385). Thomas, an African immigrant who has "run away from [his] home and [his] country . . . . [because he] would almost certainly be dead if [he] had stayed at home" (Doyle, *The Deportees* 223-225), is being coerced by Irish mobsters into running illegal packages for them. In addition to physical violence, the mobsters warn him with deportation: "He hits me again. I understand. I cannot fight this man. I cannot defend myself" (219-220).

Having an illegal status makes Thomas vulnerable, almost childlike. He gets the worst jobs: "All my work must be in secret, because I am not supposed to work" (219). He works as a as a dishwasher at a pub, and, like a child, he is given a lesson on the difference between hot and cold water and the proper way to insert an electrical plug into a socket. His co-workers teach him "dirty" words, which he parrots back at appropriate times for their enjoyment. As part of a night-time cleaning crew, he is subject to the unwanted and oddly maternal romantic gestures from his unattractive boss. When she asks him to coffee, he is powerless to refuse - or do anything else: "She will not allow me to hold the tray. Nor will she allow me to pay for two cups of coffee and one doughnut. . . .She puts the doughnut in front of me. I feel foolish. Does she think I am her son? I did not ask for this doughnut" (225). He feels even more infantilized when this supervisor tries to protect him from the mobster: "I am ashamed. The woman stands between me and the man. . . .But she cannot stand in front of me for ever, for more than five minutes. And I do not want her to stand there. I am not a child" (237). Thus, he is powerless over most of the aspects of his life.

Interestingly, his sexual encounter with Ailbhe, an Irishwoman, seems to give him the strength to assert his manhood. The day after his night with Ailbhe, he stops being intimidated:

I have been running from his type for too many years. I will not run now. I will do this myself. He is a fool because he has not seen me. He has not bothered to look. He sees a man he can frighten and exploit, and he is certain that he can do this. The men who made me fight when I was a boy, they too saw fear and vulnerability. They made me do what they wanted me to do; they made me destroy and kill, for ten years. I am no longer a boy. This man frightens me but I, too, am a man. I know what a hard man is in the language of the city. Tough, ruthless, respected, feared. This man looks at me and sees none of these qualities. He sees nothing. He is a fool. . . . .He must take control. But I will not be controlled. I walk away. (239)

Like Ellison's *The Invisible Man*, Thomas uses his invisibility as a weapon against being controlled.

Unlike Ellison's narrator, Thomas refuses to remain underground: "I will go to work. I will not let them stop me. I will go to work. I will buy a bicycle. I will buy a mobile phone. I am staying. I will not paint myself blue. I will not disappear" (241). He will not allow himself to be treated like a child - to be rescued, to be bullied, to be patronized, or to be ignored: I am not a child. I am not a man who will hide behind a woman. Or another man. I will not hide" (237). He is a man and has decided to act like a man, no better or worse than any other man.

Alhibe's treatment of him as an equal makes him realize how he has been allowing others to treat him. Thus, his pride, similar to the pride exhibited in "The Deportees," *The Commitments*, "New Boy," and "Dinner," enables him to exist in this strange new world.

Finally, Doyle mocks his countrymen's extraordinary xenophobia, extreme clannishness, and blatant mistrust of anything not-Irish by questioning the exact nature of "Irishness." What, indeed, is a real Irishman? What do they look like, act like, and sound like? (For a more complete discussion of this theme, which runs through many of the works discussed in this text, refer to the Prologue.)

In the farcical "57% Irish," Irishman Ray Brady is hired to design a citizenship test. The test, commissioned by the Minister of Arts and Ethnicity, is supposed to "make it harder to be Irish. . .[but it must] look easier" (106). Realizing that "an old-fashioned quiz wasn't going to work. A Nigerian could become an expert on all things Irish without leaving Nigeria; he could be quiz-perfect Irish before he'd even packed" (108), Ray invents a test which measures the physical reactions to certain visual stimuli. The initial images are all Irish, ranging from Michael Flatley of *Riverdance* fame to Shamrock Chambers, an Irish porn star. When Ray's mother and brother, both fully Irish, score 19% and 38% respectively, Ray, realizing that no test can accurately measure love of one's country, rigs The Failte Score, so that, as he explains to his boss, "Your response to one image or sound can send you to a series of images or sounds that will bring your score up, or down. . . .Depending on whether *we* want to bring it up, or down" (115). His boss, the nineteenth most powerful man in Ireland by his own admission, scores 57%, and is thus considered "the average Irishman" (115). Interestingly, this average Irishman, for whom "average has always been good enough" (115), has a drunken, promiscuous wife, loves foreign food, and owns several flophouses tenanted by immigrants. In other words, he is an unsympathetic hypocrite willing to use the immigrants for gain but not willing to grant them citizenship. He is, however, an equal-opportunity hypocrite, and warns Ray to "go easy on the racial. . . .—We can't be showing anyone the door because of their skin" (107). Thus, although Doyle is again acknowledging racism, it seems as if it isn't viewed as much as a problem as immigration in general..

Throughout the story, Irish characters are shown as monetarily focused, inept, and ineffectual. The more inane, greedy, dishonest or crass a character is, the more Irish he is. Indeed, in the story's final lines, we see Ray and his brother, sometime far into the future, looking at "an Irishman. . . Scratching his arse. . . .Haven't seen one like him in years" (129).

The immigrants, on the other hand, are a depicted as forceful, forthright, resourceful, and not to be ignored. For instance, Ray, incapable of kicking down a door himself, has his Nigerian roommate do it. Ray has fathered a child by a beautiful Russian woman, who both captivates and commands him. Lust, not paternal feelings, causes him to re-rig the Failte Score in order to keep his lover in Ireland: "And, if he was honest, he wouldn't have messed with the Failte Score if it hadn't been for the sex that night. Although maybe he would have; he wasn't sure—he was rarely honest" (127). His rigged test ensures that his girlfriend and eventually "over 800,000 Africans and East Europeans" pass the test. The inept government bureaucracy continues to pay his wages for another thirty or so years, despite the fact his department has been disbanded and Ray has virtually "disappeared" (128). Ironically, this full-blooded Irishman is economically manipulating the Irish government just as the immigrants do in the urban myths Doyle relates as having heard.

The story illustrates how moot the discussions of Irish identity are. What is an Irishman is, after all? If such a creature truly exists, then what are his characteristics? Real Irishmen seem to possess no special, definable, discernable, or even positive, qualities. The influx of immigrants, as we see in Ray's case, has actually improved his life dramatically and much more than he deserves. Ray, married to the beautiful Russian, has a large family, and becomes "a happy man" (128). Ireland, too, because of the number of now legal immigrants, has prospered as well, as the unflattering picture of the almost extinct "true Irishman" shows us. The new blood has been good for Ray and for the country, the story implies. By reconfiguring and expanding our concept of Irishness, Ireland can open itself up to undreamt of possibilities.

In "Home to Harlem," Doyle again makes us question the true nature of Irishness, implying that if we can't come up with a concrete definition, then the concept of ostracizing people for not being Irish is inane. In this story, Doyle takes on racism directly, showing how the Irish equate "authentic" Irishness with being white.

Declan's grandfather is an African-American GI and his grandmother, an Irish maid; thus, he is one quarter African American. Although he is born and raised in Ireland and has no ties to America, Declan doesn't feel comfortable in lily-white Ireland: "He lies back on the bed and gets dug into Langston Hughes. . . .America was never America to me. . . .Take out America, put in Ireland. That's how Declan sometimes feels, how he's felt all his life. A great little country, all the shite, but not his" ("Doyle, *The Deportees* 191). Thus far, his experience with being Irish has been uninspiring and alienating, as he explains to the director of his research project: "I've never felt Irish enough. . . .You can be less Irish. I am. At least, I used to be. . . . I'm black. . . ..That's not Irish. Or Irish enough. And my dad used to say there was a Dublin thing too. Dublin wasn't really Ireland. And there's the language. The fuckin' *cupla focail*. You're not fully Irish if you can't fart in Irish" (211-212). The attitudes his mother faced - "You were Irish or you weren't, one thing or the other. You couldn't be both; you couldn't be black" (203)— he feels he faces.

He wants to belong but is faced with the double consciousness W.E.B DuBois describes in *The Souls of Black Folk*:

> Then it dawned upon me with a certain suddenness that I was different from the others; or like, mayhap, in heart and life and longing, but shut out from their world by a vast veil. I had thereafter no desire to tear down that veil, to creep through; I held all beyond it in common contempt, and lived above it in a region of blue sky and great wandering shadows. . . .The history of the American Negro is the history of this strife, this longing to attain self-conscious manhood, to merge his double self into a better and truer self. In this merging he wishes neither of the older selves to be lost. He would not Africanize America, for America has too much to teach the world and Africa. He would not

bleach his Negro soul in a flood of white Americanism, for he knows that Negro blood has a message for the world. He simply wishes to make it possible for a man to be both a Negro and an American, without being cursed and spit upon by his fellows. (694-95)

As does DuBois, Declan feels that the barrier of his black heritage marginalizes him and strips him of his sense of belonging.

Declan's anger at being different compels him to kill, symbolically, his Irish self, and he tries to hurt Ireland as much as it has hurt him:

He just got sick of it one day. Sitting in a tutorial. . . . The lecturer droning on about Irish writing and its influence on the world—Joyce, Yeats, little country, big prizes. And the other around him nodding away, like they were part of it. Nod nod, pride pride; the smugness. It had got on his wick. . . .Ireland's gift to the world? Bollocks to it. Declan would prove that Harlem had kick-started Ireland's best writing of the twentieth century—or at least some of it. And, if he couldn't do it, he'd cheat; he'd make it up. (Doyle, *Deportees* 181)

Like a child's whose feelings have been hurt, he wants to lash out against those closest to him: an "if-you-don't-want-me-then-I-don't-want-you" reaction.

In America, Declan, despite himself, feels very much Irish, even becoming angry at his project director for joking about "the Irish and their famous profanity" (184). Declan feels the pain of Irish history:

That was the same that the Harlem Renaissance writers had had to face and fight. And the Irish writers too— the Punch cartoons, the drunken Paddy, the ape with the shillelagh, the picture that the Irish had been given and the shame behind the grinning acceptance of

166

them—this was the shame that Yeats and the lads had taken on and, sometimes, beaten. There are links here, parallels, but. . . . That's what being Irish is a lot of the time, passing for something else—the Paddy, the European, the peasant, the rocker, the leprechaun. It's sometimes funny; it's sometimes dangerous and damaging. And then there's black and Irish (201).

Although he rails against stereotypes and labels, he travels to New York City, not to study the influence of the Harlem Renaissance writers upon Irish literature, but really to find someplace he feels comfortable and to find some aspect of his history that will enable him to define himself and find "his group." He wants to find a box to tick on the registration form (179).

However, throughout the story, Declan is not above using these stereotypes for his own advantage. In his mind, being Irish is performative. A real Irishman speaks Gaelic, drinks a lot (and drinks a lot of Guinness in particular), uses Irish idioms like "grand" instead of "fine" and "howyeh" for "hi," and is white. Declan doesn't like pubs or getting drunk, hates the national drink, and the idioms hardly roll off his tongue. However, he does get drunk on Guinness and uses Irish slang to impress a girl. He even has an urge to attend Mass, something he ridicules at home. Finally, when he discovers "about twenty-eight different kinds of milk" in an American milk section, significantly, "all he wants is white" (180). Like his scratchy green cap with the map of Ireland, he longs to put on an Irish face - sometimes consciously, sometimes unconsciously.

Interestingly, Doyle says that he also feels most Irish when he is visiting the United States: "At home, I don't think about being Irish, but in the States, I become Irish because of all the topical issues that people want to talk about—clerical abuse, politics, and so on" (qtd. in Sanai 4).

As much as Declan loves New York City, he still doesn't feel African American. He distinguishes between himself and African Americans: "All the black people here are neat. Not just on Sundays. Their jeans, Jesus. They're not just ironed. It's like they've been dry-cleaned. Their fuckin' jeans. Even the homeless lads. He feels scruffy walking past them" (186). He is desperate to belong, however: Declan prefers to take a recent picture of a man who loosely fits the description of his grandfather instead of one of him as a GI because Declan doesn't want his grandmother to fail to recognize the young GI. He prefers instead to keep the illusion of having a family.

When he realizes that his original thesis is doomed, he decides to compare the Harlem Renaissance experience with the Irish experience, concentrating on the latter: "I'm going to study writing that questions the *we* in *we're fuckin' great* [Irish writing]. . . .The Harlem Renaissance questioned the same kind of *we*, here. I'll compare the two" (213). Thus, he is learning to reconcile the two warring sides of himself—discovering that they aren't warring at all. In the stories final scene, he tells his love interest the revised title to his project: "*Who the Fuck are We?*" The girl responds straightfacedly, "Love it. . . .It's *so* Irish" (214). Despite his realization that he isn't at war with himself, this response indicates that Declan will always be different— Irish when in America, black when in Ireland. The story "does not have the feel-good ending of many of the other stories— Declan never experiences the expected emotional or biological connection to the African-American relative he tracks down— but there is a heartening truth often absent from the other stories in the student's ultimate acceptance that he would never feel fully at home in either heritage" (Burke 14).

Thus, in *The Deportees and Other Stories*, Doyle directly confronts xenophobia, racism, and nationalism. Doyle wants to open up society, as he believes diversity will keep Ireland strong. Being closed off to the world fosters a backwards, corrupt and unfeeling country. Despite his writings about falsity of the concept of Irishness, Doyle believes in a better Ireland. Writing is ultimately an act of love—we don't bother to communicate with or educate those whom we don't love. Through this series of short stories, Doyle is communicating this vision directly and solely to the Irish public.

CHAPTER 7
THE DEAD REPUBLIC

The Dead Republic (2010) is the final instalment in the *Last Roundup* trilogy. Henry Smart, although still alive at the end of the novel, is 108 years old and, not even Doyle, stretching reality's boundaries as he does in the trilogy, could eke out another Henry Smart novel. At the beginning of *The Dead Republic*, Henry is emotionally crippled. He battles days-long black outs which make him uncertain about parts of his life. He knows at least that he has been a puppet, although he is unclear as to the identity of the puppeteer. Much like Paula Spencer, whose battle with alcohol obscures the facts of her life, Henry's lifelong battle with the violence and poverty make his present a mystery and his past inaccessible. As age makes Henry increasingly infirmed physically, this novel chronicles Henry's labored return to emotional and mental stability. It shows the process through which Henry reconstructs himself from the disintegrated man upon whom *Oh, Play That Thing* closes. Although he doesn't know exactly what shape into which to re-form himself, he tries to resist others' often self-serving input. At the end of the novel, we see a Henry Smart with a fixed identity, although given the covert nature of others' influence on his life, we aren't sure exactly how much this Henry Smart is of his own making.

Similarly, he tries to re-construct Irish history, only to discover that he can't fully resist others' beliefs because he has never been able to see the entire picture. He thinks he can expose the puppeteer only to discover a second puppeteer controlling the first and a third controlling the second. As he begins to figure himself out, he also figures out that "Ireland" is a created and pimped out concept. As Henry regains his sanity, he also is increasingly capable of managing the competing versions (and authors) of himself and his country which constantly barrage him.

Plot Summary

The novel, which is divided into four parts, opens on a 49-year-old, one-legged Henry Smart accompanying famed Hollywood director John Ford to Ireland, after a 29-year absence, to shoot *The Quiet Man*, which Henry believes to be a story about his life as an IRA assassin. At the end of *Oh, Play that Thing*, a dying, 44-year-old Henry has wandered into the desert to die and is saved by Ford. Ford, whose strong Irish roots beckon, recognizes either Henry or his type, and is immediately intrigued, wanting to film his story. He retains Henry as a writer/consultant for the project.

As previously mentioned, part of Henry's character is based upon Ernie O'Malley, who is listed as an IRA consultant in the credits for *The Quiet Man*: Doyle thought, "If Henry could be Ernie O'Malley, that would give me my excuse [to get Henry back to Ireland]" (McCann interview). Doyle also loved the idea of an IRA consultant: "I can imagine the exchanges: 'Where would I put the gun?' 'There.' But the IRA's presence in *The Quiet Man* is subliminal" (qtd. in Sanai 1).

Henry's position as consultant, however, is a glorified way of saying that Henry occasionally meets with Ford and his secretary, Meta Sterne, and tries to remember his past, a task difficult both because of Henry's frequent black outs and his natural reticence, engendered from years of working for or hiding from the IRA. Additionally, Ford's frequent alcoholic binges and infamous irascibility make him difficult to work with. The two men's purposes are often at odds: Henry, trying to remember and order his real past; Ford, trying to recreate and refashion that past into a story appealing to movie-goers. The process is further delayed by production companies' refusals to finance the project, as they believe *The Quiet Man*, based on a short story by Maurice Walsh of the same name, to be a small Irish film with little or no moneymaking ability.

Because of all the delays, Henry lives for three years in boarding houses and hotels, presumably at Ford's expense.

Henry suffers numerous blackouts during this period, losing track of time, events and people. He considers it a victory, for instance, when he remembers one of the names of his siblings. However, Henry does come out of his fog eventually, and he and Ford write the script of the movie, not exactly Henry's story but near enough. During his partnership with Ford, the reader is subject to interesting insights into the back story of *The Quiet Man*.

During the flight to Ireland, Henry inadvertently finds a copy of the finalized script, which is an entirely different movie from the one he authors with Ford. The new script, which is the movie we know today as *The Quiet Man*, based closely on Walsh's short story, is a bucolic love story between John Wayne, a rich American returning to rural Ireland, and Maureen O'Hara, a beautiful, albeit strong-headed, spinster. Incidentally, Doyle is a huge fan of the movie and has "watched it all my life. . . .I love it" (McCann interview). The few nods to Henry's script and Ford's original vision are almost unrecognizable.

Henry is incensed by Ford's betrayal, and, once in Ireland, argues violently with Ford, after which he walks off the set and across Ireland, winding up in the village of Ratheen on the outskirts of Dublin. It is 1951. The novel slows down here:

> For most of the remaining novel, Doyle himself abandons the Hollywood conventions that made *A Star Called Henry* and *Oh, Play That Thing* more like popular entertainments: an escape-artist hero, manic pacing and seat-of-the-pants plotting, rapid scene shifts and a 'Zelig'-like collection of historical walk-ons. . . .[Doyle] tailors the narrative to Henry's failing physical powers, contenting himself with muted suspense, allowing the characters to have long talks with and against one another and giving readers time to think about the brutal intersection of religion, economics and politics in Ireland (LeClair 1).

Henry has left his violent past behind him and works quietly as a gardener for twelve years before, just as quietly, becoming the caretaker for a boys' school. Despite his infrequent but still recurring blackouts, Henry looks after the school grounds and buildings, as well as appointing himself guardian of the boys, threatening teachers who too eagerly inflict harsh corporal punishment. He develops a relationship with the Widow O'Kelly, whose garden he tends, surreptitiously spending the night with her once a week. Sometimes he believes her to be Miss O'Shea, his revolutionary wife whom he has thought dead in America; other times she appears as merely a respectable widow.

Doyle says that parts of this section of the book are culled from some of his own experiences in school:

It was a pleasure for me to bring him back to a mile from where I live so I didn't have to read books to research other places anymore. . . .When I was a teacher, I knew that if I wanted something done I didn't go to the Principal but to the caretaker—he holds the real power. It's something the other teachers didn't seem to know although some of the pupils did. When I was about seven, the caretaker at my school was an ancient man with a limp. He dragged his foot around. I gave him a history he may not have had—I gave him a bullet lodged in his leg. . . .I went to a Christian Brothers school—it was a state school but was run by the Christian Brothers. My time there coincided with Bloody Sunday. The Christian Brothers were very angry men and were very sympathetic to the cause of the IRA. We were actually given the newspaper of the IRA and Sinn Fein to read (in one regular class.) It was a very black and white time. Everything Irish was 'good,' and everything British was 'bad.' Luckily I was old enough to make my own decisions, but when I was writing the book, I could imagine that several of the staff in the staffroom in the school in which Henry worked were IRA sympathisers " (qtd. in Sanai 2-3)

Things change dramatically for Henry, however, in 1974 when he is severely injured in an Ulster Volunteer Force bombing in Dublin during the Troubles, a period in which the IRA used escalating violence to further their cause of unifying the 32 counties of Republic of Ireland and Northern Ireland. When a local newspaper reporter interviews him, he breaks his silence about his past and winds up a local celebrity.

Almost 25 years of peaceful existence end with his newly found fame, and Henry is thrust back into the violent political arena. First, he is approached by a member of the Provisional IRA's Army Council. They revere him as a survivor of the Easter Rising and mistakenly believe him to have been a member of the First and Second Dail. Several years later, they begin to use Henry, "a slightly fraudulent symbol of the revolutionary past" (Leclair 1), as a spokesman to further their cause of a unified Ireland. They claim that he, as a member of the First and Second Dail, voted for a unified Ireland, and his imprimatur thus gives the Provos and their cause legitimacy. As the link that keeps the chain of belief in national unification unbroken, he is "their route back to Connolly and Pearse. Their link to the Lord God Almighty in heaven (Doyle, *The Dead Republic* 232).

Prompted by the public revelation of Henry's past, the Widow O'Kelly reveals that she is indeed Miss O'Shea, although, for the sake of respectability, they continue to keep their relationship hidden. Four years later, Miss O'Shea has a serious stroke which paralyzes her, and she, unable to communicate at all, is moved into a nursing facility. Henry now publicly admits their marital bond and visits her daily, where he meets Saoirse, his sixty-year-old daughter, who is married and living in America. Miss O'Shea, whose first name he finally learns is Nuala, remains in a coma until 1986, when Henry, acting on a hunch that she is staying alive only to see a united Ireland, lies to her and says that the British have evacuated Ireland, after which she dies peacefully.

The final disruption to his previously peaceful existence occurs in 1980, six years after the Provo's initial contact and two years after he begins being a spokesman. He is approached by the Special Branch of the Irish police and forced to become an informant, although the relatively sheltered Henry knows little about the IRA's inner workings. Henry is now a real "quiet man about his actual past and about his activities as a double informer (Leclair 1).

During this period, Henry is interrogated by the Provos to prove his loyalty, to which he responds, "I don't want to join the I.R.A. . . .I never left. . . .I've been in the I.R.A. since 1917. . . .I never left or resigned, or anything. And I was in the Citizen Army before that. Before there was an I.R.A." (Doyle, *The Dead Republic* 244). Interestingly, Doyle's father, Rory, says something very similar about his Fianna Fail membership: "I became involved in Fianna Fail because I was born into Fianna Fail. I never joined; I was born into it. I never joined and I never left" (Doyle, *Rory & Ita* 161).

Eventually, the Provos discover Henry's informer status, and, instead of being killed, he is used to leak certain information to the Special Branch, which ultimately results in his becoming something of a peace broker. For a brief period, he is relaying messages at an alarming rate, signifying to him that a change is about to occur, which we never see, although we do hear about it. In one of the final scenes, Henry's Provos contact explains everything to him: "Although the violence will continue, a deal has been struck and the war for the unification of Ireland has been won. . . .it'll need time. There's a lot to do" (Doyle, *The Dead Republic* 318). Although only a privileged few know, in 2016, on the anniversary of the Easter Rising, the unification a 32-county Republic will be complete.

In the last scene of the novel, Henry, prodded by his Provos contact, publicly supports the motion that "Sinn Fein should drop its longstanding and consistent opposition to running candidates in the elections to the Free State parliament, the so-called Dail" (328). In effect, as his Provos contact says, "It's time the dead handed over to the living" (327), from which statement comes the title. We leave Henry in 2009, a 108-year-old man with a 90-year-old daughter, still a republican icon but expecting every night to die peacefully. Doyle said that he was "tempted to drag in another chapter with the recession" (McCann interview) but decides instead to let Henry rest.

Argument

People need an uninterrupted narrative arc in their lives. Emotionally stable people are able to understand their present lives in the context of their pasts: They can trace Point A to Point Z without skipping too many points along the way. Photo albums, family stories, and grandparents' recollections can help them fill in the gaps of their childhoods in order to explain aspects of their adulthoods. While their lives might not make sense (who's does, after all?), their lives do, paradoxically, make sense.

Henry cannot trace his life. His narrative arc is interrupted numerous times for numerous reasons, which is one of the barriers to rebuilding his life. First, he has no validation. At the novel's beginning, he has no one to fill in the gaps, with no one to ask, "Did this really happen?" The few people who would be able to validate his experiences are dead (Victor, Jack Dalton), missing (Miss O'Shea and his family), or out to murder him (his IRA contacts).

No physical evidence of his life exists either. When John Ford is trying to get a passport so Henry can return to Dublin, he discovers that "there were no records in Dublin; I'd never existed" (86). The one artifact from his life, his wedding picture, which he calls "the record of the years hidden in a fugitive's wallet" (Doyle, *Oh Play That Thing* 337), is destroyed in *Oh Play That Thing.* When it is burned, Henry says, "I watched the thin flame turn them all to nothing" (337), signifying the destruction of the certainty of his memories along with the picture. The photo is the only real proof he has of his previous life, and when it is burned, he has nothing.

Secondly, Henry's past is slippery. The IRA has so many faces that Henry can't be sure what is true and what is false, who is guilty and who is innocent, whether his actions are heroic or criminal. The many layers and levels of the organization make his connection with it full of ghostly innuendo and suspicion. Similar are his memories from the Great Depression. Once Henry loses his leg and his family, reality and fiction merge. Henry knows Miss O'Shea is alive only through stories, stories that "came from the people who told them. Desperate men made up their desperadoes. . . .Men like themselves, just bigger. . . .The teller was part of the story, and so were the listeners, and that was one of their own out there, doing all the winning. . . .She was their story" (359-60). As is discussed in the chapter 4, Henry knows Miss O'Shea largely as a projection of himself; after he is separated from her during the Depression, Miss O'Shea becomes a projection both of Henry and of the storytellers.

Thirdly, Henry's life is disreputable. Although the neurotic acutely remember the bad and embarrassing (I can attest to this), others tend to forget the ugly, or at least, try to pretty it up a bit. His childhood is fraught with poverty, shame, and loss. As a child, he lives on the street, steals to survive, and sees his brother die of tuberculosis. As a young adult, he easily murders people, their innocence or guilt never established. He has no fond memories on which to dwell. He doesn't want to share his memories. Indeed, it could be dangerous for him to tell his stories. Thus, he must suppress them, hide them, and run from them.

Finally, Henry has always felt marginalized emotionally by being given the same name as his deceased brother, whom his mother claims is a star and whom he calls "the other Henry. The first and the real. He glowed proud and angry. He stared at me. He'd pinned me to the slab. He could have killed me—he was going to. A sudden shaft would slice and burn me up to nothing. I'd be a shadow left on the rock. I tried to stare, tried to match him. But it was hopeless. . . .He was still up there" (Doyle, *The Dead Republic* 55). Because our Henry is the "second and the false" Henry, he is constantly trying to convince himself of his value by shouting "I am Henry Smart," begging for some response indicating that he is important. He never gets that response, and on some level, he must feel that his memories are second-rate and not worth remembering because he is second rated.

Henry has also been marginalized historically. Not only is he the eternal blip on the fringes of famous events, but, as impoverished, oppressed, and Catholic, he is devalued by the Protestant ruling class. For instance, look at his reaction to the landscaping of the luxury hotel near the set of *The Quiet Man*:

> The Prods had always managed to convert their own patches of hell into some sort of England. Trees grew where none could, hedges flourished in places where finding muck to cover the spuds was the yearly struggle for the Catholics. I knew: it was the history of the place. The conqueror had taken the land that could support the trees and left the shite for the natives, and had even taken rent from them for it. I knew all that. But it was easy to fall for the alternative story: the conqueror was just better at it, more industrious, there because he deserved to be. Plants grew because he planted and tended to them; he told them to fuckin' grow (104).

Henry is told he is inferior on both personal and national levels. Thus, he must overcome many barriers in his search to reclaim his life. At the novel's beginning, Henry says, "I wasn't sure, myself, what I believed—if I believed" (7). He believes he "used to be heard;" that his "hand had once held guns and women;" and that he "was once a man called Henry Smart" (7). He can see through the glass darkly, and he can intuit what he used to be, but he doesn't know what he is. The scene in which Henry, about to die in the desert, is discovered by a urinating Henry Fonda prepares us for Henry's search. "Baptized" by Henry Fonda, he is arises from the dead, with his apostle John Ford ready to create and proclaim his Gospel. The artificiality of the scene—with building facades, a costumed Fonda, a massaged and censored Gospel—ironically prepares us for Henry's battle to find the truth about his life hidden underneath the many layers of lies.

How does Henry overcome these obstacles and find himself and his past? Henry has lost a year of his life due to frequent blackouts, but because of his relationship with Ford, he is beginning to find his past and his past is beginning to return: "It had happened before. I'd gone missing, more than once. And this guy finding me; there was a routine. But the curiosity was new. The collapse of proper time was getting on my wick and I didn't like the stupid man it made me" (16). Ford's insistent and impudent poking and prodding begins to remind him of the man he once was: "He was making me angry; he was making me think. . . . The anger felt like fingers, straightening me, pulling and prodding me into shape" (18-19). The emotional maturing Henry "wanted to put my life together, to tell my story. But I didn't want to crawl back into it, or even think that I could do that. I wanted to live properly. I wanted to keep going" (Doyle, *The Dead Republic* 57). [Interestingly, Doyle's use of Ford to jar Henry into reality is deliberate: "I've always admired John Ford. . . .I've read a lot about him. He strikes me as the kind of guy Henry would knock foreheads against" (Doyle qtd. in Sanai 1).]

Primarily, though, Ford is allowing Henry to own his past. He isn't appalled by Henry but fascinated. His acceptance gives Henry the impetus to remember: "I came to his meetings and felt myself being put together" (26). He remembers his wife and his children: "I was watching my own broken film, and Ford was watching me" (27). He begins to write down names and facts in a pebbled notebook as he remembers them. However, like the "burnt rubber lines, left where the cars had gone off the road. . . .There were hundreds of the lines, but none of the cars" (43), the names that Henry lists don't immediately bring back the people. The process takes time.

His return to sanity, although encouraged by Ford, is paradoxically hampered by Ford, who lives in a surreal, celluloid world. Ford himself is surreal. His numerous nicknames "mask a lot; the old prick hid behind them" (31). Ford's home has hidden rooms in which he barricades himself during drinking binges. He wears black spectacles even though he can see. His surroundings are artificial, made up of false deserts, Indian reservations, and towns. Ford works with actors who are English but who pretend to be Irish (51) and who attend boating parties dressed in Cumann na mBan uniforms (73).

His meetings with Ford contain a surreal, *Alice in Wonderland*, quality as well. During drunken stupors, Meta Sterne talks on behalf of the unconscious or incoherent director, and during belligerent outbursts, she gives him calming notes he has previously written for himself. During one meeting, a third man is present, who is holding, oddly, a much-too-large pen. The unintroduced man coughs, and Ford asks him "That a real cough?" (26). In another meeting, Ford talks about the movie set on which Henry was found: "That was Tombstone. . . .It got taken down after we were finished with it. . . .The real Tombstone is south of here, at the other end of the state of Arizona. . . .The real Tombstone doesn't exist" (44). Nothing makes sense in these meetings.

Ford exercises his power to make Henry's world surreal as well. No matter how many times Henry disappears, Ford's chauffeur always finds him. Additionally, the issue of *The Saturday Evening Post* containing Walsh's story "The Quiet Man," which Ford wants Henry to read, can never be destroyed:

> I left *The Quiet Man* behind me on the floor. But the fuckin' thing found me every time. And once, it got there before me. It was waiting on the bed when I unlocked the new door and walked in. I burnt it. Bits of paper broke away from the cover and rose in the heat. . But it was back on the bed the next day. . . .Could I trust my own head? I'd been falling in and out of the years, for years; I'd even forgotten who I was. I was only

getting the hang of living day to day. I'd already lost track; I didn't know the date. . . It hadn't happened. I'd wanted it to happen. I'd wanted to burn it. But I hadn't. I breathed deep. I took it in. I accepted it. (37)

Shortly thereafter, however, Henry finds a small chard of burnt magazine on his pillow and realizes that his initial memory is correct. Episodes like this, coupled with the outrageousness of Ford's life, make it extraordinarily difficult for Henry to retrieve his past.

The primary danger of Ford, however, is that he massages Henry's memories to make them more cinema-ready. He "names" Miss O'Shea "Mary. . . .Or Kate. I like that one. Something Irish. . . .Don't worry. . . .It's your story. We just need to call her something, for the script" (30). He decides to ignore the fact that Miss O'Shea is Henry's schoolteacher because it "won't get past the censor" (46). Ford needs "to take shortcuts" (58) in order to tell Henry's story. "It's a picture, Henry. You keep forgetting. You're a writer now. You make decisions. . . .In my pictures you fall in love once and you don't fuck at all" (62). Henry feels the pressure to "remember" his past in cinematic moments. "He was forcing me to fill the hole he was digging. And I wanted to. It was on my back—I was the writer. The words were on my tongue. . . I wanted to save the story" (69). If Henry doesn't remember something, Ford advises him, "Then make it up, for Chrissakes" (70).

Henry's search for the truth of his past is a metaphor for what should be Ireland's search for the truth of its past instead of its complacently accepting a mythologized version of it, a theme which I discuss in the chapter on *A Star Called Henry*. Trying to fit Henry's life into "The Quiet Man" is yet another symbol for "the failed promises of post-Independence Ireland and of the tenacity of a particular narrative: the nationalist version of twentieth century Irish history. . . .Doyle's novel testifies to the necessity of adapting this narrative—being neither too deferent nor too dismissive of it [essentially a postrevisionist historiography]—in the interests of gaining a more nuanced understanding of the period (Moynihan 1).

We see a continuation of this theme with the discussion of Ford's other films. Ford makes up more than characters in his movies. In his Westerns, Ford creates an America for Americans: "He was inventing America while he tried to get away from it. He was defining the place, and I'd reminded him of that. . . .He was building America, with John Wayne and the desert. He was giving Americans the history they wanted" (92). Ford says he "made some of the best pictures ever made. I conquered the West single-fucking-handedly. I gave them John Wayne and a brand new history" (121). Ford does the same thing for Ireland, which also inhibits Henry's return to emotional stability (and presumably, Ireland's as well):

> He made *The Quiet Man*. . . .To show a place worth fighting for. . . .Something beautiful that was going to be destroyed. . . .De Valera's Ireland. . . .Comely maidens and the rest of it. . . .It's beautiful and funny and carefree. . . .It's Ireland. . . .As far as millions of people were concerned. And they travelled here to see it with their own eyes. And we tried to live up to it. . . . *The Quiet Man*. . . .It's the story of Ireland. Catholics and Protestants side by side, in harmony. Fishing and horse racing. It's every German's idea of Paradise. And it's sexy as well. . . .Heaven on earth. . . .The Ireland your generation fought for. . . .And the Brits went and destroyed it. (316-17)

Ford wants his Irish movie to perpetuate his Ireland:

> I love this country. . . What I grew up with. I was Irish from the start. It was the stories my parents told. And the dancing and music and the drink. We were never really American. We were Irish but Ireland was thousands of miles away. And fifty years away. I grew up loving a place that didn't fucking exist. I just knew it

was a hell of a lot better than where I actually was. . . . .
Without our nostalgia we would die. . . . We'd be
nothing. Landless. The place mightn't exist, Henry, but
we need it. And the Italians, and the Swedes, the
Russians, and all of those people. They need the home
in their hearts. . . . I'm doing the right thing. . . . Making
this leprechaun Ireland. I'm doing the right thing here,
Henry. . . . It's what happened after we won the war.
Paradise. (119-121, 126)

We learn later that Ford has been asked to create this version of
Ireland by the Provos, the same people who are forcing Henry to
perpetuate his own falsified version. [Doyle in a rare boast, says,
"If I say so myself, there's a very clever twist at the end"
(McCann interview)]. This twist not only shows the theme of
demythologizing the heavily mythologized past but also
corresponds to Doyle's recurring theme of the definition of
Irishness, as well as confusing the issue of the true creators of
the Henry Smart (and the Ireland) of the novel's end.

While Ford's revisionist's version of Ireland is attractively
appealing, Henry tries to fight against it initially: When he
dreams of his daughter kissing his forehead, which he briefly
thinks might have happened "in my own Ireland," he
immediately undercuts his temporary pathos by thinking,
"sentimental shite" (122). But he soon realizes that Ford's jaded
idealism has won: "I'd tried to tell the truth but I'd ended up
inventing another Ireland. Just like Ford had done to America. . .
I'd let the blarney in. . . . My daughter had kissed my forehead.
I'd invented a place where that could happen. Ford had
invented a place where the Irish could be at rest. Where fists
didn't hurt, where drink did no damage, where there was no
real pain to hide. A monstrous fuckin' lie, but a nice one" (123).
Henry is trying to keep his past truthful but fiction slips in, often
disguised as truth, which is precisely why over-exposure to Ford
is so dangerous to Henry's stability.

Despite the obstacles posed by Ford's desire to "invent
Henry" (Fitzgerald-Hoyt 24), and later Ireland itself, the

validation he offers enables Henry to grow healthier and to become increasingly able to distinguish the present from the past, fiction from reality: "And I knew what he was doing. He was making me up. There were two stories being dragged out of me. He knew what I was doing: I was reclaiming my life. . . . He'd fucked up. . . .I was becoming the man he'd been trying to get out of me. I was more than he could handle "(Doyle, *The Dead Republic* 30, 64). Henry begins to remember his past, even if only in terms of what it isn't: He finally marshals the courage to read "The Quiet Man," something he has been loath to do: "I'd been terrified that I'd be in there, with Miss O'Shea, my life already told. It was the fear that I wouldn't know it, that I'd read it and not know myself, no matter how often I read, or coaxed and battered my memory. But it wasn't about me at all. I felt that certainty, and I stretched. . . .I could relax; I could rest; I was still intact" (80). He knows his life is not Maurice Walsh's story.

His return to sanity is marked first by small decisions: "It was years since I'd felt in charge, since I'd felt the slight swerve that was the act of deciding. I recognized it one morning, when I made up my mind which way I'd have my eggs. . . .I'd decided to shave and stop being the oul' lad. . . .You had it, or you didn't. I insisted: I had it" (63). Then, Henry demands to be officially on the film's payroll, and he buys a pair of custom-made alligator-skinned boots with his first paycheck, signifying his donning of a new, tougher, skin: "The new man, the old man. I was Henry Smart. I wasn't a ghost or a shadow, a leaking bag of memories and bitterness. I was living. I was breathing in and comfortably out" (67). The more he remembers, the stronger he becomes, ultimately taking ownership of the movie: "The picture would be made, because I wanted it to be made. It was my story. . . I wasn't waiting. If he wanted the picture he'd have to come after me. Because I was more than the writer. I was the plot. . . .I wasn't doing it again, listening to him force my life into *The Quiet Man*. I told him I wouldn't give him bits of my life to make his picture a bit less of a travesty" (74,86).

Thus, months later, when Henry reads the script of the charming romantic comedy, entirely different from the love-amid-tommy-guns piece he authors, he feels as if his story and history are both being erased. The rage this betrayal, which erases not only his past but his present, raises in Henry enables him to free himself from what could become a crippling relationship with Ford.

He is able to confront Ford on the movie set also because he finds physical validation in Ireland. Immediately upon disembarking from the plane in Dublin, he leaves the movie company and revisits the house in Roscommon in which his wife's mother has lived. "I'd come to see the wall, maybe put my hand against it, break off a piece of whitewash, put it in my mouth and taste it. But just to see it—that would have been enough. . . .Proof" (7). Tangible evidence is scarce, however:

> It wasn't there. The house was gone. . . .I was standing in the right place, but there was nothing. I wasn't there to find anyone; I wasn't that thick. But it felt like another death. . . .But it was as if the house and the outhouse had never been there, or the well, or the low stone walls that had kept the cows out of the bog. . . there was no wall, no hint of dry clay where the wall had fallen, or hardness in the ground where it had stood. . . .Not the edge of the field, where there'd once been a wall surrounding the kitchen garden. (6)

A single gate, however, is extant, which is enough to ground Henry: "it felt like sanity" (6). The gate provides validation for a host of memories.

After the fight with Ford, he undergoes another type of baptism. He climbs over the luxury hotel's high security wall - the celluloid, revisionist version of Ireland keeping out the real Ireland - walks into the lake and "climbed back out twenty years later" (128). Henry leaves the messy world he has lived in and hibernates in small village near Dublin. Forty nine years old, he works as a gardener and school custodian, and he lives in his own cottage and "begins to recover some coherence as a character" (Walton 39). "It was boring, but maybe freedom was supposed to be boring" (Doyle, *The Dead Republic* 133), Henry says. He spends more than two decades in the suburban comfort of "black prams [that] were pushed by well-fed mothers, and they were pushing babies, not coal. No one begged, no one hugged the walls" (133). He even goes to church. He says, "The quiet life was mending me" (139).

The quiet life is also validating the sacrifices he makes with the IRA: When he sees the "good house for each family; a house full of kids, and a brand new school just up the road" (133), Henry sees signs that his fight for independence has been successful, and "I began to wonder if my fight had really been a total waste" (133). He finally believes, "I'd created the land that fed them. . . .The smell of idle Irishwomen—it was my victory" (227). His past finally begins to become acceptable and respectable to him.

Further validation comes in 1966, the fiftieth anniversary of the Easter Rising, during which the country is honoring those who fought for independence. Massive celebrations occur throughout the country, and Henry, although not a part of the celebrations, nevertheless follows them closely on the television and radio. He only recognizes a few faces and knows that many of the celebrants have never fought for anything, much less for independence during the famous insurrection. He gets a secret satisfaction out of knowing that he is not a poseur. He knows he is a true veteran, and while he doesn't want parades and awards, he "was tempted" (160). At the very least, however, Henry realizes that he no longer has to hide his past and that he is no longer in danger because of it. His past finally becomes acceptable and respectable to others.

Paradoxically, his narrative arc also gains stability when he realizes that he isn't living in an entirely new world—and that the new Ireland is similar to his old Ireland. He notices sick boys at the school being taken away:

> I thought the boys were like me, and that they loved the place. It took me a while to calm down, to notice the shivers and malnourishment, the ringworm, the bruise.

It took me a while to accept that poverty could also be suburban. And it was a while before I noticed the disappearing boys. That last lesson came with a cough. . . .It was called consumption when it got Victor. Now it was T.B. And it was under control, well on the run. There were sanatoriums. . . .No one coughed to death in the new Ireland. . . .But I knew I wasn't in a republican heaven. Bad lungs weren't left at the gate, and bad bastards occasionally crawled off the farm and became teachers. (142-43)

Sadly, the continuation of illness and violence makes his past less horrible and less unique. He has a frame of reference with which to understand this new world.

Henry, an adult, refuses to be as impotent as Henry the child. Although he can't do anything about illness, he can do something about the physical abuse of the young boys. He attempts to protect these boys as he tries but fails to protect his brother Victor. He creates a republican heaven by threatening the most brutal teachers with violent reprisal for excessive corporal punishment. He succeeds: "For fifteen years the boys' national school in Ratheen was the most civilized place in the country. No child was slapped, except on the days when I stayed at home. I'd made my own republic, inside the railings of the school" (151). He uses the notoriety of his former IRA affiliation to force his will upon the worst offending teachers, and it works. Their acquiescence and fear validate his belief that he is a man to be feared, "who still had it" (63). The man that he was gives life to the man that he is.

Ironically, Henry doesn't notice that he escapes the walls of the Ford's luxury hotel room only to enter another set of walls. Within the school walls, however, Henry believes himself to be the one in control, a benevolent dictator. He has created his own world just as surely as Ford creates his own world. Even though he says, "I couldn't ban reality, the hard knocks and grief that were waiting beyond the railings" (151), he is trying to alter reality in hopes that students would remember "there was another way and they [would go] through their lives knowing that" (151). Again, he doesn't realize that his "other way" is as unreal as Ford's. Ford creates movies which inspire people to believe in a different world; Henry frightens teachers to allow the boys to believe the same thing.

Despite his increasingly firm grasp on reality, however, we get a sense that Henry is not, in fact, the sole maker of this reality. For instance, he receives a mysterious visit from the village priest, who mentions that "there are people who'll be very happy to hear" (156) of Henry's satisfaction with his job. When he awakens from his periodic blackouts, he finds fresh food in the refrigerator and knows that "someone—people were looking after me" (161). He is content to be ignorant, just as he is during the early parts of the revolution. Just as Mr. Strickland, the school's principal, pushes away doubts about the impetus behind the school's decline in corporal punishment, Henry pushes away doubts as to the reason for his peaceful, well-cared-for existence.

He is thrust out of the 23-year, womb-like existence in 1974 when a bomb explodes in Dublin. His artificial leg is anonymously recovered from the rubble, polished and cleaned, just as Henry's image is about to be. Henry receives the final validation he is unwittingly craving after a reporter writes his story for the newspaper: "I was Henry Smart again. I was side by side with the boy I'd been in the G.P.O. People knew what I'd been and what I'd done. They looked at me and saw their country. . . .I was Celtic mythology walking towards them. I was fuckin' biblical. I was the quiet man, and suddenly a fine man" (174). His Provos contact calls him: "A prophet" of "our own religion" (192) and then corrects himself, "You're more than a prophet, Henry, he said. –You're our direct line. To God" (193). Henry believes they think of him as "Moses, someone who'd actually spoken to God. . . .The eleventh commandment" (186). Now, finally, Point A is leading directly to Point Z—the Alpha points straight to the Omega. Even *The Quiet Man* has its place in Henry's journey, as Henry discovers at the novel's end.

To digress temporarily, although Henry actively disbelieves in God, he nevertheless is too Irish not to be attracted to the religious rhetoric. He transfers a belief in an omnipotent God onto the Provos. Henry gets swept up by the religious language, despite, or perhaps because of, the fact that he has no faith. As a child, Henry renounces God and organized religion. Not only rejected at the Catholic school, he feels rejected by God at every turn because of the poverty that is his life. He is rejected by the Mother Superior of the Miss O'Shea's school; he sees the hypocrisy of the praying rebels in the GPO; and finally, when he desperately turns to prayer as a means to find Miss O'Shea, he winds up alone and dying in the desert. Henry begins going to Mass only in order to secure and retain his custodial job. He bluntly says to the dying Ivan, "There's no God" (229).

In comparison to Henry's concept of an indifferent, uncaring, ineffectual, or unreal God, the Provos seem omnipotent; indeed, they have manipulated aspects of his life and Irish politics even more directly than even Henry suspects. They have taken care of Henry, and they make him feel special. They even acknowledge the presence of their divinity within him, an orthodox Christian concept.

Getting back to the argument; Henry intellectually knows that the line from Point A to Point Z is not actually a coherent one. The man he is believed to have been and the man he really has been are different. The paper runs a picture of the young Henry that isn't the young Henry at all: The boy in the picture isn't even wearing the correct uniform. Henry also isn't a hero. He joins the Rising either to die or make money, not to liberate his countrymen. Indeed, Henry is more intent upon liberating Miss O'Shea's knickers than fair Eire. Also, Henry is not and never has been a member of the Dail. Henry is being validated by a past that isn't his, one that is as false as Ford's *Quiet Man*. At least, however, this is a version of himself of which he approves. He accepts the adulation of the Provisional IRA members because he wants it: "I wanted to be who they thought I was" (186). Being involved in another struggle would validate his past immeasurably, even if, ironically, he has to lie to do so.

Thus, he doesn't correct them and tell them he was never at the First or Second Dail. He fully realizes that "I was a hero and a fraud, elated and a bit terrified" (185).

Henry finally can begin confirming his memories when he learns that the Widow O'Kelly is, in fact, Miss O'Shea, his wife. His questions about her activities during the American Great Depression are answered, as well as are his memories about the IRA. He asks Miss O'Shea repeatedly about incidents from the war: "It was a real question. I wanted to know" (211). He finally has the luxury of discussing and reliving his memories. After their retrospective bicycle ride throughout the countryside, Henry sleeps without nightmares: "No dreams—no fingers" (208). Henry has peace of mind. He has become emotionally whole.

He needs this strength because suddenly, his life becomes chaotic. Miss O'Shea suffers a severe stroke and is both alive and dead for Henry. He visits her every day, although he doesn't fully believe she is alive. He tries to establish a relationship with his daughter, who refuses to forgive him for abandoning her. He lies to the Provos on two counts: He is neither a member of the first Dails nor is he loyal to them currently, as he has become an informant for the Special Branch. Henry discovers that his wife has listening devices affixed to her by the Special Branch and that her nurses are Special Branch plants. His daughter, whom he believes to be a somewhat boring housewife obsessed with her dogs, turns out to be a revolutionary herself. Ireland, itself, has also become a source of stress for Henry and no longer seems worthy of his sacrifice, as the country is stalled with a slow economy and infected by the drug culture: "I saw it while I waited for the bus and decided that the place was worse than it had been when I was the young, hungry king of Dublin's corners. Poverty then had seemed natural, but this was just atrocious" (229). Life is no longer being lived within the protective and protected walls of the boys' school.

When Henry loses his outside validation, he looks back and begins to see patterns, imaginary or not, sewn by the IRA: "It hit me. . . .They'd been waiting for me when I got off the bus in

Ratheen the first time; they'd been keeping an eye on me all those years, when I was gardening. And before that—back to when I came down off the plane at Shannon with John Ford. . . ." (205). Once again, he has no yardstick for measuring truth—the usual methods, namely, reported news, documentation, and conversations with family and friends, are cut off for him. His Provos contact even tells him, "Ignore what you hear. On the news or from any other source. It's a smokescreen. The armed struggle. . . .Behind the armed struggle, Henry, there's another struggle going on" (214).

Henry often gets confused in his newly chaotic world. He is unaware of most of the politics involved in the Troubles, including the hunger strikes and Ivan's involvement in gun smuggling. His confusion is evident when he misreads the police's intention for him. Not only do they not want him to decry violence, they don't care what role he plays with the Provos. Henry admits, "I'm lost" (236). Indeed, after Henry says he will not be an informer, one of the men responds, "You already are, Henry" (237). Although he feels confident when he is picked up by the IRA again, the IRA's inquisition about the police's visit totally surprises him, and his confidence soon leaves: "I'd had enough of everything. I was tired and still terrified. . . .I wondered what was going to happen this time, when I walked into a packed room or climbed onto the back of a lorry" (250).

However, despite the confusing circumstances of his present life, Henry is able to keep his wits. This Henry doesn't try to escape; this Henry actively tries to learn what is going on and remain a player in the game.

Henry is able to navigate successfully the choppy waters of his political involvement because his past and present fully merge now, and his past is repeated:

Once I started paying real attention to Ireland beyond the parish, I realized it was 1920 again. Every stupid decision, every shooting, every rubber bullet— internment, Bloody Sunday, every strong rumour—

British collusion in the planting of my bomb on Talbot Street and the other bombs that afternoon—all of these sent young men and women queuing up to join. . . Reprisal and counter-reprisal, terror and retaliation—it had gone on for three years, in my day. It went on for decades this time—and it was still my day. (203)

The British, specifically Margaret Thatcher, react in the same way that they do during the revolution, namely, making people hate them:

People voted for starving men because they hated Thatcher. She'd done this to us. . . .She was the Provisionals' greatest asset. She was living, breathing evil and she was on the telly every night. . . .Thatcher had united the country more than anyone else had ever managed. People who didn't give a shite about the north felt the sweat climb out of their necks whenever they heard the voice. . . It wasn't just the message. . . .It was the voice, the reminder of who and what we were. . . .We were nothing and Thatcher told us that every time she spoke. (263, 284)

Henry recognizes how history has come full circle with the discussion over the reaction to the British retaliation:

Political ambition and armed struggle are mutually exclusive. . . .I remembered thinking that he was saying nothing new, that Ernie O'Malley had argued the same thing, whenever I'd been too slow to see him coming. . . . I knew the story. I was the story. I knew how the stupidity of 1916 had been turned to glorious success. The British had helped there too, when they'd executed the leading men instead of kicking them in their holes and sending them home. The new story had the same plot—but it was different. (260, 284)

At the funeral of Bobby Sands, which is reminiscent of the 1917 funeral of Thomas Ashe, he "recited the lament I'd written with Jack Dalton in the Gravediggers pub in Glasnevin after we'd buried Ashe" (252). Henry is also deemed not fit to run in the general election, just as he is when he is younger. And, just as he when he is younger, initially he's having the time of his life: "You're enjoying yourself, Henry. . . .I thought about this.— Yeah, I said. - I am" (261). However, just as when he is younger, he tires of the escalating bloodshed, and his body forces him into another great sleep.

Henry is able to survive this period only by using the lessons he learns during his early time with the IRA. In *Oh, Play That Thing*, Henry seems determined to forget every lesson he learns and thus makes the same mistakes throughout the novel. In *The Dead Republic*, however, Henry reaches back and begins to remember things he learns as a young man. Only because he has been able to order his past is he able to order his present. The first major piece of information he gives the Special Branch men is something he learns during the revolution: "And, basically, I told the G-men on the bus the same thing. I shifted the geography from Dublin to the north, but I told them what I'd seen and known—or thought I'd known—in 1920. I changed the tense from past to present and informed on men who were long dead" (255). Henry is able to act on his own during the final stages of the novel. We believe him when he says he is "a big man today, not the ghost of one. I was all clear, in front of me; I knew what I was going to do" (301).

Henry's first action is to save his daughter. He agrees to be trotted out across the country, encouraging people to stay hopeful, after his daughter disappears. Next, he purposefully lies to his wife and tells her that Ireland is united, freeing her from her earthly prison although leaving him alone, which is his one selfless act toward her. Finally, he gives his own opinion in the meeting in the Mansion House: "I'd done the right thing" (329). Henry's ability to act, however, does not convince the reader that on Easter Sunday, 2016, totally unity and peace will be achieved. Doyle has his own personal doubts about that: "A year ago I'd have said the violence appears to be over. . . .But all it takes is a couple of mad bastards capable of planting a bomb. Many of these don't go off but inevitably over the coming years one or two will. We just have to remember to be calm" (qtd. in Sanai 3).

At the age of 79, Henry is given the chance to relive his life. He is able to become a devoted husband and father, to serve (both parts of) his country, and to be the face of the revolution. At the novel's beginning, he is in no shape to shoulder these responsibilities. Only because he is able to come to terms with his past—to stop running from it--is he able to make his second chance count. We leave him an old man, reconciled with both his impending death and with his fully lived life.

CHAPTER 8
BULLFIGHTING: STORIES

Doyle's most recent publication, *Bullfighting: Stories* (2011), is a collection of thirteen short stories dealing with the various challenges faced by middle-aged men, most of whom are married and who have achieved various degrees of success, financially and personally. The stories, some of which were published previously and are fairly brief, are primarily the ruminations of men facing sterile marriages, disease, unemployment, or family revelations, and fluently "tack back and forth between the hilarious and the heartbreaking" (Shone 1).

Doyle, born 1958, is about the same age as the men in the stories. In an interview years ago, a younger Doyle warned against writing strictly from experience:

> I think if it's taken literally, [writing what you know] is a dreadful piece of advice. Because none of the books I've written have been about what I know, in the literal sense. If it's taken in the broader sense, yeah, that's fine. But I think that piece of advice, which probably started off as a good, benign, piece of advice, has become something of a tyranny. This idea that you have to go out there and live and then come back and write about it—that's one way of writing, but it's not the only way of writing. (Sbrockey interview 551)

This book is one of the first in which he has been able to relate to many of the experiences of his characters. These short stories "are more autobiographical than I've ever done" (McCann interview).

> One of the great things about being a writer and growing older is that everything is easily reachable.

Inevitable really. I can't remember what age I was when the first book came out—28. I'm now 52. So quite a lot of living has been done. Living that in many ways I would have liked to have avoided. You know, the death of a close person is something that I never wanted to see. And that's something—a matter of growing up. It brings me knowledge of grief that I wouldn't have had beforehand. Watching your children grow up brings pride, anxiety, the form of grief that is watching them become independent. These things go into the work. [*Bullfighting*] is a collection of stories that's largely about middle age. And I don't think I'd have written it without being middle aged. It wouldn't have occurred to me. (Personal interview 16)

Thus, Doyle has felt some of the same angst that his characters experience, especially concerning children: "When you're walking through town with kids when they're very young, you start looking at what they're looking at. You begin to see things that you never saw before, or just at ground level. . . .You end up seeing things at angles that you didn't anticipate seeing. There are routines and habits that become very funny in ways and great material for stories, like pets and funerals for animals, like goldfish" (Dwyer 2).

The unifying theme of the collection is the awakening from the routine of habit and the loss of its strangely innocent and secure stupor. As Samuel Beckett famously writes about Marcel Proust's "creatures," Doyle's less successful characters:

Are victims of this predominating condition and circumstance—Time. . . .victims and prisoners. There is no escape from the hours and the days. Neither from tomorrow nor from yesterday. There is no escape from yesterday because yesterday has deformed us, or been deformed by us. . . .Yesterday is not a milestone that has been passed, but a daystone on the beaten track of the years, and irremediably a part of us, within us, heavy and dangerous. We are not merely more weary because of yesterday, we are other, no longer what we were before the calamity of yesterday. (2-3)

Time works on Doyle's (and Proust's) characters unawares, and they wake up to a changed world and to a changed self: "But the poisonous ingenuity of Time in the science of affliction . . . [results] in an unceasing modification of his personality" (4). Instead of confidence, security, and stability, middle age in *Bullfighting* most often brings harsh reality in the form of boredom, impotence, and routine, this last of which is the most insidious, continues Beckett:

Habit [is an attribute] of the Time cancer. . . .Habit is a compromise effected between the individual and his environment, or between the individual and his own organic eccentricities, the guarantee of a dull inviolability, the lightning-conductor of his existence. Habit is the ballast that chains the dog to his vomit. . . . A minister of dullness. . . an agent of security. (7-10)

Not to disagree with Beckett, but habit is not always bad. Routines are necessary to remain sane, for goodness sakes. However, a habit of habit, almost the inevitable product of middle age, dulls us to the beauty of life. *Bullfighting* illustrates just this—that habit "has both positive and negative aspects. On the one hand, it covers over change, making [us] unaware of time passing and allowing [us] to live in the present without grieving over a past that has largely disappeared. On the other hand, it makes [us] miss things and is therefore responsible for the moments that pass unnoticed while [our] minds are occupied elsewhere" (Elkins).

Doyle's characters awaken to the direness of their situations. "This is a book filled with stragglers and loners, men who have come loose from the pack and don't know how to get back. . . .The immobilized bull [in "Bullfighting"] is a fitting figurehead for the men in this collection, most of them becalmed in middle age, guarding ever emptier nests, beset by mysterious aches and pains" (Shone 1). *Bullfighting* examines how characters handle the sudden awareness of the crisis of middle age, when characters are faced with "periods of transition . . . [that] represent the perilous zones in the life of the individual, dangerous, precarious, painful, mysterious and fertile, when for a moment the boredom of living is replaced by the suffering of being. . . .[and] Habit may [be]. . . sleeping" (Beckett 8-9). The characters "for a moment free, [are] exposed to that reality—an exposure that has its advantages and its disadvantages" (Beckett 10). The characters handle their periods of transition differently, sometimes gracefully, sometimes fearfully.

For those that rue this moment of awakening - who are paralyzed and incapable of action - the early adult years, those in which careers are uncertain, children are helpless, and money is tight, are often viewed in retrospect as protected and idyllic, before the ennui brought on by the religion of routine. The characters see their early lives as filled, almost de facto, with both unusual and alluring excitement.

The more successful characters proactively attempt to appreciate and learn from this awakening. They see these moments as "enchantments of reality. . . .when [their lives are] . . perceived as particular and unique and not merely the member of a family, when it appears independent of any general notion. . . . Unfortunately Habit has laid its veto on this form of perception" (11). The most successful characters in the collection have consciously decided to counteract the opiate of habit. Thus, these characters accept the challenges life brings and learn to temper the routine of life with change. Their lives are like rivers, always moving but always constant.

I choose to group the collection into two categories, those dealing with marriage and those that don't. In the former, the characters are, obviously, primarily dealing with issues centered on their wives and marriages. While the characters may have other issues, for instance, their health, children, or unemployment, the stories focus on their relationships with their wives. Interestingly, Doyle, an active supporter of the 1995 divorce referendum, seems to have very hopeful views of the resiliency of marriage, as each story offers a glimmer, albeit sometimes small, of hope.

"Recuperation," the first story in the collection, offers us such a glimmer of hope for a dying relationship. Hanahoe, whom we follow on one of his daily walks, is thinking about his marriage, which, after many years, has become empty and lonely. His early memories of his marriage are good: "He used to go there with the kids. She'd come with them. They laughed when they realized it: it was a family outing. Nearer than the zoo. Ice cream on the way home. The kids were delighted. The innocence. It was lovely" (Doyle, *Bullfighting* 8). The innocence, not only of the children but also of his wife and himself, is compelling. His life then, from his present perspective, seems idyllic, uncomplicated, and rich. He and his wife are partners, two people who, with their gaiety, are able to turn a trip to a pet shop into a family occasion.

Over the years, he has been "deformed" by the endless repetitions of "yesterdays" (Beckett 2). His marriage dissolves, and the innocence ends: "He's been living alone for years. He doesn't know what happened. There was no shouting, very little. There was no violence. No one was hit. No one played away from home" (Doyle, *Bullfighting* 8). Hanahoe sees no resolution to the sterility of his marriage:

> What went wrong? He could never say that. What happened? She'd look at him. He'd have to explain. Where would he start? He hadn't a clue. And the question would announce it - the end. They'd have to admit it. And one of them would have to go. Him. But he's alone already. . . .Who's to blame? No one. It just happened. It's too late now. He can't pull them back, his wife, the kids. They have their own lives. She does; they do. . . .He doesn't know. He knows nothing. He feels nothing. He doesn't even feel sorry for himself. He doesn't think he does. He's fine. He copes. (9)

Finally cognizant of his situation, he is at a loss how to fix it and feels a victim to habit.

While Hanahoe cannot consciously discern the reason for the state of his marriage, the reader can posit a guess. Hanahoe seems a man of strict routine. He walks the same route every day and dislikes interactions with people and interruptions to his order. Notice how he refuses to stop walking or change course during a sudden downpour, abhorring the thought of a variation in his routine. Ironically, he is aware enough to realize the destructive quality of his routines: "It's depressing, a life, laid out like that. Mass, driving the kids to football, or dancing. The pint on Friday. The sex on Sunday. . . .The routine. One day he knew: he hated it" (6).

In the story, however, the ferocity of the storm forces Hanahoe to stop his walk and wait under a bus shelter, although it "annoys him, giving up" (10). With him is a gang of rowdy adolescents who jostle him and make him so uncomfortable that he almost leaves, despite the rain. After the group leaves in a taxi, however, he reacts very differently to a precocious little girl who remains behind. In a brief exchange, she tells him that she is waiting for her mother to come home from work and remarks that the rain "was badly needed" (11). Hanahoe agrees, and once the rain stops, he leaves the shelter, walking towards home and smiling.

The rain - as well as the divergence from his routine that it brings - is badly needed. He wakes up and thus temporarily becomes free of habit: "Our current habit of living is . . . incapable of dealing . . . with any circumstance unforeseen in [the] curriculum" (Beckett 9). He discovers that this first deviation from his route is somewhat pleasant: "But he's—not sure—reassured, or something. He can change his mind. He's prepared to" (Doyle, *Bullfighting* 10). His first interaction with strangers also ends well: Despite the initial discomfort and annoyance he feels because of the teenagers, talking to the young girl is pleasant. When the sun comes out and he opts to return home instead of continuing with his walk, the reader is left with a feeling of optimistic expectation. Perhaps Hanahoe is "awake" enough to be able to revitalize his marriage. At least, we feel, he will be able to endure the changes that a divorce would bring.

"The Joke" is a remarkably similar narrative. The unnamed narrator is also faced with a dissolving, long-term marriage.

> Something had happened. Nothing had happened. It had just happened. The way things were now. . . .And the partnership had stopped. Somewhere. He could never have pinned it down. He'd no idea. There'd been nothing said. Nothing done. As far as he knew. But, who knew. . . .Something had gone wrong. Something small. Something he hadn't even noticed. It had changed. . . .he didn't know her. He knew her, but he didn't know her. It had been a slow thing. Very gradual. (71)

This man, however, is different from Hanahoe in that he is more actively worried about his marriage, not numb. He has many feelings that he admits—he loves his wife and wants to save his marriage, although he is angry at her for taking him for granted. He is even mad at himself for letting the marriage disintegrate. He feels the loss of innocence and wants to recapture that feeling of partnership. He thinks about reverting to old methods of connection, namely telling her a joke: "And it wasn't the only way he'd made her laugh. Words used to do it. Jokes. Play-acting, acting the eejit. She'd like it. She'd loved it. She'd moved closer to him when she was laughing. He could give it a try. Now. A joke. . . .He'd see if it worked as he told it" (76-77).

Oddly, he decides upon a rather vulgar joke and is prepared to tell it when his wife ends her phone conversation. The story ends, however, not with the joke, but when his wife comes to the door of the den, and he looks at her. The rain is pounding outside. We never see him tell the joke.

This story is different from "Recuperation" in that the rain doesn't end. Besides wanting his marriage vibrant, the man doesn't show any ability to change. Yes, he is aware and awake to reality, but his only solution is to revert to a previous routine. The story's "happy" ending rests on the ability of the narrator to tell a joke. Although at least he is trying, sadly the story documents only his inability to act. Hanahoe has more wherewithall to restore the vitality of his marriage. Despite his adherence to routine, he is capable of change: For instance, he has taken steps to improve his health by walking daily. The main character in "The Joke," alas, never leaves his chair throughout the story. Although he is actively worried, he isn't active in any other way. We doubt his ability to marshal his resources to save his marriage.

Much of his marriage's success depends upon his wife's perception and reception of the joke. We know she is able to perceive need in her friends and family; can she perceive the need in her spouse? Will she recognize the off-color joke as an olive branch? And, if she does, will the best case scenario be that the couple will fall back into their old patterns, the same patterns that have disintegrated into the situation we encounter in the story?

These two male protagonists realize the inexorable erosion time brings. Both marriages are on the brink of dissolution, and habit is the only obvious culprit. The couples grow apart gradually; there is no distinct point of no return, no action one could wish undone. Age here does not bring about wisdom but ignorance. Age does not bring comfort but only distress. The struggles of the past seem like childlike innocence to these world-weary, lonely men. The terror lies in that, were these characters able to do it over again, they do not know what they could do differently.

"The Dog" features another at-risk marriage, although this protagonist is able to trace the path of disintegration. He believes their difficulties began specifically with their aging bodies. His wife Mary is disgusted by his gray chest hair, he by her "four decades of arse parked inside a piece of string" (142). The distance grows until she gets a dog, Emma, and suddenly, "there was a child in the house," and the two grow closer. They both enjoy walking her, taking her to obedience classes, and caring for her, although the narrator isn't as attached as his wife. The dog, in a sense, introduces change to each character personally as well as to them as a couple. The narrator walks along the beach and bird watches with the dog: "He'd never have been comfortable by himself, walking along the empty beach in the morning. He'd have felt strange. . . .But with the dog it was fine. He didn't have to explain anything, to himself or to anyone else" (152). This change, which disrupts their habit, draws the couple together. Their closeness introduces a feeling of safety into their home. For instance, the homeless Romanian family they pass on the way to obedience classes makes them more appreciative of their own security and stability.

The dog, ironically also is the cause of their marital difficulties. The dog runs away one day, after which they become the clichéd couple driven apart by the death of a child. When Emma disappears, that sense of change, the enchantment of reality that she brings, is shattered. Because Mary has emotionally invested in Emma, she withdraws when the narrator doesn't grieve as openly or as much as she does. He later realizes later his mistake: "But he'd failed. He could have pretended. Cried a bit, let her console him, take over—he didn't know. . . .It was about grief. She grieved. He didn't. Simple as that. He should have pretended. It would have been a different kind of honesty" (157). Their sorrow could have been bound them together as another type of enchantment, and they could have come together as a united front against it. However, the husband fails to realize this until it is too late. This miscommunication is fatal, and the marriage is irrevocably damaged: "The walking out stopped. The rows stopped. The talking too; it was a wordless life. They'd drifted. But, actually, they hadn't drifted, and that was another problem. One of them should have gone. . . .But that wise moment had never happened" (157). Instead, the two are in a marital purgatory. After experiencing the enchantment of reality, habit fails them as an "agent of security."

The next stories show more successful relationships, ones in which the marriage is fluid yet steady. "Ash" refers to an event, namely, the 2010 eruption of the Icelandic volcano Eyjafjallajokull, which spilled ash all over the surrounding area and crippled air traffic for weeks. A week or so before, Kevin is jolted out of his routine, when his wife, Ciara, announces, with no explanation, that she is leaving him. Hours after the pronouncement, she returns home and initiates passionate and drunken sex, only to leave again suddenly. Kevin, confused and hurt, is trying to hide her absence from their two children by keeping their lives as normal as possible. However, he does face the possibility that Ciara is gone: He even makes plans to go to a singles bar.

After only a few days, Ciara returns home one evening, and Kevin retains some of his dignity by refusing another alcohol- or guilt-driven sexual encounter. The next morning, as he makes breakfast for his children, he tries not to feel bitter but fails. The tension between Ciara and him is dispelled by the news coverage of the volcano, during which one of the children asks, "What's ash?" (89). Ash, they learn from the news, "killed planes. . . .It was an act of God. . . .It had nothing to do with climate change or the economy. No one was to blame" (90).

Doyle then makes the connection with ash as a metaphor for the marriage. Ciara explains that ash isn't permanent: "It's just for a while. Things will get back to normal after the ash drifts away. Or falls. . . .It won't [hurt]" (90). Thus, she is apologizing to Kevin and reassuring him that she won't leave again. Ciara, obviously, has had an awakening and has reacted. Her actions force Kevin to abandon his routines as well, although he doesn't quite understand what is happening. Kevin is flexible enough to change his routine without disintegration. He is steady enough to maintain a healthy routine, yet he allows Ciara her freedom, although not at his own humiliation. Their life has routine but it doesn't paralyze them. Growth and exploration for both partners is allowed. These periods, while painful, are acts of God. Eventually, the story indicates, the ash will settle down—only to be disrupted again—which is a good thing. Routine happiness will return, but the routine stupor won't. Kevin and Ciara, because of the give and take of their marriage, will survive this volcanic eruption.

"The Plate" shows another flawed but strong marriage. Jim and Maeve spend most evenings drinking too much wine, eating dinner, and talking. Some evenings, the talking escalates into fighting—fights "they drank into" (134). One night, Maeve hurls a plate at Jim, which refuses to break, even after he stomps on it for effect. Soon after that incident, Jim has a medical emergency, and Maeve, too anxious to wait for the ambulance, drives Jim to the hospital. Only a few moments from the house, they both realize that they have forgotten their infant. They immediately turn around to get her, and Jim, despite his agony, has an epiphany: "And he knew something, in the minute it took to get to the house: they were happy" (139).

Their marriage, while seemingly at risk, is oddly healthy. The passion inspired by their fights—albeit drunken fights— keeps habit at bay. The couple's love for each other—seen when Maeve is so distressed over her husband's pain that she forgets her child—has not been dulled by habit. Life and marriage should be like the plate—messy, perhaps chipped, but unbroken.

"Blood" is undoubtedly the oddest story in the collection, with its forty-one-year-old narrator suddenly developing a penchant for drinking raw blood. The yearning becomes so overwhelming that eventually one night he decapitates a neighbor's chicken and sucks down its blood. The narrator's primary concern is not his odd urges but hiding them from his family: "He remembered—he saw himself—attacking the meat, hanging over the sink. He closed his eyes, snapped them shut— the idea, the thought, of being caught like that. By a child, by his wife. The end of his life" (120). He is terrified that this bloodlust will destroy his normal, protected life - with his normal job, kids, wife, sex life, and hobbies - and he spends most of the story describing how he surreptitiously satisfies his ever-increasing thirst.

After the chicken incident, however, his wife discovers the evidence of his nocturnal activities and confronts him. The reader expects a series of implausible lies, followed by his wife's disgust and the irrevocable dissolution of the marriage. Instead, he tells her the truth, which she, strangely, readily accepts, even asking, "What was that like?" He replies, "Great" (130) and the story ends.

These two strange bedfellows make a strong marriage. Again, we see a marriage that has enough consistency—dinners at home, children's routines—but also enough flexibility to prevent habit from mummifying it. Both he and she are open to the enchantments of reality, no matter how peculiar these enchantments are. While we don't know that she will embrace drinking blood, she isn't appalled by it or him, and she may be a little intrigued. At least, she is willing to ask questions, to listen to answers, and to talk. Thus, curious culinary cravings aside, this couple is every bit as healthy as and even healthier than the other couples we have examined.

The final story in the collection, "Sleep," is a beautiful retrospective from the perspective of a man, married for more than twenty-five years, who is lovingly watching his wife sleep. Because he has just received news of a cancer diagnosis, her sleep, unconsciously reminding him of death, makes him look back over his life. He thinks about the early days of their relationship when, as a teacher, his anti-bourgeois ideals manifest themselves by his living in a grungy apartment, refusing to eat in restaurants, and perceiving an incident of sexual harassment as "politics, saying yes to a working-class woman with an unemployed husband" (209). He loves being surrounded by "the little sons of men and women who'd never known work. Giving them that bit of power" (209).

However, he allows his wife Tara to teach him to enjoy life instead of futilely avoiding its goodness in false sympathy for anti-bourgeois ideals. He learns: Although she never expects it, he moves out of his apartment and concentrates on his writing. He takes what she offers and changes for the good of the relationship. Thus, they can exist together.

But they can also exist apart. She also has the ability to sleep for days, literally: "But even then he'd loved to look at her while she slept. There was something about it that made him feel lucky, or privileged. Or trusted. She could do that beside him, turn everything off, all the defenses, and let him watch her" (203). Each of their differences he sees positively. When she sleeps, he tends to himself. He allows her space of her own, and instead of begrudging that space, he focuses on how it reflects upon their relationship: Her sleeping makes him feel trusted, not ignored. He appreciates what her sleep means about their relationship. Instead of getting annoyed at what could, admittedly, be seen as a rather annoying habit, he embraces it.

The story ends with his reminiscing about a time he takes their young son to the hospital for an asthma attack. Initially, unaware of the severity of the attack, they bicker about who should take him back to his room and put him to bed. After they sense the danger in his labored breathing, they work as a team to get him to the hospital. When Tom comes home with his son, she welcomes them both to bed, covering them all with the duvet as if to ward off the evil. Tom knows, as he lies there, that the next morning, together, they would clean the house to rid it of any dust catchers and read up on how to deal with asthma. Again, the give and take in the relationship reflects this alternating space and closeness. Time is spliced in the last paragraph of the story, and Tom both foreshadows and recollects how they raise their son together and how wonderful their lives will be and have been.

This is a beautiful love story, a love poem dedicated to a sleeping woman, who is completely unaware. The love the two share transcends consciousness and habitude and has provided a real bubble of safety in which the two operate instead of habit's false sense of security. Tom is gifted to be able to see things—his wife's somnolence, his recent diagnosis of cancer— with a freshness that crushes the power of habit. Just as "so much depends upon a red wheel barrow glazed with rain water beside the white chickens" (Williams), so much depends upon Tom's ability to resist habit's erosion of his ability to perceive beauty. Tom's appreciation for the ebb and flow of each other results in a successful marriage.

Thus, the marriage group proceeds from examining at-risk marriages to loving, stable yet fluid ones. We see that the inexorable slide from stability to stasis demands constant vigilance.

Marriage is not the only source of stability or instability in people's lives. The next grouping of stories examines men, many with solid marriages, but who are grappling with awakenings brought on by disease, family revelations, or personal epiphanies. Again, the most successful characters in these stories strike a balance between continuity and fluidity. They accept the changes time brings, not always gracefully, but they ultimately embrace the change instead of hiding in habit.

The themes in "Teaching," of impotence, ignorance, and gradual dissolution, dovetail with the themes of the previously discussed stories. The main character, a veteran teacher on the first day of a new school year, thinks back on his life the few minutes before a class. Over the past 23 years, he has begun to drink too much and has lost his "status as one of the nice teachers" (32); he views "a kid stopping at the desk, a boy or a girl . . . [as] something to be wary of, almost to dread" (31). He misses his one chance at marriage primarily because he is repulsed at the thought of bourgeois respectability and routine, "the happiness that was Southside, Catholic respectability" (40), that he believes marriage would bring. He pretends that he has not succumbed to middle class in middle age. However, his quiet, alcohol-supported existence reeks of bourgeois (vastly different from the life of the ex-girlfriend he almost marries, a foreign correspondent in a poverty-stricken country). During his reverie, he thinks back to an incident with one of his own grade-school teachers, a Christian Brother named Flynn. Flynn shows marked preference for him, for which his young peers ridicule him. Once, when he is sick, Brother Flynn takes him next door to the Brothers' quarters and tucks him lovingly and paternally into bed. This innocent and charming memory is jaded by the teacher's adult perceptions: Ironically, the teacher seems almost disappointed that no sexual abuse occurs, something which would, at least, make his story different. He knows his life has been staid and unremarkable—very different from the life he envisions as a young, innocent man. His youthful idealism isn't corrupted by sin or evil, merely by routine and habit.

When he thinks of his students, however, he begins to feel more hopeful and wakes up from his disappointment and stupor: "And it reminded him—now; he could feel it—of why he'd loved teaching: Empowerment. He'd loved that word. He'd believed it. Giving power to working-class kids. He could get worked up about poverty, and why he was there in the school" (39). He remembers his former enthusiasm and thinks about stopping drinking and even forging a type of Brother-Flynn relationship with someone. His plans excite him and he changes his lesson plan for the day: "He could already feel the buzz, the energy" (42).

As with the other stories, we don't know how long this feeling of regeneration will last. The cynical (and former teachers) would say his first lethargic, post-prandial class will squash it. Perhaps, however, allowing the new students' energy into his life will be enough to destroy the middle-aged ennui that is destroying him. He looks forward to the coming year with trepidation. Although he thinks, "he was fine" (42), he is scared of the change it could bring.

In "The Photograph," Martin enjoys middle age and no longer being "on call" (13) as a father. While other characters in the book look back on their children's childhoods with unabashed sentimentality, Martin seems relieved it is over:

He'd love it, mostly, the whole family/kids things, and he'd ignored the throb above his left eye that had often felt like too much coffee or dehydration, too much or too little of something, that he thought now had probably been the pressure of life. For years, the throb—the vein. Everything he'd done, everywhere he'd gone. Every minute had been counted and used.

He had four children, and there were eleven years between the oldest and the youngest. It was over now—it seemed to be over—and the throb had gone away. (14)

While he misses his children, he nevertheless loves the freedom that comes with age. Seemingly, for him, fatherhood has been too intense an experience for him to have become dulled by routine. In fact, he welcomes a dull security. That security is postponed when one of his longtime friends, Noel, is diagnosed with cancer and slowly dies. Shortly before Noel's death, Martin gets his own health scare when he notices blood in his stool, which turns out to be diverticular disease, a non-life-threatening condition in which the bowel contains pus-filled abscesses.

Martin is aghast, not from the fear of dying but from the fear of ridicule: "Why him—why Martin? What had he done to deserve perforations and pus? Cancer was dignified, something nearly to be proud of—a fuckin' achievement, compare to this" (21). Martin spends days constantly worrying about the indignity and unsexiness of his condition. Diverticular disease becomes his raison d'etre, making him see himself as old, ineffectual, and embarrassing. He is so humiliated he doesn't initially tell his wife of twenty-nine years.

At Noel's funeral, placed on the coffin is a picture of a healthy Noel, which makes Martin remember the young, virile Noel:

He'd forgotten that Noel used to look like that. A big man with a big grin and a big collar on his red shirt. . . The last two years, they'd watched Noel get smaller. And, in the last months, the smaller version became the man. . . .he'd forgotten about the real man. The full man. . . .He felt guilty. He'd let himself forget. He'd let the sick man become the man. He'd forgotten why Noel had been Noel, why they'd been friends. (27)

He suddenly realizes that time has eroded his perceptions, both of Noel and of himself. Just as we see in Proust's *In Search of Lost Time*, involuntary memories are "triggered by sensory experiences that bypass the . . . usual, rational conception of the world. . . .[and]show that [one's] past and present self are intimately connected" (Elkins). Martin is having a Proustian *madeleine* moment, "when he is suddenly made aware of time made invisible. In these brief moments, past and present reveal deep correspondences that affirm a continuity of self in spite of time's flow" (Elkins). Martin has been jarred into remembering himself and his friend as young, virile men. He also has been jarred into recognizing that his young, virile self is intimately connected to the closet hypochondriac and that he can consciously stop this downward slide: "He wanted to laugh. He wanted to stop being the man with diverticular disease" (Doyle, *Bullfighting* 28). Handling change gracefully is a willful act.

In "The Slave," the unnamed narrator also has a more abrupt awakening, his effected by finding a dead rat on his kitchen floor. This narrator loves routines: "I'm a bastard for routines. The slightest excuse, everything become a routine, and I've always tried to fight it" (66). The narrator's life routine is irrevocably broken by finding the carcass. For instance, his purchase of house slippers, speciously to avoid stepping on another dead rat, signifies more: "I never wanted to be a man who wore slippers. . . . Get into a pair of slippers and you're fucked; your life is over. That's what I've always felt, since I was a teenager and my father got a pair from our granny and he put them on, sat down in his chair in the corner and never got up again. . . .And everything I hated about him, about myself, about everything, I aimed at those slippers" (52-3). Although he knows he is middle-aged, the slippers, resulting from the rat, make him feel it.

More significantly, the rat brings up fearful "what if" scenarios for him, such as, "What if the rat had bitten his child?" Hundreds of "what if" scenarios flood his mind and remind him of his utter impotence at preventing life's "what ifs": "But I've thought about nothing else. And it goes way beyond that.

Everything. Fuckin' everything is polluted by it" (58). His outlook is completely altered: "What I used to take for granted, I can't take for granted any more" (57). The rat incident creates "the miserable poor shite you're looking at. I'm just so tired, you know. . . .it's middle age. I know that. It's getting older, slower, tired, bored, useless. It's death becoming something real" (62, 65). The security of habit has been destroyed, and reality terrifies him.

Inspired by a novel in which the main character, a Jewish slave, must struggle against circumstances, environment, and community to retain his religion, the narrator becomes determined to fight reality to retain his feeling of well-being. He refuses to become contaminated. By the end of the story, he makes a concerted effort to "taking the house back. I'm repossessing it. . . .I'm guarding it against nature. The only reason life can go on in this house is because we managed to keep nature out. . . .Life is a fight between us—the humans, like—and nature" (64). He is not consciously trying to descend into the stupor of habit; instead, he is trying to embrace reality and live consciously. Life is a fight between consciousness and unconsciousness, between acceptance and fear. He is awake now. He just needs to overcome the terror it inspires.

We can change nothing in reality: None of us can stop time or reorder chaos. Middle age and the dead rat just awaken the narrator to that fact. However, as in the other stories, trying to mask or dull reality is ultimately harmful. Our narrator is attempting to establish a balance between sudden, chaotic disintegration and slow, routine disintegration. He wants to go back to the time in which "the world was a straightforward, decent place that could be simplified into a line of words running down a blackboard. . . .Only, it has to be protected" (66). The story is telling us, as do others in the collection, that the feeling of being simultaneously aware and protected, which we see in "Sleep," has to be consciously fought for.

Bill, in "Funerals," initially doesn't have a rude awakening as do some of the other characters. Instead, reality, with its threat of fiscal difficulties, has slowly intruded upon his heretofore uncomplicated, banal, but secure, existence, not wrecking it but disturbing it. Bill doesn't actively seek to confront this changing reality. Instead, he tries to avoid it by allowing himself to be seduced back into a comfortable security when he begins to escort his elderly parents to the funerals of their various acquaintances. Hardly macabre, emotional, or sensational, the outings are cheerful. Bill enjoys being with his personable and loving parents, seeing people from his past, and sliding back into a more protected time. Bill looks forward to entering his parents' uncomplicated, orderly world - a world with no immediate financial worries, with grown children, with better than average health, with a stable and solid marriage - a world in which one can sigh, "We've made it." When he is with them, his only concern is not getting lost on the way to the funerals. His parents seem protected by the easy routine of life - not burdened by it - and Bill is eager to soak in this world. He is experiencing mini-*madeleine* moments, as does Martin in "The Photograph," in which the past merges with the present in a blanket of security. Even though Bill is technically chauffeuring his parents, in effect, they are chauffeuring him out of his insecurity.

During one funeral, his mother mentions, almost as an afterthought, that Bill's father, as a young boy, was abused by a priest. Bill panics as reality intrudes. He realizes his parents' lives are not and never have been protected by an easy routine and thus the safety they exude is a false ideation. "Bill tried to get rid of the terror, the fierce guilt that had a sore hold of his stomach. . . .Bill sat between them, afraid to let his arms and shoulders touch either of them; the contact would push something, a button" (107). He is suddenly aware and terrified that nothing can really protect him and that reality will not be avoided. These sacred and secure outings—and by extension, every sacred memory or secure feeling—have been infiltrated.

His parents, cognizant of what has happened, offer him a way back in to security: On the car ride home, they begin to talk in nonsensical terms about the past and allow Bill the glimmer of hope that his mother has misspoken, a narrow crack through which to squeeze back into his protected bubble. Bill, his refuge of temporary innocence burst, at first thinks of his parents as elderly and senile, and the world and its "decline, the slide" creep in. Then, when his father catches his eye in the rearview mirror and gives him a reassuring wink, Bill, desperate, is assured that world hasn't crept in yet. "Something had happened. Suddenly. . . Bill knew he didn't have to believe this. He didn't have to change his past" (113). His father is still protecting Bill, and innocence, albeit forced, is still intact. Unlike the narrator in "Slave", Bill wants to pretend that his moment of clarity hasn't occurred and he allows himself a cowardly escape.

"Animals" introduces us to George, a good father to several, now-adult children. George, redundant emotionally and fiscally, is depressed and feels useless. Just as in "Recuperation," we see George's thoughts as he takes a walk, this time with a dog, a rescued Cavalier Spaniel. (Doyle also has two rescued Cavalier Spaniels). His reminiscences, which center on the plethora of pets his children have had, range from joyful (convincing his young children that their lost finch has merely flown back to the pet store) to traumatic (finding a pet rabbit dead after being mauled by the family dog) to guilt-ridden (accidently running over the family dog but pretending an unknown, careless driver is responsible). His past, as opposed to the uncertainty and unhappiness of his present and future, feels solid and secure: "When he could hold Sandra and tell her they'd be fine, she'd be fine. The first miscarriage, her father's death, his own scare—he'd never doubted that they'd be grand" (166). However, these memories are incapable of recreating positive feelings. He can't will himself to feel better by remembering the good times: "Voluntary memory . . . is of no value as an instrument of evocation. There is only one real impression and one adequate mode of evocation. Over neither have we the least control" (Beckett 4).

Despite the impotence of his voluntary memories to change his present circumstances, George dwells on the past because the present is too unpalatable: "He's walking the dog because he likes walking the dog and he has nothing else to do. His kids are reared and he's unemployed" (Doyle, *Bullfighting* 163). The economic crisis has shaken George. "The Lost Decade. . . .He hadn't been talking about the last decade; it was the next one. It already had a name, and George knew he was fucked. . . . Suffer, your man Krugman said, when he was asked how Ireland should deal with the next ten years. Well, this is George, suffering" (165, 166). Although he has endured many crises, empty-nest unemployment is almost too much and strips him: "Gone. That certainty. It wasn't arrogance. Maybe it was—he doesn't know. It doesn't feel like a sin or a crime" (167). His hope has disappeared. Even though he is "making her [the dog] one of the kids" (171), he can't envision adopting any more pets after her, reflecting his dire feelings for his future: He is shutting out the world as he feels he has nothing left to offer and sees his usefulness as over.

On the walk, George visits his son at work and impulsively confesses to running over the family dog years before. In a sense, he is trying to purge his past of negative memories, thus making it an entirely safe place in to which to escape. He apologizes and explains his deception as an attempt to protect his young children from the devastating truth. His son says, "It would've been alright. . . .We all knew we had a great da" (173). George is overwhelmed by this reply. He can't respond: "His heart is too big for him . . . .The blood's rushing up to his eyes and his mouth. Him and the dog, they'll both explode together" (173).

George is another character experiencing a madeleine moment. His past memories suddenly flood his present and overwhelm him. George's past and present merge, allowing him to recapture the feeling of security and innocence, the feeling of mattering. Additionally, he realizes that his past is not confined to his memories but is alive still in his children and in their respect for him and in the feeling of security that they obviously had and still have. Thus, he is able to find that feeling momentarily by seeing himself through his family's eyes instead of through his own, jaded, helpless ones. He finds the feeling of confidence, which most of the men in this collection are trying to recapture, in his son; Bill, from "Funerals," finds it in his parents: Both find it in their pasts.

The work from which the collection derives its name, "Bullfighting" centers on Donal, another devoted father who is just as wrapped up in paternity as is George from "Animals." He dreads the day when his youngest becomes an adolescent, embarrassed by his parents: "And when that happened he'd die; he'd lie down on the ground. . . . After twenty years. Independence, time to himself—he didn't want it" (174).

Donal is a man of routine: Every Thursday he meets his childhood friends at a pub for drinks. He turns down an exciting promotion because he likes the familiarity of his current job. He vacations with his family, always at the same location in France. During the story, when he breaks routine and vacations with his friends for a week in Spain, they ignore the local customs and take their Thursday night custom with them, frequenting local pubs and idling about the rental home: "That was their week in Spain. Their routine. Like heaven, in the Talking Heads song. Where nothing ever happened" (192-3). Routine pacifies Donal, and he is in danger of being faced with the previously discussed stupor.

In the past, Donal's family saves him from his overdependence upon routine. He is a storyteller, and all his stories center on his children, through whom he enjoys living vicariously. When his children become older and start leaving home, his stories and excitement leave too: "The stories—twenty years of them. They already seemed stale. . . .The stories, his memories, were wearing out and there was nothing new replacing them. His whole fuckin' life was going" (176). The excitement and change that he personally has lacked is about to be cut off. Up to this point, Donal's children have provided the energy and unpredictability his life has needed to protect him from habit. At this point in his life, however, he must learn how to provide that change for himself and get fodder for his stories without his children, a difficult task for such a predictable man.

Until the story's final pages, Donal seems destined for an orderly and slowly eroding life that one day, he will suddenly notice, has become untenable. However, when Donal stumbles upon a bullfight and "enjoys an eerie *morituri te salutant* moment" (Shone 1), things suddenly change. Although Donal is in the ring when the bull is released and its horns ignited, the bull does not charge towards him but flies out another gate. Donal does trip and fall in the ring, but he injures nothing and is in no real danger. Thus, nothing extraordinarily exciting happens. However, Donal's perception changes. He is shocked by the sudden change in himself: "What he'd just seen. What he'd just done. . . .The feeling he'd had, before the bull moved. Not caring. But knowing he was safe—it hadn't felt stupid (Doyle, *Bullfighting* 201). This feeling of safety and excitement, chaos and control, routine but reality, is what most of Doyle's characters are striving to rediscover. Like the opening chapters of *To Kill a Mockingbird* in which Jem and Scout explore their protected neighborhood, Donal experiences a controlled rush. He is so overwhelmed by the feeling, the first time he has experienced it personally, that he vomits when he returns to the rental home. Then, lying on the ground with his friends nearby, Donal feels "good—clear. . . .He was fine—Fuckin' brilliant. This was living, he thought. This was happiness" (201-02). Donal is back in the "bubble." He has the safety of routine but now knows that he is able to add his own excitement and change. He has his story.

This collection, while at times repetitive, is nevertheless interesting in the variety of ways Doyle shows the same middle-age angst and the same fight between habit and the enchantment of reality. No two men face the same exact crisis, yet each story deals with the crisis of middle age. The collection proposes that surviving the trauma of middle age is a continual act of will. There is no "hump" to be gotten over. For many, middle age is Eden immediately after the apple—painful because the proximity of innocence is so close, merely but unalterably a change in perception. Unfortunately, there is no directive to follow to prevent the change, no fruit to cautiously and conscientiously avoid. Thriving in middle age takes a conscious balancing between letting life in and keeping life out, something akin to a loosely tethered hot-air balloon, grounded but not aground. I wish he'd write a collection of similar stories depicting middle-aged women.

CHAPTER 9
CONCLUSION

Doyle has been a figure on the literary landscape since *The Commitments* was published by Vintage in 1989. Although some critics initially disputed his works' literary merit and thus denied him status in the literary elite, winning the Man Booker Prize for Fiction in 1993, after being short-listed for it two years earlier, earned him a seat at the literary table, from which is he is not likely to be asked to leave any time soon. While his recent work is not always liked, it is taken seriously.

In more ways than his experimentation with different genres, over the years, Doyle and his style have changed a great deal. Firstly, Doyle's characters are mirroring the altering Irish landscape. Doyle has begun to look outside of stereotypical Dublin for his subjects, and immigrants feature more and more in his works. Indeed, already are they becoming a staple of it. No longer will we see the lilly-white Barrytown-esque areas.

As the problems created by the influx of the immigrant population are relatively new (the Celtic Tiger began less than twenty years ago), his treatment of them has been largely superficial. He has tended to idealize the immigrant population, elevating it over the native Irish, and has proposed rather simplistic answers to questions of racism and xenophobia, indicating that problems between races and nationalities will disappear with sustained contact. Alas, sustained contact hasn't eliminated the problem in America, and I don't see it doing so any time soon in Ireland. The problems will remain for the foreseeable future and perhaps even intensify. Additionally, after racism fails to disappear and more overtly hostile forms appear, his perception of "casual racism of some Irish people" (Sanai 4) is bound to change, and he will see racism itself as more of an issue. Thus, Doyle has got to address the issues faced by the new population in something more substantive than 800-word installments. I can see that he would eventually base a novel on an immigrant family in order to expose further the racism and xenophobia in Ireland.

Doyle also seems to be fascinated with the idea of truth and history, specifically both whether we can ever be able to know the truth of our pasts and whether, indeed, there exists such a thing. This search for truth is a theme in the Paula and Henry novels, as I have noted. Doyle says,

> It struck me years ago that if two people witness something, then they see two different things. So, it struck me forcefully at one point years ago. I was naively walking through the area I grew up as a journalist. You know, I hadn't yet established what the dos and the don'ts as far as journalism and privacy. So I was walking through this park, and I saw a parakeet flying close, you know. As I was walking through this place and having grown up in the place myself and being very warm towards it, I thought, "You know, you could do a lot worse than live here." But the journalist wrote about it as a slum. He was seeing something completely different. . . .Entirely different. . . .Yeah, it's not only that we witness the stories and live through them, but we make them up as well, and we actually edit them as we go along. . . . You know, we remember things differently--I don't know why-- I suppose in that way we are all created the same. In that way, I wouldn't lie awake at night wondering about the nature of reality. It's there. There's ground. We walk on it. It's the way it's perceived, I suppose. It's a story waiting to be told, lived, and we all do it differently. Anybody. You have siblings? Then you know yourself that none of you remember the same things exactly. You know. I've got three. And I am quite taken aback at how we've all lived different lives under the same roof. We haven't all lived the same story. That's reality. Everybody recognizes it.

Although the unreliability of memory is a theme in his novels, he sidesteps the question of exactly how unreliable memories are by creating extraordinarily unreliable narrators. Certainly, Paula, with her alcoholism and abusive marriage, could not be expected to fully remember her past; and certainly Henry, in the middle of the many layers of the IRA, beset by poverty and illness and braggadocio, couldn't either. Doyle takes baby steps with the theme in *Rory and Ita*, using reliable narrators, namely, his parents, to dispute the validity of various memories. Perhaps he will explore this theme more fully in a novel with a reliable narrator, although, if he believes that none of us is ever truly reliable, he may consider that topic explored.

Because of the immigration Doyle has also explored the definition of Irishness, which I predict he will continue to do. Although he gives this theme ample time in the Henry novels and in some of his short stories, he does so in a negative form. He tells us what Irishness is not. He never tells us what Irishness is. He says he does so on purpose:

> The definition of what it means to be Irish is the root of much of the political difficulty in Ireland--the idea that one person or one group of people has the right to call themselves Irish. I suppose [this debate is furthered] particularly with the arrival of people from Africa, you know, Eastern Europe too, but especially from Africa. You now have ten Nigerians on the streets of Dublin, but that's ten more than you would have anticipated ten, fifteen years ago. Even now, I'm reluctant to define what it is to be Irish for several reasons: (1) because I don't know; and (2) to say, "That's Irish" seems to be restrictive. I don't think it's about the language. I don't think it's about where you were born. I think it's about a group of people living together [in peace]--as you can see anywhere else in the world. There are things that make us distinct, I suppose. The way English is spoken in this country is one thing. I suppose that we share a similar history--although with England [and the history

of divisiveness], that may be quite different. I suppose the icons are familiar to us--sporting traditions are similar to us. . . . But I'm not altogether interested in penning down what it is that is Irish. I am much more interested in asserting my right or characters' rights to be Irish regardless of what the guidelines are for what they say isn't [or is] Irish. Even in my in my twenties and thirties, with religion for example, the big political issues were divorce and abortion, for example, and the banning of that which was already banned. That was a religious crusade really, and that was something I was very involved in. I would think, "Well, why can't you be rock-solid, one-hundred- percent Irish without following any religion or any faith or doctrine what so ever? Why can't you be an atheist and be a card-carrying Irish person?" And I would say that today, this battle is between fewer and fewer people saying that you have to be Catholic to be Irish. So, I'm not sure if I am answering your question, but I only feel Irish when I am not actually in Ireland and people ask me where I am from. (Personal interview 1-2)

Despite what he says, I do not see his defining Irishness as the United States Supreme Court Justice Potter Stewart defined pornography, namely, "I know it when I see it." There are unique qualities that make someone an Irishman, and Doyle exploits these ephemeral qualities in his early works. While we know that Doyle does not think these qualities include being white or being Catholic, we don't know what Doyle does think these qualities include. At some point, I would like to see him posit some idea about the nature of Irishness.

Doyle also seems ready to revisit more of his characters and show how the Irish are handling the ups and downs of their economy and the changing landscape of their population.

Things change. Circumstances change, and it's interesting in that they, kind of, are gone from your imagination, but you realize things seem to re-circulate from twenty years ago. You put twenty years on them, and you begin to wonder. Now, they may not be enough for a book, but I'm just sort of toying with them--just to see how they've got on in those twenty years. You know what I mean? They are twenty years older. (Personal interview 8)

Perhaps because he felt he had to earn his literary stripes, in general, he has avoided returning to his early (and which, ironically, most people would call uniquely Irish) characters. Now that he has earned his street cred, he may not shy away from them as he has. However, I don't believe he will revisit too many of his former characters just to show the new face of Ireland: It would be too easy for him, who is ever on guard against repetition.

In his ever present search to expand his repertoire, Doyle may eventually find it interesting to write about characters in a higher social class. He says he has little interest in this: "A lot of the trappings of the middle-class I'm just not interested in. And it seems, even though I live in a leafy suburb of Dublin wrapped with eighteenth century houses, well, it has inspired me to a degree, and I feel very at home and relaxed in the place. But it's not what I'm driven to write about" (Personal interview 8). I've called Doyle the champion of the underdog several times because his characters are the voiceless who need him to be heard. However, it would be a challenge, at least, were Doyle to find that the more powerful, less needy but still worthy population of the upper-middle class can speak through him as well.

Even if Doyle does none of the above, I fully expect him to continue to experiment, keeping his work fresh, new, and unable to be categorized. Although I foresaw a darkening of Doyle's perspective, I do not see that pessimism now. Instead, I see now the almost naive optimism and enthusiasm of *The Commitments* in his work and in his characters, despite their perhaps more problematic and difficult life situations. Things work out for his characters: Paula is in recovery; an elderly Henry is reunited with his family and has finally gained recognition and acceptance; even the grimmest of the *Bullfighting* stories offers a glimmer of hope. Doyle doesn't kill off his Gatsbys; he doesn't condemn his Jake Barneses to lives of solitude and fishing. He lets us—and his characters—hope.

How does he allow his characters wiggle room and still remain a serious writer? As I wrote in 2001, "His readers and his characters benefit from the 'lessons' found in his works, namely that humor, some type of [loosely defined sense of] family, and self-understanding will provide the independence and strength to live a satisfying life in today's difficult world" (146). Today's world, with its economic crises, political upheavals, genocide, and escalating violence, is arguably more difficult than the world in 2001. However, his characters still manage to survive and hold on. The unassumingly humble Doyle seems confident that his "recipe" still works. While it might not cure all ills, in Doyle's world, at least, it cures most of them. And I believe that the literature-reading public seriously needs the hope of such a cure.

INTERVIEW WITH RODDY DOYLE

Roddy Doyle interviewed by Carrie White
Dublin, Ireland, August 2010

Carrie White: What is to be Irish? Answering this question seems to be a dominant theme in your later work.

Roddy Doyle: I don't actually know. I suppose that since Ireland is an island, there is a tendency to be insular. The definition of what it means to be Irish is the root of much of the political difficulty in Ireland - the idea that one person or one group of people has the right to call themselves Irish. I suppose [this debate is furthered] particularly with the arrival of people from Africa, you know, Eastern Europe too, but especially from Africa. You now have ten Nigerians on the streets of Dublin, but that's ten more than you would have anticipated ten, fifteen years ago. Even now, I'm reluctant to define what it is to be Irish for several reasons: (1) because I don't know; and (2) to say, "That's Irish" seems to be restrictive. I don't think it's about the language. I don't think it's about where you were born. I think it's about a group of people living together and [living in peace together], as you can see anywhere else in the world. There are things that make us distinct, I suppose. The way English is spoken in this country is one thing. I suppose that we share a similar history--although with England [and the history of divisiveness], that may be quite different. I suppose the icons are familiar to us - sporting traditions are similar to us. For instance, you're right beside Croke Park, which is inexplicable to anybody outside of Ireland. I think it's the fourth biggest stadium in Europe, and the people who play their sports there are amateurs, and the sports played there aren't played anywhere else outside of Ireland.

White: I was watching hurling on television just this morning.

Doyle: Yeah, you know hurling is a huge event this time of year and actually is a mystery to anybody outside Ireland.

White: I didn't understand it at all.

Doyle: Yeah, so people say, "What's it like?" It's actually like nothing else. It's really by itself. But I'm not altogether interested in penning down what it is that is Irish. I am much more interested in asserting my right or characters' rights to be Irish regardless of what the guidelines are for what they say isn't [or is] Irish. Even in my in my twenties and thirties, with religion for example, the big political issues were divorce and abortion, for example, and the banning of that which was already banned. That was a religious crusade really, and that was something I was very involved in. I would think, "Well, why can't you be rock-solid, one hundred percent Irish without following any religion or any faith or doctrine what so ever? Why can't you be an atheist and be a card-carrying Irish person?" And I would say that today, this battle is between fewer and fewer people saying that you have to be Catholic to be Irish. So, I'm not sure if I am answering your question, but I only feel Irish when I am not actually in Ireland and people ask me where I am from.

White: Your work discusses this a lot, for instance, in *The Deportees*.

Doyle: Yeah, I suppose because the plot of the stories are from the notion that so many people arrived or had arrived here, and even though quite a few Eastern Europeans have gone back, a lot have put down roots and they're here to stay. They are like everybody else, but still, in some cases, [things] will never be the same again. I was working with a group of young people the last school year who were sixteen or so. They were all [Dubliners], except one who had just recently arrived from Latvia, I think, but they were all talking with Dublin accents. They were all Dublin kids, but when you saw their surnames, you realized that they were coming from all over the place, either they themselves or their parents. They're Dublin kids. They're Irish. They have names that end with "OV" which wouldn't have been in the roll book of any school ten years ago, but they are now, and these children will be part of the country's future. *The Deportees* was meant to bring these people into Irish stories, so to speak, to rub up against Irish born people. So when I met with the editors of the paper [*Metro Eirenann*], the short stories were to be about, at first, Irish-born people meeting new arrivals. Then I started to get a bit more ambitious and sometimes the new arrivals rubbed back against the Irish-born people as I began to experiment with the grammar a bit.

White: I was just thinking: is "Irishness" different than "Americaness"? I don't even know if that's a word. But Americans are saying the same thing: "Oh you are not really American if you're not. . . ."

Doyle: Well that's what a lot of political, philosophical, and moral arguments are about. Identity. That stamp is for some of us difficult to accept - that contradictory thing that you can be happily Irish and hate everything Irish. It's probably essential.

White: You just were talking about Christianity and Catholicism, and, during our last interview, you noted that you were an atheist.

Doyle: Still am.

White: Your parents, Rory and Ita, they seem pretty mainstreamed Catholics.

Doyle: Yeah, they are.

White: How did you become an atheist?

Doyle: It wasn't anything spectacular. It was in my teens. I wasn't at Mass or anything. I just decided I didn't believe. It wasn't that I didn't believe in the routine of the liturgy or the various routines of Mass at the end of the week. I just didn't believe anything. I was at an interview with Woody Allen ten years ago and he captured it better than anybody. He said our religion is that we live in the city. And I agree with him. It's as simple as that. When I was a teacher for example, I had to remind people that I am not Catholic, so that I wasn't going to be bringing this class down to the church. Things like that. Again, those days are gone. I'm not a teacher anymore. Anyway, nobody's interested anymore. You know I married a Protestant woman. Twenty-five years ago, or whenever we started going out with each other, this was a point of interest. Now nobody gives a damn.

White: Your work seems almost anti-Christian--like "New Boy" which has the little kid who is beating up Joseph. His name's Christian. And in *Oh, Play That Thing*, you've got Sister Flow.

Doyle: I don't think it's anti-Christian as such. I've gone past that. The name Christian I just liked. There's nothing religious about it. If I set a story in the present day, I like to use names that aren't traditionally Irish and that you don't see every day - that are more popular these days - like Britney and Anna. And names like sub-continents, Asia, India and China. The most interesting thing is the use of "Patryck" among Polish people, and seems to me it was on the list of one of the most popular children's names last year. It strikes me that they are trying to integrate by choosing a name that is Irish, but they are choosing to spell it with a "y." So I find that really interesting--that's the choice of that name. So the Sister Flow was a part of history. . What's her name McKendrick? Was that her name? [Florence Grattan McKendrick]. It'll come back to me in a minute. I came across the name and even Woody Guthrie had a song about her, and she was this outrageous evangelist who disappeared and reappeared. She was a great communicator who had a great sexual allure even though she wasn't traditionally what you would call an attractive or even a beautiful woman, but she had something going for her because people were battering each other to get into the doors of her church every Sunday. She had, as far as I remember, a big neon cross on top of the church that you could see for miles and miles - and a radio station and shop. So it was those links, what were created in the 1920s in America, that we take for granted. Religion as a business. That's really where the inspiration for that came from - Sister Flow, I mean. You know, religion, as I said, is fundamentally silly, but it's entertaining.

White: There is also Micah, who's born again. What is your view of Catholicism and Christianity? Is it kind of like Wallace Stevens's ordering principle - if it makes your life better it's a good thing - otherwise, it's not?

Doyle: No, I kind of don't think about it at all. It doesn't get into the house really, and it doesn't interfere. I look at the stories about clerical child abuse that aren't going away. The way the Vatican handles it – it's all atrocious. It's horrible and it's stupid, which is actually a surprise. And that's all. It's terrible. I don't feel detached completely. I don't feel it explicitly because I am not a Catholic, but I don't feel detached from it either. It's the country I live in, and you know, still the majority of people have their children christened even though they're not practicing. It's a cultural thing rather than a religious thing. But I do feel a distance from the church. They don't interfere with me. They don't knock on the doors. I live in a big city, so I can send the children to schools that aren't denominational. There are state schools. So it's not an issue. It doesn't come out of my pocket, so to speak. The standard of education here is very good. So I can send the kids to a non-religious school–again it's the price I don't have to pay. If I lived in the smaller place [it might be an issue]. It's not something that plants itself on my table. So I suppose it's my own choice: Most things that aren't illegal aren't dangerous - just get on with it and leave me alone.

White: On to another topic: Do you feel compelled to write about marginalized people? Your background seems pretty solid, but your characters seem very marginalized.

Doyle: It depends on what you describe as marginalized people. If you are living in a state, you are not marginalized. From somebody else's perspective you might be marginalized, but I never saw that I was marginalized. I suppose you can say that the women who experience domestic abuse are marginalized. But I suppose writing the book was to drive her [Paula] back into the center. So I never actually see the characters as marginalized. I suppose people that are born into that – if you can accept the idea [of their being] marginalized – and are somehow outcasts. I suppose there are good stories about that. But I never ask you to perceive them in that way, you know. I'm trying to think. No, I've never actually. . . .I decided to write about working-class characters. But what does that mean, and how do you measure it? It seems so much easier to do it now than five years ago because poverty is back and unemployment is back in a traditional way. So probably measuring these things is easier than it was five years ago, but working-class people often demand a larger income than middle-class people. It was what they did with the money or what they didn't do that seemed to show us their priorities and make us type them as a class. I'm not particularly interested in marginalized people as such, but I just saw. . . .Say, for example, if we decide that recently arrived people are marginalized people, somehow, that just struck me as an opportunity to tell stories that I hadn't had an opportunity to tell before. I didn't see it as shedding light on an injustice. It was more an opportunity rather than a crusade. It wasn't a crusade at all. I just wanted to write what I saw.

White: It's not Edith Wharton, New York, high-class society.

Doyle: No. Again, it may be an Irish thing. I grew up on the margins of a working-class estate. I was in the fields when I was a little kid, but by the time I was a teenager, the fields were all working class and public housing, and project-housing estates, I suppose. So I grew up on the margins, on the out looking in, and I got a job teaching English, grammar, etc., etc. My parents owned their own house, but my father's background is solid working-class, and my mother's is solid middle-class. But I think the vast majority of people who have been educated in the '60s and '70s came from that background - familiarity with both. And the middle class, besides a small core, is still very recent. It's almost now assumed that your child will continue his education or her education up until they're eighteen or nineteen and then go on to college or some sort of third level. I think that's almost assumed, and it's almost a surprise when you hear somebody's child say that he's just looking for work. Going back twenty-five, twenty, fifteen years ago, it was not as assumed, you know? Things change. It's less easy to see the border between one thing and another. I have written about more working-class than middle-class people. But when it comes to actually getting down to the grind of it, how do you assert middle-classes in a country like Ireland when it is not immediately apparent? You could have a large car stopping outside of this café and a couple coming in, and you know by their car and that they are middle-class. So a lot of the trappings of the middle-class I'm just not interested in. And it seems, even though I live in a leafy suburb of Dublin wrapped with eighteenth century houses, well, it has inspired me to a degree, and I feel very at home and relaxed in the place. But it's not what I'm driven to write about. I'm writing about what goes on a mile down the road. It's only a mile, you know. And actually it's in some of the [nearer] houses as well. It's not so much that I'm driven to the margins. It's the way we perceive it. I've only started a novel so I can't really talk about it because it's not in my head yet. I'm only revisiting all of the characters. But not for a second do I see them as marginalized.

White: What are you writing?

Doyle: The Rabbitte Family.

White: What? I thought you said "no more Rabbittes?"

Doyle: I did yeah, but then things change. Circumstances change, and it's interesting in that they, kind of, are gone from your imagination, but you realize things seem to recirculate from twenty years ago. You put twenty years on them, and you begin to wonder. Now, they may not be enough for a book, but I'm just sort of toying with them - just to see how they've got on in those twenty years. You know what I mean? They are twenty years older. So the story is there that I like, but….

White: Which story?

Doyle: Uh, I don't really want to talk about because I've only just begun. And I haven't really started when I say that either.

White: Well, that is another question: I would think it would be very difficult not to write about a character about whom you obviously cared.

Doyle: Yeah. I mean, it's not just about caring about them when you're writing about them. Paddy, for instance - I'm not interested in him at all. It's gone. So I don't want to bring him back in any shape or form. I really can't. I wouldn't. I suppose as you get older, you're more reluctant to say never. I suppose you should always allow yourselves the right to change your mind. Like I said I'd never go back to the Rabbittes - I think I was trying to clear my desk and move on to other things. And I have. I don't know how many novels I've written since then. Six, I think. Yeah, I think it's six. [It is six.] So now that decision doesn't seem—well, it shouldn't be written in stone. But I can't see myself going back to Paddy now. It's just that character doesn't seem to live beyond the confines of a book. You know the reason I went back to Paula Spenser was that she seemed to be a good guide through the changes that had occurred in the ten years between the two books. And I think I was right. Kind of a wise, interested observer, who may not be gaining overtly from the boom and who wouldn't be feeling bitter either - and who would actually bring me back to street level. So the decision to write a book from her point of view was a good thing. I may well have said after that, I will never go back to that character again, but I probably will go back to that character again, if there is an interesting story to be told. The same with the Rabbittes. I decided I'd never go back, but once I got that out of my system and wrote *Paddy Clark* and opened the doors and the trilogy - and then, last year, it made sense just to look in the window and see if there was a story there or just to leave them alone.

White: Your reluctance to go back to Paddy may be because he is so young and his voice is so young. Maybe you want to keep him at that age.

Doyle: Well it's the boy, and the words are chosen by a ten-year-old boy. There's no book or story that can be summarized by a sheet of paper. It's all about the boy's words. And the notion about writing about the teenage years - I have no interest in it. I have no interest in changing the perspective. So, I think it's that one book and no more. The others I suppose, they have eventually added some shape or form to their vocabulary - vocabularies are written to take on other words--as we all do. But basically, they are fully formed. You know we have to take on the language of technology, whether we understand it or not. You know, even geography - countries shift, disappear, form, and reform. You know. So things happen all the time and our vocabulary is added to all the time.

White: What about how your books play with reality? Paula goes back in the first book and says that happened and no, that didn't happen, and Henry does the same thing. Henry and his father create the story of their lives—and are storytellers, you write. What do you think about memory and reality? Is there a reality or are you trying to make everyone out to be a storyteller without a solid sense of reality?

Doyle: Yeah. To an extent I have to say yeah. It struck me years ago that if two people witness something, then they see two different things. So, it struck me forcefully at one point years ago. I was naively walking through the area I grew up as a journalist. You know, I hadn't yet established what the do's and the don'ts were as far as journalism and privacy. So I was walking through this park, and I saw a parakeet flying close, you know. As I was walking through this place and having grown up in the place myself and being very warm towards it, I thought, "You know, you could do a lot worse than live here." But the journalist wrote about it as a slum. He was seeing something completely different. And his language was too flowery. I mean, it wasn't good writing. But it wasn't that he was being dishonest. But he was seeing something completely different. Entirely different. So, little things like that remind you that a story that makes a man laugh can make a woman squirm, and vice versa. For instance, something my wife was telling me last night about somebody sounded so boring and so personal-- that's just life. I just wasn't engaged. I just couldn't care less, but she did. Yeah, it's not only that we witness the stories and live through them, but we make them up as well, and we actually edit them as we go along. So, you know there are many things, bad marriages, whatever. You know, we remember things differently - I don't know why - I suppose in that way we are all created the same. In that way, I wouldn't lie awake at night wondering about the nature of reality. It's there. There's ground. We walk on it. It's the way it's perceived, I suppose. It's a story waiting to be told, lived, and we all do it differently. Anybody. You have siblings? Then you know yourself that none of you remember the same things exactly. You know. I've got three. And I am quite taken aback at how we've all lived different lives under the same roof. We haven't all lived the same story. That's reality. Everybody recognizes it.

White: Is that why you wrote *Rory & Ita*?

Doyle: No. Not particularly. I don't know why exactly at that point, I just thought it would be a good idea. For my kids, I suppose. My father had been very ill. He had a series of heart attacks. Luckily he had a series of successful bypass operations in 1992, I think it was. He's done very well since. He's 87 now. I suppose we can all drop off of the planet at any time, and I suppose I knew a fundamental part of my mother's life was that her mother died, as you know from the book, when she was three. There's only one photo. She didn't know her. She didn't even know her surname. Nobody spoke about it. I suppose those days are over. If anything, people have too many photographs. If you are at an event with children, parents are climbing over each other to record it. It's ludicrous. I think it's calmed down in recent years. Capturing everything, everything, and everything. But nevertheless, I thought my kids now are old enough to have very clear memories of my parents. I just thought it would be a shame that, if something happened, there would be a mystery attached. So, as a personal thing, as a family record. And quite early on, I decided, because I know the way the dynamic works - they are very much a team - that I wanted to isolate them and talk to them and look at their lives before they were "Rory and Ita"– because even though strangely they were born very, very close to one another, they didn't meet until they were in their twenties because of their backgrounds. That became Chapter One and Chapter Two, and I thought, "Well there's a book there." There is a coincidence of their ages as well. My dad was born a year after the foundation of the state. So he's been around for a long time. His life has belonged to the state. I suppose in the late '90s he went from being a blue-collar worker to a white-collar worker living in a commercial house to living in a private house. He left school when he was fifteen, and all of his children went to secondary school. So there are definitely those steps involved that were bringing wealth and stability to the country. So it's a good story, and I was more convinced the more I looked. So it became a book even though it didn't start out that way. It's just a personal thing to keep a record. You know, we just like pictures of them and such.

White: Right now, can you write anything you want and get it published?

Doyle: No.

White: Oh really?

Doyle: Yeah. I've had stuff rejected.

White: Really? You've had stuff rejected?

Doyle: Yeah. I won't go into details because it was a bad experience. But yeah. No, I'm not in a position like that. In fact, it's just that my books don't sell in the same numbers as they used to at all. My last novel, which did quite well in this country, was on the best-seller list every week and it went to number four. And the paperbacks do okay. And the Trilogy books - when they come out, they will do okay. But the days when I was on the best-sellers list in Ireland and Britain as well are gone. So, it's hard to sell a book these days as well. So there's a pressure to it. I'm safe in that all my books are in print and remain in print. Actually my children's books do better than my adult books these days.

White: I loved your children's books. My husband said this is because I love to talk about poop. Well since we're talking about it - children's books, not poop - are your children's books easier to write? Compared to your other highly researched books, it seems like they'd take you a day to write.

Doyle: Oh no, it's actually a slow process. They're not easier. They are, in as they aren't so many words. But they are not easy. They are not realistically based. Things happen in the stories that aren't feasible but they have to be within the context of the story. They have to be realistic [and feasible.] In particular, in the three children's books [the Rover series], the idea was to play with reality and imagination. You know? It's hard to let your mind go and not damp the ideas down. The other books that I've written - when I've given them to my editor - they are finished. He would probably agree with me and say that they are kind of one work day. Not his work, but the work of, say, us coming together and making final decisions about a sentence here and a paragraph there. You are talking about hours, maybe, a day. In fact, the last one we did online because for me to go up to London was a waste of time rather than doing it just online. You know? The children's books - my editor [in New York] always thinks they can be funnier. So by the time they are finished, the books are always longer in matter. And I have to be willing to adapt. I've written five books for children, and he's the editor for all five. I've just finished a new one.

White: The book about *Wilderness*, about dog sledding. Did you actually go dog sledding?

Doyle: Yeah, it was a holiday that became an idea for the book.

White: With your children?

Doyle: Yeah with my wife and two boys, who are now nineteen and seventeen. They would have been eleven of nine at the time. It was great holiday. It was a week. And the husky and dog sleds. On the first day, we went kind of slowly because they drag you wherever. You have to learn the motion and how to keep yourself under control. You make them stop by putting your foot on the brake. They follow the lead of the pack. You know if they turn the corner, you turn the corner, and it's your job to stay on. But there's a point where in the first hour, it's very tiring, surprisingly. I suppose you are using muscles you don't normally use, and, considering it is really, really cold, you are perspiring quite a lot. And it's hard to see. You're sliding through trees and past lakes. Because it had snowed the night before, it looked like we were the first people who had ever been on that lake. And it struck me, then, that there's a story to write. I suppose it's because we lived the story you know. But it was so easy to write. So easy to imagine. It's so glittery and so simple, white. It's just so pristine. On the way home I suggested it to the boys while we were waiting on the train. I just got a notebook and wrote down all I needed to remember. It was a long ride. The problem with my career as a writer of children's books is that I've always written them for my own children, whereas, the adult books, I write for someone out there that I don't know exists. The children's books, that have always somehow been aimed at my children, I've got wrong on several occasions. And that one I got wrong. By the time I got around to it, the boys were older, and I had to start again and write something. So that's why it ended up being a book for older kids. They were older. By the time I finished with it, the older boy was [too old for it], and he's never read it.

White: Oh, it's a really good read.

Doyle: Well he's not interested. He's read other books of mine. But maybe he will read it with his own kids or something like that. I wrote another book for my daughter and I finished it. I've been to India and dramatic places like that that are inspiring. But I've never had a book jumping up and down. But I think the fact that, although it was a foreign country, Finland, it was virtually uninhabited. It was like a blank page. It allowed me to think, as a foreigner. I still got away with writing a book about this place. Whereas you go to India, you're mobbed. You go to Finland and you've got a couple hundred people and you go to India, and you've got millions.

White: You've got a million people in one square.

Doyle: Yeah, exactly. And you feel really under qualified-- whereas, in Finland I didn't feel that way.

White: Going back to what you were saying about the decreasing sales of your more recent books. Your style's gotten a lot harder to understand. The language with The Rabbitte books was easier to follow - more user-friendly - whereas the Henry novels are much more difficult - the narrative jumps around and there are all the historical and political references as well. Does this have anything to do with the sales? Why has your style changed?

Doyle: It's the story telling, I think. Henry, at first, his personality is larger than life. He perceives himself in that way so the words that have to go with that the story are fatter, so to speak. And because I never saw it as strictly fiction as such, and I'm not even sure what that is. But Henry is still alive and is describing a world that has basically disappeared. Parts of Dublin he describes aren't there. In fact even the street scape has changed so that you need to fill in gaps that you wouldn't if you were writing about the contemporary world. So the books are bigger and in a sense more complicated. And you're bringing in big history whereas in the past I hadn't. So it's a different demand. And the liberty with the American one - I didn't want to confine him. He's an older man, but still a very young man. He's in a very different exciting place that's inventing itself every day. The jazz and the new rules and the breaking down of old rules - the form is breaking down as well even though I wanted it to be the same in four parts. And within those parts I wanted it to reflect that. *The Dead Republic* is the book of a much older man. So these things, you know, once you are committed to them, you are stuck to it. So it's not that I planned for more and more complex things. Probably the most complex of the books structurally is the *Woman Who Walked Into Doors* yet people don't draw attention to that. It's a story that is shown on parallel tracks, the present, recent past and the distant past. And I've broken them up, you know. And it's rare enough that people say that's very complicated. It's just, I suppose, that taking up the structure was a big decision to make--but having made it, then it's easy. So, I suppose as well, I like the challenge--you know, not necessarily wiping the slate and starting something completely new. But I do like to the challenge myself. And again though, maybe I got that out of my system and I don't know what the next book will look like. And the vocabulary will be a different kind of challenge - trying to make sure if I write about the Rabbittes I'm not trying to use the dialogue that they would have used twenty-two years ago, but that they'd be speaking like people who have lived through the last twenty-two years. And there will be changes and differences. The thing not to do is to be too stupid to read the old books and to start underlining things and to start being slave to it. That's not the way to achieve it at all. Each book has a different challenge really. The way things are marketed as well - if I was to ask a marketing person what are the mistakes made along the way, probably the writing of *Rory and Ita* would be a mistake because it confused things. It was the one that came after *A Star Called Henry*. Ideally, the next one on the list should have been *Oh, Play That Thing*, the follow up. *Rory & Ita* sold in very small numbers, as that's the type of book that it was. And then when people go up there to the shop - they just look at how much the last one sold and *Rory and Ita* sold only a few. These are things that have nothing whatsoever to do with the work - and shouldn't. But they do have consequences.

White: Some of the critics say that you are trying to reshape Irish history - putting your spin on it.

Doyle: Oh yeah, I'm just playing with it, really. Well, you know any film, really. I'm trying to think of an impressive sort of a film recently. Not just recently but anybody who tries to con you know.

White: Like *JFK*?

Doyle: Yeah, *JFK* is a visionary about one person's life and must fit, in order to entertain society, in a film of two or two and a half hours; it's always going to take liberties. So this is doing the same thing. And I think when I was a kid, less so in secondary school but definitely in primary school and before the IRA started planting bombs and stuff like that, Irish history was presented as doctrine, as religion. These men must have been complicated human beings with their egos, you know, their ideologies and their egos. They were men who decided, and they were mostly men, to engage in this hopeless war, say, in 1916, who locked themselves in a building in order to jump out. They were there to sacrifice themselves. And one or two of them did. That's what their poetry was about, blood and sacrifice. In a different context, it's pessimistic. Yet this was all presented to us as deep membership. They belonged to Ireland. But there is a continuity from the mythological figures, you know like fictional characters like Finn [Fionn mac Cumhail, anglicized to Finn McCool] and Saint Patrick, historically based, but fiction as they are. Right up to these historical figures who shaped the Ireland that we live in now. But they're all presented as being good guys, saints in some shape or form. And I suppose a changing society can allow yourself to poke fun at that and to reinterpret that and satirize it. I'm not interested in satire - taking those old things and making them modern. I wasn't doing it in a way of putting it in paper. But people, satirists, comedians - Neil Jordan was doing it with *Michael Collins* movie - things like that will happen anyway. I wasn't attempting to re-write history. I'm not a historian. I suppose I was telling the story from a different angle.

White: What about Louis Armstrong?

Doyle: Oh! That's a simple enough answer. Because I was still writing about America with Henry. Still thinking I had to. I was in New York. I can tell you it was around about Halloween, 1997, and I was there with my family, and we were at the Sunday reception of the *New York Times Book Review* section, and there was a book about Louis Armstrong. I can't remember which one it was. And it seemed like a good book. I'd never been interested in him particularly. I remember when he was on TV, he was on *The Andy Williams Show* or something like that. Everybody loved him. Looked like Muhammad Ali really. Everybody loved him. And I liked the little stories and incidents about his childhood - particularly reading about it. So I decided I would read the book. And did. And there were interesting coincidences between his own life and Henry's. Self-defined, mythological - he created his own mythology really. Telling lies as well. I just got interested. There was a story in there around when Armstrong was about 19 or 20 and was leaving New Orleans for Chicago to become the world famous Louis Armstrong, and he knew a bouncer, a night club bouncer from New Orleans. And he told Louis that when he got up there to "make sure and get yourself a white man to put his hand on your shoulder and say, 'This here is my nigger,' you know." And there is a lot in that story. It's kind of funny, but it's shocking and kind of sad. And I thought, "That's interesting." So Armstrong was going up to Chicago with that advice in his ears, between his ears. So I wanted Henry to meet him off of the train, so to speak. I put that kind of behind my ear like a cigarette or something for future use to see if it worked out. And then gradually he became part of the story.

White: Would you consider yourself, like Henry, a self-made man creating your own story?

Doyle: Oh yeah. We realize through the choices we make what we will be, the way we dress. Sometimes it's more obvious than others, people who try and transcend their backgrounds. I always thought of my father like that. He always dressed up. We always dressed up. He won a competition when he was an apprentice so, even though he wasn't smoking cigarettes, he bought a pipe. So, in a kind of obvious way, I would have grown up with that mentality. He was a very elegant man in a place that wasn't at all elegant. I think up there they are all self-made. I think that town is very useful. He must have felt smothered by other people who were making a lot of money. So yeah, they are all self-made. I think that term is very useful. But its usefulness has been somehow kind of shattered because it has come to refer to those with a lot of money. You know, lifting them up by their bootstraps. But in a way we all are, within conventions, really.

White: Henry seems to end up like Ellison's invisible man. Have you read the *Invisible Man*?

Doyle: I've read it.

White: Ellison's narrator disappears underground several times, and there is the whole issue of names and being used by an organization. Is that just me or did you mean that reference?

Doyle: I think it might be you. But no, I think that's fair enough because sometimes we're not consciously aware of the impact a book can have on you. Now I read the *Invisible Man* in my twenties so we are talking about thirty years or so. If you ask me what the plot is I can't remember, but I do remember being very, very impressed. I don't remember the opening chapters, but I remember liking it a lot. And I remember feeling a bit let down because it was his only novel at the time. But I'm not sure about its overt influence on me. But on the other hand, I've just been reading a new translation of the *Tin Drum* [by Gunter Grass], and I read that originally, and then I was sent by a friend of mine a new translation. He sent it to me about a year ago, and I hadn't read it in quite some time. So, I reread it. I was really quite taken aback by how much Henry seems to be in that book. The perspective, the political situation. And I noticed a coincidence down at the post office and the rebellion taking place in the post office, and I noticed that was the start of events. I knew the book was based on historical events, so it was purely coincidental. Maybe at the time I was reading this book, it struck me how striking the similarities between these two books was. So, there are many similarities that I wasn't aware of when I was writing these two books. But now when I reread *Tin Drum*--to say to somebody that wasn't an influence on me--if I had answered the question last year that the book wasn't an influence on me, I would be coyly dishonest. I have to say, yeah, it did have a powerful influence on me. So, *The Invisible Man* might be the same.

White: You should go back and reread it.

Doyle: I will, yeah. I might read a few short ones between then and now.

White: Why is Miss O'Shea's first name such a mystery?

Doyle: Well, names are quite arbitrary. They seem to be very vital but they're quite arbitrary, and I think that in part would be my Irishness. You know, from the very first day of school you're allowed to give a different version of your name. So, I was Roddy Doyle. But by the day three, I was always Roddy O'Doyle because they have to have an Irish name. That was the stupid way things were done back then. How they manage now with the Irish names and the Nigerian names I don't know. So I was Roddy O'Doyle. And then somewhere along in primary school I had a teacher reading off the roll calls, bringing them up to date, and he had in the roll books the name of our parents. So, Rory O'Doyle, the name of my father, was called. The kid sitting next to me thought the name was hilarious. And it became a nickname. Nobody knew it because it's a family name. There are only a small group of people who call me Rory and as far as they're concerned that's my name. It's not really used anymore but it was when I was in school. You know when I was filling in one of those examination forms I had to put in that and not my real name. So, I think there is a sense that names can be really arbitrary. People go and get new names all the time. Yes, it is a stamp, you know. Some names are even pronounced differently like the Louis Armstrong name with the "LEWIS" pronunciation instead of "LEWEY." So, I was intrigued by that. That was the name he was known by but he absolutely hated it. It was a lack of respect if you didn't know and you called him by that. And I think that's the complication of being a black man in a white world. Instead of being a term of affection, it's an insult. So, there are lots of things going on. And then there are actors.

White: Like Marilyn Monroe.

Doyle: Yeah, yeah. You know Marion Morrison [John Wayne]. It's hard to imagine being called Marion and being the star of anything. So, I like that opportunity. But then there are people who are adopted and begin looking for their roots - coming here and looking at their roots. It reaches a point, in my case, where your children get older and they're going to hit thirty pretty soon and you have more respect for it. People are feverishly looking for their roots. So, it's clearing in a way but it's arbitrary. And then you think, if somebody had been given a different name would they have been the same person? Or would they have lived up to something else?

White: Yes, that's interesting. And Henry Smart's always proclaiming, "I am Henry Smart!" And he has to share the same name with his dead brother. What about *Forrest Gump*. Did you think about Forrest Gump and Henry?

Doyle: I have never seen *Forrest Gump* from beginning to end. No, the parts I saw I just couldn't stand– I just couldn't sit through it, so I've never seen it.

White: I'd have to agree with you on that. On a totally different topic, Henry is really sexual. There is a lot of sex—almost graphic at times - in the Henry novels, especially the first two. Why?

Doyle: Henry is actually a very passive character even though he's a man of action. Things happen to him, and women discover him. And he is found in women so to speak. It's a part of his personality. And I think part of growing old is it's a shadow. It's still there but it's not there. I was intrigued by a man called Ernie O'Malley. He would shoot soldiers so that they would cry when they were dumped on the street. And he was a strikingly tall and handsome man. He was captured and shot and tortured. Maybe even thirty years on. But to me there is no similarity between the young man and the over-aged man. Something similar happens to Henry. There is a shooting. He never settled into the new Ireland; he went to America. Ireland was a disaster after the revolution. O'Malley died around 1957. So there's also things like that. And again, it's in an Irish context and that really began when I was a kid. The official thing was sex was something around that you had to endure. It wasn't to be a recreation. And it never got a reference in public. When it was referenced on television it was a huge controversy. In my lifetime things have changed dramatically. A politician said that there was no sex in Ireland. Obviously it's a silly thing to say. If Henry is going to have sex with Mrs. O'Shea, then it's going to be in the middle of the GPO or that kind of place.

White: And maybe it was just my American, Catholic sensibility, but when I saw the school teacher looking at Henry when he was fourteen. . . . and then, you know, the whole pedophilia in the Church stuff coming out over here. . . .

Doyle: Yeah, you know whatever afternoon or morning I decided to do that back when or whatever - don't ask me why, It just seemed like a good idea. Again, he grew. We grow so quickly dot dot dot.

White: Why, with Paula's second book, did you switch from first person to third person?

Doyle: Yeah, I didn't want it to be….well, the first person was all right. It was the past to the present kind of thing. I didn't want it to be about those first ten years. I didn't want it to be in sequence. And also I wanted it to be fresh. If I was to go first person to first person then inevitably you're going to be falling back into the character. But, if I wrote it in third person second tense – that was a bit of an experiment. I could distance myself from the first book also. I could stay close to it, but I could write alongside it. With first person, I use the analogy that she's holding the camera. In the third person, somebody else is holding the camera. It helped with a different perspective and a different vocabulary. It helped me to stay close to her but not be her.

White: Do you reread your work after it's released?

Doyle: No. Again though, never say never. I read *The Commitments* recently for the first time since it was published. But I have to for professional reasons. For the heck of it, no. I haven't reread them since. I'm not curious. I reread *A Star Called Henry* when I was finished and it was out to the public, but only to make sure that my characters and situations were current. I had this horrible misgiving from the first about a character [in *Oh, Play That Thing*] - I had a horrible idea that I'd killed him [in *A Star Called Henry*]. And I wanted to double back and make sure that I hadn't before I kept on writing. But actually, I hadn't, so it was fine. So, I reread those two just to make sure there were consistencies in the stories.

White: When I write something, I never read it once it's in print because I'm afraid it'll have mistakes in it.

Doyle: No, I'm just happy to get rid of it. I don't think I hate it, just am sick of it to an extent. Because, you know yourself that you do one draft, two drafts, three drafts and you know the last and then the book and then a round of interviews. It's the same thing again and again and again. So, there's eight of them. I suppose it's some sort of intellectual nausea. You just want to move on. Oh yeah, I was saying that I don't get the urge to reread them. No, I feel I can relax after I've written it.

White: Of all of the stuff that you've written, what is your favorite? Is it a "the most recent work" kind of thing?

Doyle: No. I think for the reasons that have nothing to do with the plot of the book really, *The Snapper*.

White: Oh, why?

Doyle: It was the second book, so I put more thought into it than the first one. It was more difficult to write because of that really. It took longer to write. A short book, but within that time I did an awful lot of living. I suppose we always do. But a lot of things happened in my life at that time. A lot of exciting things. A lot of changes. So, I associate those years, '86-'89, with things that were happening. I was writing *The Snapper* at the time I met my wife, and we were married by the time it was published. So a lot of things went on and then my family and the children as well arriving. So, there are things in the book and movie that are directly related to experiences and things. It's always been my favorite book.

White: I think it's my favorite too.

Doyle: Yeah. It's not one of those things that would leave me awake at night, though. I'm content enough with all of them, but I think it will always be my favorite, you know. And then, like my children's books, the first, for very simple reasons.

White: *The Snapper* seems really optimistic.

Doyle: Yeah, it's kind of strange in some ways. It's about a fundamentally emotionally successful family. And that's quite rare. Not just in Ireland but anywhere. I mean rare in fiction not rare in reality.

White: Oh, I was thinking rare in reality. Do you think you've grown as a writer?

Doyle: Growing. I don't know what it means really. One of the great things about being a writer and growing older is that everything is easily reachable. Inevitably, really. I can't remember what age I was when the first book came out….. 28. I'm now 52, so quite a lot of living has been done--living that in many ways I would have liked to have avoided. You know the death of a close person - that is something that I never wanted to see. And that's something that's a matter of growing up. It brings me knowledge of grief that I wouldn't have beforehand. Watching your children grow up brings pride, anxiety, the form of grief that is watching them become independent. These things go into the work. My next book will be out next year. It's a collection of stories that's largely about middle age [*Bullfighting*]. And I don't think I'd have written it without being middle aged. It wouldn't have occurred to me. So, I don't think I've necessarily grown because, I suppose, when I wrote *The Commitments* I didn't feel the urge to rewrite it. It just seemed to me fine. So, you'd think now that I've grown, I'd feel a bit of embarrassment for its naivety and its enthusiasm, but I don't because that's a part of the book. And I think that enthusiasm and naivety are choices, but you don't have to use them. So, I don't think I've grown. I'm just older so I've got more to write about in some ways. It seems like not a nice thing to say about a young writer--you know, to dismiss them as having not done so much living. That's not the case at all. It's just the fact. I suppose that to me is the key. The difference between me the writer now and me the writer twenty-five years ago: I've written more based on experience and I've lived more; therefore I have different things to write about.

White: Do you think, as some people have said, your novels are increasingly pessimistic? I assume you don't think that?

Doyle: Not really. If we measure a twenty-five-year chunk, it's probably darker in the later books.

White: See, I don't think that your work is dark. There is always a light at the end of the tunnel.

Doyle: Yeah. There is in all of them really. I don't see the pessimism, but I don't argue the case.

White: What is your biggest regret? Do you have a biggest regret?

Doyle: I do have two professional regrets really. One is about a piece of work I decided not to do and the other is about a piece of work I agreed to do. And one is easier to deal with. A friend with the BBC contacted me at the time. I'm not sure about how long ago. He's been dead about five years. But he contacted me and invited me to write a modern version of *Peter Pan*. They had the rights to do it at that time. And it was a great idea. It was a lovely thing to be asked to do. But I persuaded myself I was too busy. But a few years later, I realized you're never too busy. And I do regret having said no. That type of invitation doesn't come anymore. So, it's not that I'm bitter as opposed to then. Today, I really would jump at the invitation. However, I couldn't do it because I don't think the invitation would be made.

And the other thing is more recent and it's difficult to talk about. I co-wrote a play [a rewrite of Synge's *The Playboy of the Western World*] with Nigerian writer Bisi Adigun. And we wrote it back in 2006, and the writing was difficult but it went very well. Line by line, we kept the structure of the play. And it went very, very well, but after that he claimed that I've breached the contract. He's on the warpath. And if I could go back and just— well, when he suggested I write with him, I'd just say no. I really would. . . . But we will see how it goes. I was very happy with the play. When I saw it on stage it was really good. I was happy that it gave me a job and the director is now a solid friend of mine. It's not off the record as such because it has been in the newspaper.

White: What kind of father are you?

Doyle: I'm not qualified to answer that.

White: In *Wilderness*, the daughter and her mother switch roles, which seems to indicate a vision of what a good parent would be.

Doyle: That's the novelist. I've never ever written a book about parenting. I don't know what sort of father that I am, other than a loving father. We're all that, because we're all men - the vast majority of us anyway. But I don't feel like I have anything to say, you know. I don't have anything to say. Not that I'm trying to be abrasive - I just don't have anything to say. Because if I start talking about it I fall over. I'm always stunned by the number of people who think they can write books on how to raise children. You know? I just find it quite funny. No, I have nothing to say, I suppose, like most people who try to answer that. And I rarely do. But in a casual use of the language if you ask me, I'd answer.

White: Sorry. I'm not a mom so I had no idea how difficult a question that would be. How about this: What are you politically?

Doyle: Well, I suppose in a left/right spectrum, I lean towards the left very much. But again I live in Ireland and that raises questions and issues. When I was much younger I would have gone through a communist phase. And I'm kind of wary of "isms" now. Anything that ends in an "ism." But I suppose I am—um, somebody said I was socialist, and I guess I would say that I am--but without going into the various reasons because it's a term that's as bland as the terms "right" and "ice-cream." But my politics always lean towards the left in a European sense. I don't have anything interesting to say politically that thousands of people in this country couldn't say better. I'm not affiliated with any political party. "Fighting Words," which I cofounded, is as concrete of my political expression as anything is. [Doyle and Sean Love opened Fighting Words, a creative writing center which, as its website asserts, "helps students of all ages to develop their writing skills and to explore their love of writing." In the unfashionable neighborhood outside of Croke Park, multi-aged children can practice writing and editing and creating projects, can receive one-to-one tutoring on projects, and get encouragement for their creativity. Doyle is a presence in the school, despite his status as a nationally recognized figure.] It's very deliberate and in the city of Dublin. It's deliberately bright and new for working class. It is not second-hand or charity, although some people are surviving on a wing and a prayer there. I have made years and years of work there. And it's open to anybody. It's an open invitation. The vast majority of people who go in there are working-class kids. They are from the locality around Dublin, so I am very pro-European. And that means nothing coming from your side of the Atlantic. You know, there is this notion of [Ireland being] little Britain, and I've always voted against that. I like being able to call ourselves European and having another angle to look at. Even though we are not able to speak different languages, it has opened us up and made us less insular. I think it's huge and has had a great impact on us. But a lot of the left, union people are pro-European. In an Irish context I hate the word "republicanism". I am a republican under the notion of electing our leaders and such. I hate the idea of having a head of state that is born. It seems so absurd and silly. But yet most of the other European countries have exactly that sort of system. But "republicanism" in the Irish sense has violent affiliations. And in America, Bush and Palin seem almost fascists. That's what I feel like saying today.

White: What is your writing technique like?

Doyle: It's pretty mundane really. I'm not working this week. It's roughly about 9:00am to 6:00pm Monday-Friday. But when I began writing, my children were very young and it didn't make sense to work countless hours. The house was empty on Sunday, just me and my sons in the house. They are grown up now and independent, so I did a little bit of work on Sunday because I knew I was going to be busy this week. I don't feel the need to. I get plenty done and I think it's no harm to take a few days off. But it's really mundane and boring on paper. I don't work into the night unless I have an urgent deadline and they're very rare. The kids are grown, and I don't have to drive from place to place, so I don't have to be anywhere.

White When I interviewed you fifteen years ago you told me the same thing - I tell my students that now - to set their time to write. I can never do it though - set my writing hours like a job.

Doyle: I do that. Once I'm working on more than one project I find writing into the day more than enough, you know.

White: When you finish a novel is there a decompression period - you know, "Leave me along for two weeks or three weeks" - or not?

Doyle: No. When I finish a novel it's back to work the day after. Uniquely, I finished *The Dead Republic* and everything to do with *The Dead Republic* - when did I finish it? Probably around this time last year - and I'm only just now thinking about a new novel. And that's very strange for me. I'm usually starting a novel very soon after because I like working on a lot of things. It's a good thing I've been working on a novel, and I've been itching to work on a few little things, but I'm also itching to get back to the novel. But there is no creative decompression, no. Not really, no.

White: I figured as much--when I was writing my first book on you, I would think, "Could he please stop writing so much so I can go ahead and finish!" I kept on having to add chapters because you kept on publishing stuff.

Doyle: There will be two books out next year.

White: Oh, really?

Doyle: Yeah. Two children's stories.

White: Where did you learn to write for kids? Was it when you were telling your kids stories?

Doyle: Yeah, it's as simple as that.

White: Ok. When you look back at your life. . . . It's funny because I haven't interviewed you for fifteen years and now you're "Roddy Doyle," icon. Are you like, "Holy cow, I can't believe I've done this?"

Doyle: No, it doesn't seem to make sense from that perspective. A question like that invites an unbearable answer. You know what I mean? So, I either don't answer it, and that in itself is an answer, or I just feel I needn't answer the question. But I walked here, I live about half a mile in that direction, but I walked here this morning and I looked around exactly the same way I would if I worked for the Department of Agriculture and I did the same stuff when our dog was sick over the weekend--and the fact that I'm a world-famous novelist didn't make cleaning up easier. So, in fact, one's position doesn't impact life. Sometimes, in a casual day-to-day living, if I go somewhere I don't normally go, it's a different measure. That is rare because outside of having a new book out, I keep myself to myself. Of course, ten percent of the people who now live in the country weren't born here and a lot of these are in positions behind counters. Ten years ago the people behind these counters wouldn't have known who I was. They couldn't care less here, you know. That's the same in most counter situations and one of the big benefits. But it doesn't really get in the way. I love what I do, and I suppose it's easier to love what you do than see what you do being published and people reacting to it. So, to that degree, yeah it has an impact. I would still be a writer whether financially I'd have to do something else or not. If I had to do something else, I'd be a teacher or something - I don't know. I gave up teaching when I was still a very enthusiastic teacher. And I gave up teaching seventeen years ago. So whether I'd still be an enthusiastic teacher or not is hard to imagine. The school where I taught was shut down about four years ago so I'd have to be teaching somewhere else. It would be very hard to go to a new place. So I'd probably be quite different. Again, it's not something that you can imagine.

White: You know, this is a little random — but, with all the dogs in the children's books, I was wondering if you have a dog.

Doyle: Apparently two of them. When I wrote early on, we didn't have dogs. We've had several since then. So yeah, I do. Two dogs at the moment. I've had them for two years. They are rescue dogs but they're Cavalier Terriers. They're beautiful dogs. Really lovely, lovely dogs. But they are rescue dogs. But yeah, we've had a series of dogs.

White: Who are you reading now? What authors?

Doyle: At the moment, tonight or tomorrow morning, I'll be finished with *The Tin Drum*. I don't know what I'll read then. I don't know. I've read a lot. I took all of July off and went to a place where we stay for the summers - south of here - and I read a lot. I read *Alone in Berlin* by Hans Fallada which was written in 1947, the year he died. Very quality. Thought it was great. I like to keep up with contemporary fiction. I think the best contemporary fiction book that I've read in a while is by an Irish woman [Emma Donoghue] called *Room*. If you casually Google it, it's about children never seeing daylight. It's absolutely brilliant and funny. The circumstances are really funny, but it's really exciting. And it's just wonderful. A brilliant piece of writing. That will be what I'd say when asked what my books of the year are - if not the book of the year from my point of view. Really great. And Per Patterson, a Norwegian writer. He has a new book out. I read *Out Stealing Horses* which was out about five or six years ago and now he has a new one out. Can't remember the name of it [*I Curse the River of Time*].

White: Well, I know it's time for you to go. Thank you so much for agreeing to speak with me.

Doyle: Thank you.

Bibliography

Agundo, Juan. "Demystifying Irish History in Roddy Doyle's A Star Called Henry." *ABEI Journal* 7 (2005):125-134. Print.

Alford, Steven E. Rev. of *Rory & Ita* by Roddy Doyle. *Houston Chronicle* 15 Dec. 2002: 23. Print.

Adigun, Bisi. Arambe Productions. 2 Nov. 2011. Web.

Ball, Magdalena. "A Review of *Oh, Play That Thing* by Roddy Doyle." Rev. of *Oh, Play That Thing*. *The Compulsive Reader*. Web. 4 Aug. 2011.

Beckett, Samuel. *Proust*. New York: Grove Press, Inc., 1931. Print.

BookLounge. "Roddy Doyle, Author of The Deportees." 06 Nov. 2008. Online Video Clip. Accessed on 27Aug. 2010 >

Broughton, Trev. "Taking a Battering." *Contemporary Literary Criticism* 178 (1996): 15-17. Print.

Burke, Mary. "Roddy Doyle." *Irish Literary Supplement*. 2009. 14. Print.

Callil, Carmen. "Fiction—The long road to recovery." *Financial Times Weekend Magazine* 26 Aug 2006. ProQuest. Web. 12 July 2011.

Charles, Ron. "A Bright Light in Ireland's cloudy Sky." *Christian Science Monitor* 91.204 (16 September 1999): 16. Print.

Clancy, Luke. *Bisi Adigun's (and Roddy Doyle's) Playboy. The Loy.* 04 Oct. 2007. Web. 19 Aug. 2011.
Connelly, Cressida. Rev. of *The Deportees* by Roddy Doyle. *Spectator* 15 Sept. 2007: 51. Print.

Cremins, Robert. Rev. of *A Star Called Henry* by Roddy Doyle. *Houston Chronicle* 10 Oct. 1999: 15. Print.

Crompton, Sarah. Rev. of *Rover Saves Christmas* by Roddy Doyle. *Daily Telegraph* 1 Dec. 2002. Print.

Cummins, Steve. Rev. of *The Playboy of the Western World* by Roddy Doyle and Bisi Adigun. RTE Ten. Web. 2 Nov 2011.

Dawson, Janis. "Aspects of the Fantastic in Roddy Doyle's *A Star Called Henry*: Deconstructing RomanticNationalism." *Journal of the Fantastic in the Arts* 12.2 (2001): 168-185. Print.

Deignan, Tom. "Maeve Binchy: 'Aches' to Break Retirement? Meanwhile, Roddy Doyle takes Aim at Harry Potter." *Irish Voice* 14.27 (4 Jul. 2000) Web. 12 July 2011.

Deignan, Tom. Rev. of *The Deportees and Other Stories*. *American Magazine*. America Press, Inc. 2008. 2 Nov 2011. Web.

Doyle, Roddy. *A Star Called Henry*. New York: Viking Penguin, 1999. Print.
---. "Ash." *New Yorker* 24 May 2010. Print.
---. *Bullfighting: Stories*. New York: Viking Penguin, 2011. Print.
---. *Mad Weekend*. New Island Open Door: Dublin, 2006.
---. *Her Mother's Face*. Illus. Freya Blackwood. New York: Arthur A. Levine Books, 2008. Print.
---. *Not Just for Christmas*. Boston: Gemma Open Door, 2009.
---. *Oh, Play That Thing*. New York: Penguin Books, 2005. Print.
---. *Paddy Clarke, Ha Ha Ha*. New York: Viking, 1993. Print.
---. *Paula Spencer*. New York: Viking Penguin, 2006. Print.
---. Personal Interview. 20 August 2010.
---. *Rori & Ita*. New York: Viking, 2002.
---. *Rover Saves Christmas*. Illus. Brian Ajhar. New York: Arthur A. Levine Books, 2001. Print.

---. *The Commitments*. New York: Vintage Contemporaries, 1989. Print.

---. *The Dead Republic*. New York: Viking Penguin, 2010. Print.

---. *The Deportees and Other Stories*. New York: Viking Penguin, 2007. Print.

---. *The Giggler Treatment*. Illus.Brian Ajhar. New York: Scholastic Children's Books, 2000. Print.

---. *The Meanwhile Adventures*. Illus. Brian Ajhar. New York: Arthur A. Levine Books, 2004. Print.

---. *The Snapper*. New York: Penguin Books, 1990. Print.

---. *The Van*. New York: Penguin, 1991. Print.

---. *The Woman Who Walked Into Doors*. London: Jonathan Cape, 1996. Print.

---. *Wilderness*. London: Scholastic Children's Books, 2008. Print.

---. *Yeats is Dead!* New York: Alfre A. Knopf, 2001. Print.

Doyle, Roddy, et al. *Finbar's Hotel*. Ed. Dermot Bolger. New York: Harvest Original, 1999. Print.

Drewett, James. "An Interview with Roddy Doyle." *Irish Studies Review*. 11.3 (2003): 337-49.

Dwyer, Ciara. "Roddy opens his door." *Sunday Independent*. 25 April 2010. Independent.ie. 2 Nov. 2011. Web

Du Bois, W. E. B. *Souls of Black Folk*. *Norton Anthology of African American Literature*. 2nd ed. Eds. Henry Louis Gates, Jr. and Nellie Y. McKay. New York: W W Norton & Company, 2004. 692-766.

Elie, Paul. "Ireland without Tears." *Commonwealth* 126.20 (1999): 57-8. Print.

Elkins, Katherine. "Proust: *In Search of Lost Time*, Part One." *The Giants of French Literature: Balzac, Flaubert, Proust, and Camus*. Recorded Books, LLC: Prince Frederick, MD: 2010. 34-37. Print.

---. "Proust: *In Search of Lost Time*, Part Two." *The Giants of French Literature: Balzac, Flaubert, Proust, and Camus.* Recorded Books, LLC: Prince Frederick, MD: 2010. 38-41. Print.

Engall, Priscella. "Roddy Doyle. The Cinematic Man." *Australian Screen Education* 29. Print.

Engelfried, Steven. Rev. of *The Giggler Treatment* by Roddy Doyle. *School Library Journal* Nov. 2000: 119.Print.

Farrey, Brian. Rev of *Click* by Roddy Doyle et al. Teenreads.com. Web. 2 Nov 2011.

Fitzgerald-Hoyt, Mary. "A Republic Called Henry?" *Irish Literary Supplement.* 2011. 24. Print.

Fraze, Barb. "Archbishop says Catholics not Passing on Faith to Young People." *The Catholic Virginian.* 30 May 2011: 11. Print.

Gordon, Edmund. "Dark Side of Ireland." *New Statesman* (5 Apr. 2010): 58. Literature Resource Center. Web. 15 Sept. 2011.

Hall, Pauline. "Mother Courage." *Estudios Irlandeses—Journal of Irish Studies* 3 (2008): 197. Gale Literature Resource Center. Web. 14 July 2011.

Henry, Rick. Rev. *of The Woman Who Walked Into Doors,* by Roddy Doyle. *Contemporary Literary Criticism* 1997: 26. Print.

Holden, Stephen. "Unlocking the Esprit of the Irish with Sex." Rev. of *When Brendan Met Trudy. New York Times.* 9 March 2001: 24. Print.

Hopkin, James. "Mired in History." "Roddy Doyle." *Contemporary Literary Criticism* 178 (1999): 37-38. Print.

Howard, Sandra. "An Exercise with Jerks." *The Spectator* (2004): 49. Print.

Hoyt-Fitzgerald, Mary. "A Republic Called Henry?." *Literature Resources Journal* (2011): 24. Print.

Hutchings, William. "Memoir: Rory and Ita." *World Literature Today*. May-Aug. 2004. 82-83. Print.
---. Rev. of *A Star Called Henry*, by Roddy Doyle. *World Literature Today* 74.3 (2000): 594.

"Roddy Doyle." *Contemporary Literary Criticism* 178 (1999). 44-45. Print.

Jacklein, Charlotte. "Rebel Songs and Hero Pawns: Music in a Star Called Henry." *New Hibernia Review* 9.4 (2005): 129-143. Print.

Jay, Ann. "A Personal Response to: *The Woman Who Walked Into Doors by Roddy Doyle*." *J Med Ethics* 26 (2000): 58-59. Print.

Junyk, Myra. Rev. of *Click* by Roddy Doyle. *Resource Links* Dec. 2002: 37. Print.

Keen, Suzanne. "Irish Troubles." *Contemporary Literary Criticism* 178 (1996): 25-26. Print.

Lacey, Colin. "Roddy Doyle: Ruffling Feathers, After a booker." *Publishers Weekly*. 25 March 1996: 55-56. Print.

Lanters, José. "Demythicizing/Remythicizing the Rising: *Roddy Doyle's A Star Called Henry*." *Hungarian Journal of English and American Studies* 8.2 (2002): 245-258. Print.

Leclair, Tom. "Henry Rising." *The New York Times Book Review* (2010); 11. *Literature Resources from Gale*. Web. 15 Sept. 2011.

Levi, Jonathan. "Beauty and the Beast." Rev. of "Roddy Doyle." *Los Angeles Times Book Review* 3 Oct. 1999: *Contemporary Literary Criticism* 178 (1996). 40-42. Print.

Lewis, Michael. "How the Financial Crisis Created a New Third World" by Terry Gross. *Fresh Air. NPR.org.* NPR, 4 Oct. 2011. Web. 7 Oct 2011.

Lusembo, Matthias. Homily. Christ the King Catholic Church. Christ the King Catholic Church, Norfolk, Va. 19 Nov. 2011.

Marsh, Kelly. "Roddy Doyle's 'Bad Language' and the Limits of Community." *Critique* 45.2 (2004): 147-159. Print.

McCann, Colum. PENamericancenter. "Roddy Doyle in Conversation with Colum McCann." 04 May 2010. Online Video Clip. Accessed 18 July 2011.
<http://wn.com/Roddy_Doyle_in_Conversation_with_Colum_M cCann>

McGlynn, Mary. "The Protean Character." *Irish Literary Supplement* 2004. 23. Print.

McGuire, Matt. "Dialect(ic) Nationalism?: The Fiction of James Kelman and Roddy Doyle." *Scottish Studies Review*. 80-94. Print.

McMahon, Regan. Rev. of *Rover Saves Christmas* by Roddy Doyle. *San Francisco Chronicle* 16 Dec. 2001: 4. Print.

McMullen, Kim. "New Ireland/Hidden Ireland: Reading Recent Irish Fiction." *The Kenyon Review*. 126-148. Print.

Meany, Helen. Rev. of *The Playboy of the Western World* by Roddy Doyle and Bisi Adigun. *The Guardian*. 6 Oct. 2007. Print.
Monahan, Barry. "Playing Cops and Robbers: Recent Irish Cinema and Genre Performance." *Genre and Cinema: Ireland and Transnationalism* (2007): 45-57. Print.

Moore, Charlotte. "In Their Own Words." Rev. of *Rory & Ita* by Roddy Doyle. *Spectator* 30 Nov. 2002:54. Print.

---. "Mother Courage on the Wagon." *Spectator* 30 Sept. 2006. Print.

Moynihan, Sinéad. ""The Ghost of the Real Leg": Maurice Walsh, John Ford, and Adaption in Roddy Doyle's *The Dead Republic*." *New Hibernia Review* 15.1 (2011): 49-63. Print.

Murphy, Andrew. "'White Chimpanzees': Encountering Ireland." *But the Irish Sea Betwixt Us: Ireland, Colonialism, and Renaissance Literature.* (1999, 2009). Cengage Learning. Web. 14 July 2011.

Myers, Kevin. Rev. of *A Star Called Henry* by Roddy Doyle. *Spectator* 4 Sept. 1999: 32-33. Print.

NYSWritersInstitute. "Roddy Doyle at the NYS Writers Institute in 2004."16 May 2009. Online Video Clip. Accessed on 04 Nov 2010.<http://wn.com/Roddy_Doyle_at_the_NYS_Writers_Institute_in_2004.>

O'Grady, Thomas. "Playing Now: Roddy Doyle's New Boy." *The Boston Irish Reporter* 20.6 (Jun 2009) ProQuest. Web. 23 June 2010. 12 July 2011.

O'Tool, Fintan. "Working-Class Dublin on Screen: The Roddy Doyle Films." *Cineaste* 24.203 (1999): 369. Print.

Piroux, Lorraine. "'I'm Black an' I'm Proud': Re-inventing Irishness in Roddy Doyle's *The Commitments*." *Contemporary Literary Criticism* (1998): 26-34. Print.

Playboy of the Modern World. The Independent. Web. 19 Aug. 2011.

Prose, Francine. "Molly Bloom Said 'Yes', Paula O'Leary Says 'Maybe'." *Contemporary Literary Criticism* 178 (1996): 17-24. Print.

Quinn, Anthony. "Out of Ireland." *The New York Times Book Review* (14 Nov. 2004) *Literature Resources from Gale*. Web. 15 Sept. 2011.

RandomReads. "*The Dead Republic*.-Roddy Doyle-Speaks Exclusively About His New Novel." 31 May 2010. Online Video Clip. 26 Aug. 2010.
<http://wn.com/The_Dead_Republic_Roddy_Doyle_SPEAKS_E XCLUSIVELY_ABOUT_HIS_NEW_NOVEL>

Reddy, Maureen T. "Reading and Writing Race in Ireland: Roddy Doyle and *Metro Eireann*." *Irish University Review*. 374-388. Print.

Rev. of *The Giggler Treatment* by Roddy Doyle. *Publishers Weekly* 24 Jul. 2000: 94. Print.

Rev. of *Yeats is Dead*! by Roddy Doyle. *Amazon.com Review*. Amazon. Web. 2 Nov 11.

"Roddy Doyle." Contemporary Authors Online. *Literature Resource Center*. 25 Mar. 2010. Web. 14 Sept. 2011.

"Roddy Doyle." *Contemporary Literary Criticism* 178 (1996). 1-47.

"Roddy Doyle." *Spectator* 290.9095 (2002). Print.

Rourke, Mary. "When Irish Eyes Were Smiling, Laughing, and Crying." *Los Angeles Times* (15 Nov. 2002): E31. Print.

Salis, Loredana. "Immigrant Games: Sports as a Metaphor for Social Encounter in Contemporary Irish Drama." Irish Studies Review 18.1 (2010): 57-68. Print.

Sanai, Leyla. "Roddy Doyle at Edinburgh Book Festival." *Rock's Backpages Writers'*. 27 Aug. 2010. Web. 19 Aug. 2011.

Sbrockey, Karen. "Something of a Hero: An Interview with Roddy Doyle." *The Literary Review*. 1999.537-552.

Schwarzbaum, Lisa. Rev. of *When Brendan Met Trudy*. *Entertainment Weekly*. Issue 587. 16 March 2001: 44. Print.

Shepherd, Allen. "Never the Same Again." *New England Review* 16.2 (1994): 163-167.

Contemporary Literary Criticism. Ed. Janet Witalec. 2004. Literature Resource Center. Web.

Shone, Tom. "Bullfighting." *The New York Times Book Review*. (29 May 2011):26(L). Gale Literature Resource Center. Web. 14 July 2011.

Skea, Ann. Rev of *Finbar's Hotel* by Roddy Doyle. *Eclectica Magazine* 2.2. Web. 2 Nov. 2011.

Skloot, Floyd. "Irish Myth-Making and Myth-Breaking." *Sewanee Review* 107.4 (1999): c-civ.
---. Rev. of *A Star Called Henry* by Roddy Doyle. *Sewanee Review* 1999: C3. Print.

Synge, J.M. "The Playboy of the Western World." *The Complete Plays of John M. Synge*. New York: Vintage Books, 1960.

The Quiet Man. Dir. John Ford. Perf. John Wayne, Maureen O'Hara. Republic Pictures, 1952. DVD.

Walsh, Maurice. "The Quiet Man." *Coo-ee. . .Australia Calling*.

Michael Humphrey. Web. 14 Nov 2011.

Walton, James. "Home and Dry." *The Spectator* (17 Apr. 2010): 39. Literature Resources from Gale. Web. 15 Sept. 2011.

When Brendan Met Trudy. Dir. Kieron J. Walsh. Perf. Peter McDonald, Flora Montgomery. Alliance Atlantis, 2000. DVD.

Williams Kenower. "Roddy Doyle." 11 Jun. 2010. Online Video Clip. Accessed on 08 Mar. 2011.
<http://wn.com/Roddy_Doyle_Interview>

Williams, Kevin. "Faith and the Nation: Education and Religious Identity in the Republic of Ireland. *British Journal of Educational Studies* 47.4 (Dec 1999) 317-331.

Williams, William Carlos. "The Red Wheelbarrow." *The Norton Anthology of American Literature*. Shorter 7th ed. Ed. Nina Baym. New York: W.W.Norton, 2008. 2014. Print.

Wilson-Smith, Anthony. "The Seeds of Terror." *Maclean's* 112.43 (25 October 1999): 93-4. Print.

Also Available from Glasnevin Publishing

Why Some People Succeed and Others Fail
By Samuel A. Malone
2011
ISBN: 978-0-09555781-8-2

In this inspiring and remarkable book you will discover the principles of success that have directed and motivated many people to make a significant contribution and difference to the world. You will also uncover the pitfalls to avoid in your quest to become the best you can be.

Success in any endeavour does not happen by chance. It happens through the application of sound principles and purposeful actions such as: Setting realistic goals, Making worthwhile plans, Practising good interpersonal relationships, Having confidence and self-belief, Being optimistic, Developing self-esteem, Being persistent and resilient, Being highly motivated, Developing the habit of lifelong learning and continuous improvement, Practising good personal values

This book has an entertaining blend of inspirational real life stories, quotations, practical tips, acronyms and activities to help you acquire the right habits and practise the skills of success. The book is underscored by the best scientific research currently available which is made accessible to the reader through clear simple language. By following the principles set out in this book you will become the happy and successful person you are destined to be.

Samuel A Malone is a self-employed training consultant, lecturer and author. He is the author of 20 books, some of which have gone into second editions and foreign language translations.

Visit: *www.glasnevinpublishing.com* for more titles and information

Also Available from Glasnevin Publishing

How to Get a Flat Stomach in 30 Days
By Kevin Sheridan
2011
ISBN: 978-0-09555781-9-9

You will NEVER have to go on a diet again...Are you ready to embark on the most rewarding and exciting challenge of your life? The weight loss technique shown in "How to Get a Flat Stomach in 30 Days" has proven to be virtually 100% successful for those who genuinely apply its principles. The good news is that this book gives you all of the tools to obtain a flat stomach in 30 days and keep it! You will discover the secrets that others have paid thousands to learn.

This book will show you: How to lose weight easily using the latest scientific findings. How to feel motivated and healthy, and to increase your energy levels. How to use the unique "MERC" weight loss formula. An effective 30 day program that will remove years of accumulated toxins from your body. How to identify and remove the foods and chemicals that depress your metabolism. Effective exercise techniques and programmes to remove excessive fat. Imagine, you can lose up to 15 pounds (6Kg) in 30 days... permanently! The secrets and techniques in this book will even help you to burn fat while you sleep! This book promises "your best ever shape" and you will not be disappointed, because it really works!

Kevin Sheridan is one of Ireland's leading weight loss experts. He is an NCEF qualified personal trainer with over twenty years of experience specializing in weight loss, toning and fitness. He lives and works in Dublin where he is a full time personal trainer and a frequent contrubutor to radio and TV programmes where he specialises in weight loss. He also lectures on college courses in fitness and health.

Visit: *www.glasnevinpublishing.com* for more titles and information

Also Available from Glasnevin Publishing

Steve Cummins

Where do Daddies Come From? A Pregnancy Guide for Men
By Steve Cummins
2011
ISBN: 978-1-9086890-0-9

Where do daddies come from? is a laugh out loud yet genuinely helpful book to make pregnancy easier for both of you by giving you the skills and the motivation to be a help to the woman in your life despite just how crazy she is at the moment. Pregnancy is a difficult time for a man. Everyone concentrates on the woman, and rightly so, but now here is a soothing hand on your fevered brow. This book is for you. It is filled with information and advice on what you need to know about pregnancy and some puerile gags that you don't. From breast milk target practice to protection from the "Tit Nazis" this book offers advice and support in a hilarious format which keeps the laughs coming at
breakneck speed while genuinely preparing you to help the woman you love.

Written by Steve Cummins a comedian, author and dad. Steve has appeared on TV and radio numerous times and performs stand up comedy all over the world. He is the father of two strong beautiful boys.

Visit: *www.glasnevinpublishing.com* for more titles and information

Lightning Source UK Ltd.
Milton Keynes UK
UKOW051824260712

196622UK00001B/21/P